Each experience is a window to your consciousness.

Open your heart to the immense possibilities that are awaiting you.

THINK SUCCESS

Essays on Self-help
Revised and Updated

Jayaram V

Published by
Pure Life Vision LLC
New Albany, Ohio

Think Success: Essays on Self-help
Copyright © 2010, 2014 by Jayaram V, All Rights Reserved
Published and Distributed Worldwide by Pure Life Vision LLC., USA.
Second Edition (Revised)

This book is copyrighted under Berne convention. Printed in the USA. All rights reserved. No part of this publication may be reproduced stored in a retrieval system, or transmitted in any form or by any means, electronic, mechanical, photocopying, recording, scanning or otherwise, without the prior written permission of the publisher or the author. Requests to the publisher for permission or for bulk purchase of the book should be submitted through http://www.PureLifeVision.com.

Thank you for buying an authorized edition of this book and for complying with copyright laws by not reproducing, scanning, or distributing any part of this book in any form without prior permission.

First published in the USA by Pure Life Vision LLC.

Limit of Liability/Disclaimer of Warranty: While the publisher and the author have used their best efforts in preparing this book, they make no representation or warranties with respect to the accuracy or completeness of the contents of this book and specifically disclaim any implied warranties of merchantability or fitness for particular purpose. No warranty may be created or extended by sales representatives or written sales materials. The publisher or the writer is not engaged in rendering psychological, financial, legal, or other professional services. The advice and strategies contained herein may not be suitable for your situation. If any assistance is needed, you should consult with a competent professional where appropriate. Neither the publisher nor author shall be liable for any loss of profit or any other commercial damages, including but not limited to special, incidental, consequential or other damages.

Publisher Cataloging-in-Publication Data

V, Jayaram
Think Success: Essays on Self-help
    p. cm
Includes bibliographical references
ISBN- 13: 978-1-935760-22-1
ISBN -10: 1-93-576022-X
1. Success-Psychological Aspects. 2. Success 3. Conduct of Life 4. Self-help techniques. I. Title

BF637.S8 2014
158— dc22   2014906853

Printed in the United States of America
10 9 8 7 6 5 4 3 2

About the Author

Jayaram V is a leading teacher of Indian religions, philosophy, mysticism, and spirituality. His writings reflect his composite personality and diverse knowledge. He has proficiency in various branches of knowledge, including science, business management and information technology. His knowledge comes from his academic background, personal and professional experience, self-study and observation. Through his writings, he provides rare insights into the nature of reality, human personality, yoga, consciousness and mystic symbolism. He also writes about self-development and human behavior, combining the transformational wisdom hidden in ancient scriptures with recent researches on human psychology and consciousness. Jayaram has written hundreds of articles on various subjects and authored several books, which include Brahman, an Introduction to Hinduism, the Bhagavadgita Complete Translations and the Awakened Life. Since 2000, he has been actively engaged in spreading awareness about spiritual and moral duty. Jayaram V can be contacted at http://www.jayaramv.com.

Also By Jayaram V

- The Awakened Life
- Brahman
- The Bhagavadgita Complete Translation
- The Bhagavadgita Simple Translation
- Essays on the Bhagavadgita
- Introduction to Hinduism.
- Selected Upanishads
- Brihadaranyaka Upanishad
- Chandogya Upanishad
- Thoughts and Quotations

Think Success

Jayaram V

Stretch your mind to the heavens and beyond.

What you seek in life, you will find it, if you believe in it and work for it.

Happiness and sorrow are but mental responses to the events and situations we perceive. You can change them if you have the resolve.

Contents

Preface 1
Introduction 3
Why Self-Development? 8
Effective Listening Skills 16
Critical & Analytical Reading 25
Develop Your Negotiation Skills 33
Accept Full Responsibility for Your Life 44
Coping With Fears 55
What You Can Learn From Successful People 66
How to Improve your Memory 80
Dealing with adversity 94
Success Principles Worth Following 104
A Lesson in the Art of Appreciation 108
The Art and Science of Relaxation 118
Becoming Aware of Yourself 131
The Building Blocks of Your Life 141
Career Development 150
Witnessing Your Own Fears 163
Coping With Failure 170
Planning Your Day 178
Dealing with emotions 182
Dealing with the Problem of Loneliness 190
Health and Fitness 199
The Power of Your Thoughts 208
The Power of Attraction 215
The Power of Determination 219
The Power of Positive Affirmations 221
Positive Thinking in Daily Life 226
Priority Areas of Life 231
Simple Relaxation Techniques For Your Eyes 237
15 Effective Ways to Deal with Adversity 244
How to Manage Your Self-talk 256
Mental Maturity and Adult Behavior 267
How to Cultivate Mental Peace 276
Morals from Aesop's Fables 285
Problems and Problem Solving 292
The Pillars of Prosperity 304
Planning Your Vacation 320
Positive Mental Attitude 325
Protecting Your Health 328
Simple Pleasures of Life 333

Stop Blaming Others 340
Qualities of Successful People 347
Working with Long Term Goals 352
Overcoming the Monotony of Life 359
The Power of Positive Affirmations 363
How to Improve Your Self-Esteem 366
Recommended Reading 375

For Padma

Open your heart to the immense possibilities that are awaiting you.

Whatever you do, do it with love and discipline.

Preface

The first edition of Think Success was published in 2010. This new edition is coming out nearly after four years, with some additions, deletions, and improvements. Most of the chapters are thoroughly revised and updated. In the first edition, information was arranged in two sections. That distinction is now removed. All the articles that were published in the first edition are retained. The articles deal with various aspects of self-growth and improvement. You can use them for reference, inspiration, guidance, self-motivation, or to improve specific skills.

The articles provide a lot of inspirational information, which you can use in your daily life. I do not claim originality for the ideas presented in them. However, they reflect my own philosophy and approach to life, and they are based upon my observations, understanding and analysis. They also reflect my beliefs and understanding of eastern religions and philosophies, which I have studied for over five decades and which I believe have played an important role in shaping my personality and behavior.

I am always inspired by the human capacity to excel and succeed against odds. My heroes are those who never give up and never admit defeat. They are not bound to a place or time, or even a religion, but to certain ideals and values that reflect the untiring nature of human spirit. My heroes work against odds and represent the best of human character and dignity in dealing with problems and over-coming hurdles. At times, they may fail and falter, but never lose their hope, faith, and focus. To me, they bear testimony to the fact that if we are determined we are unstoppable in reaching our goals. Through their lives and actions they prove that, despite our failings and shortcomings, we can self-craft our behavior and personalities to be role-models and the best of the species.

Unfortunately, most of us are still caught up in divisive thinking and a limited vision that refuses to see our true place in the universe. We have yet to realize the innumerable opportunities that await us beyond the earth. What gives me hope in this scenario is that progress is always achieved by a few determined individuals who aim to set new trends and think differently. They remain focused amidst chaos and sane amidst conformity. Whether we are aware or not, and whether we like it or not, the seeds of progress are sown every moment in the minds of men who are dreamers and achievers. Every day, someone, somewhere, rewrites history, and sets new limits of achievement, overcoming a problem or disability, and discovering new truths about themselves and the world in which we live. Our passion for progress never ends, as our need for self-actualization. We have an insatiable desire to extend our influence in every possible direction. While some may think that it creates problems and complicates our lives, it is a great blessing because it fuels our dreams and desires.

I have been greatly influenced by self-help books in my life. They have played an important role in my career, goals, thinking, beliefs and behavior. I have faith in what I have stated in this book. I believe that they can inspire you and motivate you to work for your growth and betterment. They reflect the knowledge and awareness I have cultivated and internalized. We know inherently what is good for us and the world. Through self-effort and inspired vision, I believe we can become better human beings. We need a little push from within to make that possible and bring out the best in us. I sincerely hope that the writings I presented in this book will motivate you and inspire you to move forward in that direction and achieve peace and happiness in your life.

Jayaram V

Introduction

The ultimate goal of life is not to have any goals. The real joy of living comes to us when we learn to flow with the world and accept life as it happens. This is the highest goal for the mankind, envisioned ages ago, by our saints, seers, teachers, prophets and incarnations.

However, not all are capable of surrendering to the flow of life and accepting things as they are. Until most people reach such an ideal and make it the sole aim of their lives they need to work on transforming their consciousness to hold the brilliance of their own divinity, without being overwhelmed by it. Until they achieve perfection, they have to remain within the realm of perceptual reality and focus upon mundane aspects of their lives to prepare for their mental and spiritual growth and evolution.

Our inner calling for enlightenment manifests in us in many ways. It arises in us as the deepest yearning to transcend our limitations and realize our true potentials. It propels us to enter the objective world, and attain permanent happiness by securing the things we love or avoiding those we detest. Sometimes, it assumes in us the form of a deep-seated obsession to achieve permanence through physical means, by controlling the natural processes such as aging, sickness and death.

Our preoccupation with materialistic life is but a disguised or even a sublimated expression of our spiritual longing to extend ourselves into the objective world and secure our lives. Having become imprisoned inside our bodies, we express our longing for freedom by trying to go beyond our physical boundaries, into forms and things to become an integral part of the creation and the world of God. For an individuality that mirrors the illusions of life, securing things seems to be a natural solution to the problem of impermanence and instability caused by the forces of Nature.

Materialism does not deliver us from impermanence and the problem of death and disease. The accumulation of things leads not to freedom, but to bondage and suffering. All religions allude to this truth and warn us against the impending dangers of excessive materialism and attachment to things. They prescribe a moral code of conduct as the divine law for the people to balance their materialistic ambitions with spiritual aspirations and safeguard themselves against the consequences of desire-ridden actions.

Using our natural faculties and intelligence we can express our deepest thoughts and make organized effort to realize our persistent dreams. Each of us has the ability or potential to achieve success. If people do not succeed, it is because they do not want to. Knowingly or unknowingly, somewhere in their minds, or in their subconscious thoughts, they create limiting beliefs about their abilities and opportunities, and deny themselves the desire to succeed.

Because of self-defeating attitude and negativity, most people fail to secure peace and happiness and suffer from negativity, doubt and despair. They focus mostly on what they do not have or what they cannot do, rather than what they can accomplish with their natural talents and skills. They may believe that they do not deserve success or do not have the ability, deluded by the notion that success is achieved by extraneous factors like fate or family background, rather than one's own ability. Other than this, they may also come to the wrong conclusion that to be successful one has to break rules and indulge in questionable acts of immorality and evil. Success does demand its own price. However, to be successful one does not have to barter away one's soul or compromise one's values.

Success and effort go together There are no shortcuts to success, while there are many to failure. In life you either make things possible with your resolve or let them happen by remaining passive and inactive. People often blame others, even God, for their failures, despite evidence to the contrary. Sometimes, there may be a real justification to blame others for your personal failure. However, when you analyze such incidents, you will realize that they could not have happened without your involvement and complicity.

Your life is shaped mostly by your thoughts and actions. We are endowed with a free will, which greatly determines the course of our lives. Sometimes events may happen without our consent or against our will, but it should not be an excuse to avoid taking responsibility. We create most of the circumstances in our lives, by our thoughts, decisions, and actions. Others may play a role to the extent we let them control our lives and actions, but ultimately it was we who let them happen. Whatever you do and achieve in your life, even divine intervention, happens because of your desires and decisions only.

Irrespective of the circumstances in which we are born or live, we have an innate ability to control our minds and bodies and regulate our lives. We have some power over our destinies. We are wired to be potentially intelligent and competitive. In the entire universe, until now, we are the only rational beings, having the skill and the ability to survive in most testing circumstances and in a very difficult, unstable, unfriendly and unpredictable world. We do have many weaknesses, but we also possess many strengths. Although, history may not recognize the achievements of every worthy individual, we know that the world would not have been where it is today without the contribution of everyone who lived upon earth. Each living being, intelligent or otherwise, sets in motion a chain of events and forces, which generations later, branch out into innumerable streams. Whether intended by Nature, or not, each being who lives upon earth has a place and role in the universal scheme of things. Without even one, the manifest universe would be incomplete.

We may not know that in our lives we influence many people and are influenced in return. Our actions and interactions grease the wheels of life upon earth, creating positive and negative consequences, while we suffer because of them. The absence of even a single person on earth will have far reaching consequences for the generations that follow. A person who was born a few thousand years ago might be an ancestor to millions of people who are alive today, while the plants and the animals he destroyed or fostered might have left their own brush strokes upon the canvas of the earth.

One of the most promising features of success is that it is this worldly. We can see it and feel it and discern it in the people we meet or the people we know through others. The world offers us innumerable opportunities to achieve success, and to experience it, understand it and manifest it in our own personalized ways. While success may mean different things to different people, we know inherently what it means and how it can be achieved. We know instinctively when someone achieves success, as we are conditioned to succeed in our lives and look for opportunities to excel in our actions. Successful people affect the world in many ways. They leave behind a great personal example and may set new standards of behavior and excellence. Their influence lasts for generations, as others follow their example and create their own successes.

Society owes a great deal to people who succeed in their lives, even if they are not well known, because with each success they achieve, they add a vast pool of knowledge to our collective wisdom. Successful people thrive in free societies where they have equal opportunities and freedom to excel by using their talents and skills and proving their worth. Countries, which discount individual success and promote the idea of collective will, ignore this fundamental fact. The life of each individual is precious, and the ultimate authority upon it rests with the individual who embodies it rather than any extraneous power. What this means is that we must promote individuality and encourage people to achieve individual success, without losing sight of the greater good to which each individual can contribute and the obligatory duties they are expected to perform.

The articles presented in this book are about how to achieve success, peace and happiness, within the limitations to which you are subject. They are meant to provide you with inspiration and information to cultivate a growth mindset, which can help you to reach your goals with commitment and determination. You can go through this book in whatever way you want. You may read the entire volume or only those articles that apply to you. You can also refer to the articles whenever you feel your motivation is weakening or you need to recharge and refocus.

My writings are meant for those who want to improve themselves, and who believe in themselves and in their will to succeed. If success or excellence is your goal, you may find this book useful and worth reading. Everything happens for a reason. If you are reading these lines, it means that you are interested in self-improvement, and know that success is not a pipe dream but a certain possibility. If you are reading my books or my writings, know that you are in communication with a person who is genuinely interested in your growth and welfare and who has himself struggled in life to overcome certain limitations and live differently. With my knowledge, abilities, skills, perfection and imperfections, I have brought these ideas to you to be molded in the crucible of your own life and experience.

In this context, I want to share with you my personal philosophy, which played a significant role in shaping these ideas. It is based upon the following seven fundamental beliefs or convictions. They influence my thinking and actions and help me to find clarity, direction and purpose and be myself in a world of diverse opinions and conflicting approaches.

1. We are part of the universe. The universe expresses through us, and we express the universe through us.

2. We have a right to safeguard our lives and interests from exploitation and intimidation, and secure peace and happiness for ourselves and others.

3. As long as we live upon earth, for our individual and collective good we have to fulfill certain duties and obligations.

4. We are endowed with certain abilities and potentialities, which we must manifest fully to fulfill the very purpose for which we are born.

5. Our lives and destinies are shaped by the choices we make. Our happiness as well as our suffering arise from our choices only. Therefore, for our own good we must exercise our choices wisely with great discretion.

6. To achieve something, we must believe in something, be it God, a personal philosophy, or a set of values that help us to deal with the problems we face and remain strong.

7. To fulfill the aims of creation and our existence, we must fully manifest our uniqueness and individuality until we rest in the ocean of life without a trace.

Why Self-Development?

Several years ago, I had an opportunity to attend a week long training program for senior managers organized by the company where I worked. During the training, one of the faculty members delivered a lecture on building effective teams by resolving emotional problems and interpersonal conflicts caused by irrational thinking. He also gave examples and suggestions about how to counter iraional arguments. Overall, it was an informative lecture, based on the speaker's own experience and observation. However, some managers in the group were not impressed. During the lunch break, they kept saying that they heard nothing new, and what the speaker said was general knowledge and plain commonsense. Some even added with scorn that self-help and management subjects helped none but those who used their high connections to secure speaking deals. The people who engaged in that thought process were not well educated. They rose to the ranks mainly by sheer hard work, operating in the same niche markets for decades and establishing a good customer base. Most of them did not possess leadership skills and ran their offices like family units, disregarding the rules set by the company when it suited them, and acting more like parental figures rather than professional heads. They would have achieved more success, if they kept their minds open and showed readiness to learn and improve.

Is self-help knowledge helpful?

When it comes to self-development subjects, you will find many people who harbor skepticism and negative thoughts. Self-help is not an exact science. It does not enjoy the same status or respect as astrophysics or quantum mechanics. However, you cannot also dismiss it as a product of speculation or common sense. Historically, self-help knowledge developed as an offshoot of spiritual wisdom, ethics, and philosophy, but with the development of modern psychology and behavioral sciences it acquired a distinct status and credibility as a reliable and practical subject worthy of study and exploration. We now know that self-help knowledge is not just commonsense or a folk science. Using reason and commonsense you can surely resolve many problems in your life. Today, self-help writers and experts derive their knowledge from various sources including human psychology, sociology, history, medicine, anthropology, spirituality, philosophy, literature, ethics, mortality, aesthetics, and religion. You may not be benefited by every self-development that has been published, but you can expect some good from most of them. Sometimes, self-help knowledge may not directly help you, but create in you a desire to understand your hidden potentials, talents and abilities and improve them through self-effort. It motivates you to become a better person.

However, whether you succeed in that effort or not depends a lot upon you only. To use self-help techniques effectively, you need a proper mindset, preparation, and training. It is also incorrect to assume that you can substitute self-help knowledge with pure commonsense. Studies prove that people are not always guided by their common sense, reason, or intelligence, but by their fears, doubts, impulses, and expectations. While we are rational beings, our thinking and actions are not always guided by pure reason. We are frequently influenced by our desires, emotions, habits, beliefs, and prejudices rather than what is needed and suitable for the situation. Even our perceptions and understanding are clouded by irrational thinking and unverified assumptions. The same pattern of behavior influences our thinking and actions in personal and professional matters. People are guided by various considerations, which are not necessarily rational or intelligent. They may read self-help books but may not derive much benefit from it due to mental blocks, wrong priorities, and reservations. Hence, it is not proper to pass a summary judgment against self-help knowledge and brush it aside as mere speculation or pure commonsense.

It is important to remember that in any effort to improve yourself or change your life you alone make the difference. The results depend largely upon your effort and involvement. The knowledge may help, but its value and importance depend upon your needs and problems and how relevant it is to your life and circumstances, rather than how great and experienced its author is. It is not necessary that the same methods and techniques should work for everyone or apply to everyone. If a particular program does not work for you, it does not mean that it will not work for others, and vice versa. What matters most is whether it serves any purpose in your life and whether you find it useful, motivating and transformational. Personality factors and individual differences and attitudinal issues also play a vital role. If you do not believe in it or if you accept it with doubts and fears, you may not try enough or find it use. If the problems are too personal, intimate, or sensitive, you may have to even customize the knowledge using your own intelligence. Hence, it is not proper or rational to brush aside any self-help theory, technique or suggestion as useless because it has not worked for you. Any problem that you may find with self-help theory and practice may not be because they are defective, but because either they are not right for you or you have not tried hard enough. Even the best self-help experts in the world cannot guarantee 100% results in every situation or in case of every individual. A lot depends upon your own effort and involvement and how far you able to apply the knowledge to your situation. Therefore, if self-help knowledge has not helped you, you must first look into yourself and see what went wrong. Based upon your findings and conclusions, you can search for alternatives.

Self-development topics show you the way to maximize your chances of success and achievement. They point to the possibilities of what you can accomplish with preparation and right knowledge and how you may overcome your limitations and weaknesses to create the life of your dreams. From them you will learn that while you are entirely responsible for your circumstances, you can train yourself to deal with them and create your own conditions and opportunities to become a better and capable human being, transcending your limitations and your self-destructive negativity.

It is difficult to tell whether a particular self-help theory, technique or principle is suitable or relevant for you. However, in a competitive world none can deny the importance of learning, growing, changing, adapting, and improving. Justification for self-help knowledge arises from the awareness that we are not born perfect and there is a lot in us that needs to be improved, transformed, or removed. Our imperfections show up in many ways in our thinking and actions. They become self-evident when we measures ourselves against the ideals we cherish. We are not only imperfect, but we also live in an imperfect world, amidst a sea of imperfections. We are pitted against the most destructive forces of Nature, which show no mercy if we are weak, incapable, or negligent. Our imperfections and insecurities are sufficient reason why we need to focus upon change and personal growth. When we know that we can accomplish more and live a better life, it becomes our duty and responsibility to work for our betterment.

Understanding how self-help knowledge works

Self-help knowledge helped countless people in the past. Millions of people followed the methods and suggestions made by the experts and improved their lives and personalities. Many vouch its importance in overcoming their weaknesses and vulnerabilities, controlling their emotions and behavior, dealing with pain and suffering, resolving conflicts, improving communication, managing relationships, developing job skills, and so on. We know from experience shows that it is not easy to change human nature or behavior. When you want to change any aspect of your personality, you will encounter a lot of inner resistance from your own mind and body and find it difficult to sustain your progress. Self-help knowledge helps you to deal with such problems by letting you know what others have done in similar circumstances and what alternatives you can follow. It is especially found effective in facilitating the following seven fundamental processes of change and growth.

1. Preventing those aspects of your behavior which interfere with your ability to function normally and effectively.

2. Preserving and promoting what works for you, strengthens you and helps you to fulfill your aims and aspirations.

3. Creating conditions and qualities both within and without which improve your ability to resolve problems, overcome obstacles and achieve physical, mental and spiritual Wellbeing.

4. Destroying or removing what is undesirable and redundant in you so that you can overcome your imperfections and limitations and improve your character, personality, and behavior.

5. Promoting attitudes, qualities and traits that contribute to your happiness and Wellbeing.

6. Adapting and adjusting to your environment and responding appropriately to the problems and situations you face in your life with an open and flexible mind.

7. Making the best use of your resources and circumstances to maximize your chances of success, and secure peace and happiness.

As stated before, there is no guarantee that self-help books and information will help you. A lot depends upon your motivation and specific needs. Your age also plays an important role. As you grow older, your thinking, priorities and behavior change. You may also find that certain types of knowledge, solutions and techniques that were useful in the past are not useful anymore. As you grow and adapt, you will develop certain likes and dislikes, habits and behavioral patterns that prevent you from being flexible, adaptable and open-minded. Whether you are young or old, your success with self-help techniques and suggestions rests upon the following four important factors.

1. Effort: Many people read self-help books but do not follow the suggestion sincerely or practice the prescribed exercises. Genuine and sincere effort is required for success in any field and self-development is not an exception. Your thoughts and desires must be matched with suitable, intelligent, efficient and goal oriented effort

2. Precision: Precision means following the methods strictly as planned without any variations. Self-help techniques work better if you are specific in your thinking, goals and approach. Your thoughts must be clear, goals must be measurable, and your actions must be pointed. Only then you can expect positive outcomes.

3. Timing: You must practice the suggestions within the timeframe as you originally planned. If the program demands daily practice, you must practice it daily. To set in motion proper chain of events, you must stick to the schedule as planned or intended and know what to do, and when. If you do the right thing at the right time in the prescribed manner, you will achieve the expected results in time.

4. Techniques: You may customize the solutions, but you have to practice certain techniques exactly as prescribed. Otherwise, it may result in negative consequences, unexpected results, injury, or personal harm. For example, if you are required to practice certain techniques under the supervision of an experienced guide, you must follow advice sincerely and not take any liberties.

Qualities for success

Apart from the above, success in self-development effort depends upon certain important qualities such as the following.

1. Focus: Focus means the ability to remember your goals, priorities, and purpose. Failure is almost certain when you are distracted or loose focus. You can sustain your focus by constantly remembering your goals and implanting them firmly in your consciousness.

2. Perseverance: If focus is about attention, perseverance is about both focus and effort. It means you must sustain your effort in pursuing your goals and should not give up or lose your courage and conviction because of failures and setbacks. You must keep learning from them and keep trying until the end.

3. Faith: As stated before, without conviction you will not be able to use self-help knowledge effectively. To continue your effort, you must have faith in your goals, in yourself and in your actions and methods.

4. Commitment: Commitment depends upon how serious, motivated, focused, enthusiastic and hopeful you are about your goals and techniques. It comes from experience, discretion, faith and correct knowledge. With commitment you can also sustain your focus and perseve-rance and earn the trust and goodwill of others.

5. Determination: Determination strengthens your desire to achieve your goals and deal with your problems and obstacles. If you have it, you will not be deterred or discouraged by failures and setbacks. You will remain in control of the situation until you reach your goals.

The commonsense scientific approach

Self-help suggestions and techniques are meant to address specific problems and situations arising from your thinking, behavior or actions. You cannot generalize them or use the same solutions for everyone and every situation. However, most suggestions, solutions, theories, concepts, and techniques are formulated based upon a common approach involving the following four basic steps.

1. Define the problem: This is the first step, where the problem is identified, analyzed, understood, and defined. This is a crucial step because everything else depends upon how you frame the problem or relate to it.

2. Find the solutions: In this phase, you focus upon the alternatives, study the consequences, weigh your options, gather information from various sources, apply your knowledge and intelligence and formulate concrete methods and solutions to resolve the problem according to your circumstances, opportunities and resources.

3. Draw the program: In this phase, you determine your goals, techniques, action plans, precautions, and standards of performance to monitor your progress.

4. Use your methods: In this phase, you check your methods and techniques by acting upon them and subjecting them to reality check, and based upon your observation and conclusions, you will make necessary adjustments and improvements to make them more effective. You may also share your knowledge and experience with others.

Self-development is neither a mystical nor a magical process. It is based upon your perceptions, experience and behavior. It does not promise to resolve every problem you face, but offers possibilities and opportunities to change and improve your thinking and behavior so that you can reach certain goals in your life and experience fulfillment. Since you cannot change every aspect of your personality and behavior, especially those that are genetically determined, you have to be realistic in your thinking and expectations, and know what you can and cannot accomplish with its help. Even in the areas where you can expect change and improvement, a lot depends upon your own commitment, conviction, involvement and belief. As we discussed, in any self-development effort you are the one who makes the knowledge useful or useless. You are responsible for the actions your take and the change you want to bring in you. You become the subject, the object and the focal point of your actions. In the end, what matter most are your thinking, attitude and effort. Others may come and join you, but ultimately the improvement or change that you desire must happen in you and with your willful participation. If self-development subjects create in you the desire to work for your improvement or transformation, it means they have served their basic purpose.

Effective Listening Skills

Are you a good listener? Do you listen attentively with concentration? Do you listen quietly, reflectively, and unassumingly, without critical and judgmental attitude? When you do speak to others, are you motivated by a desire to prove that they are wrong, or you think you know better than them? How do you respond when you listen to ideas and opinions you dislike? Do you listen at all when others speak? These questions are worth examining to know honestly whether you are a good listener. If you want to know from others about your listening skills, you should ask your spouse, a close friend, son, or daughter for their honest opinion and they will surely give you one.

Many people think that they listen well, whereas in reality they do not. They take their listening skills for granted and do not think that listening is as important as speaking. In life, we listen selectively. The more familiar a person is, the least likely you will listen to him or her attentively, unless the situation is serious. If you want to be a good listener, you have to cultivate good listening skills and become an effective listener. It requires effort and changing of a few listening habits. It is not sufficient, if you occasionally listen with full attention. You have to do it regularly to enrich your life and benefit from your communication with others.

When I newly joined as an assistant sales executive in a private biscuit manufacturing company, my immediate boss made sure that I spoke effectively with my colleagues, dealers and customers. He closely monitored my speeches and presentations, and told me where I needed improvement. For him not being able to talk forcefully in the presence of others was like losing a grim battle in the life of a sales-executive. Unless I stood for myself and spoke confidently about my beliefs and convictions, he would ask, how could I defend anything in life, stand for others in my team, or promote the products of the company? My first boss taught me how to speak effectively and forcefully and counter any objections the customers raised, but he never told me anything about listening. He assumed that I was a good listener, since I listened to him obediently and passively most of the time, or thought that I would learn it by myself with experience. In this regard, he was not much different from others. People prefer talking rather than listening because talking gives them the false sense of control and authority. In their opinion speaking is the sure way to success. The same attitude is reflected in our culture and society. We remember the greatest speeches in the history of the world with nostalgia, but do not pay much attention to anyone who listened to others and facilitated a treaty or a peace charter.

Noise vs. silence

We celebrate noise, not silence. It is a fact. We do not celebrate silence because to celebrate anything we need noise. To enjoy an occasion, we have to shout, laugh, clap, jump, sing, dance, or set off fireworks. You cannot create all that thunder when you are silent. People like to be heard, understood, approved and appreciated through spoken words. Words give them the feeling of being alive and active. We use them to build relationships and fulfill our need for belongingness, recognition, approval and acceptance. We expect even God to speak to us in our language. The Vedas hold speech as divine and suggest that we can use the power of sounds to reach out to the gods of heaven and seek their favors. We use speech to express our deepest thoughts and feelings, assert our power and position, establish control and authority, protect and promote our desires and interests, or extend our zone of influence. We use it to improve our relationships or prove to others our skills and abilities.

When it comes to listening, we believe it is secondary and not as important. We may listen to others, but do it mostly to facilitate a conversation or extend social courtesy. For most people listening is a passive and inferior activity, and a even sign of weakness and submissiveness. As every child learns eventually, making appropriate noises attracts attention, sympathy, and even rewards from others. Hence, many people resort to speech to declare their presence, extend their influence or secure their aims. In the process, the virtues of listening are rarely appreciated, except in academic and professional fields.

The importance of listening

Good communicators know the value of listening. They will tell you that in communication listening is more important than even speaking. You learn it early in your education. If you do not listen to your teacher in the classroom and follow his lecture, you may make mistakes in your responses or will have to spend more time studying and understanding the same. Unfortunately, most of us do not remember this simple virtue later in life and are carried away by the charms of speech. Effective listening has several advantages. Speaking exhausts you, whereas listening enriches you. A speaker betrays both his knowledge and ignorance, while a listener remains mysterious and eludes others' judgment. When you listen attentively, you increase your knowledge of people and situations and your chances of becoming likable, friendly, and agreeable. People prefer being in the company of sympathetic listeners rather than garrulous speakers. They want to be heard and understood, rather than lectured and dominated. Hence, they readily open their minds and hearts to those who are willing to listen to them.

Thus, active listening is the foundation of any good conversation. If you want to be friendly with others and increase your zone of influence, you must listen to them most of the time and speak only when necessary. Those who always speak run the risk of attracting unwanted public attention and even ridicule, whereas good listeners quietly mingle with strangers and find new friends. Listening helps you to know others, gather information and build relationships. It helps you in teamwork, leadership, conflict resolution, negotiations, team building, and problem solving.

Listening does not mean you have to agree with everything or submit to everyone's opinion. It only means you have to pay attention, show respect and listen with concentration. By listening actively and paying attention, you can change the tone and tenor of any conversation. When you listen attentively, others feel comfortable in your presence and open their hearts and minds. Good listeners are enablers. They empower people. They facilitate conversation, promote understanding and diffuse tense situations. When you listen attentively, you can observe and understand others and develop a better insight into their behavior. When you speak your mind will be preoccupied with what you want to say next, whereas when you listen you have a better opportunity to relax, observe and stay with the moment.

Listening styles

Just as people differ in their thinking and behavior, there are also differences in the way they listen and react. Studies show that people use four different listening styles in their communication with others according to situation and their emotional states. While some people may show preference for particular listening styles, depending upon their needs and states of mind, most people use one or more of these in their communication.

1. Aggressive listening: In aggressive listening, the listener listens selectively and judgmentally to attack the other person, further his agenda or find fault. The focus is solely upon what the listener wants to convey, or his demands and expectations, with an intention to dominate, hurt, or prevail upon the other person, with little consideration for the information coming from the other side. People who are in positions of authority, or those who are emotionally upset, angry, afraid or resentful, usually resort to aggressive listening. This attitude leaves the other person unhappy, intimidated or frustrated. In real life, aggressive listening may take place between a parent and an unhappy child, or between a resentful superior and his weak subordinates.

2. Defensive listening: Defensive listening is also selective listening, in which a person perceives threat to one's self-esteem or pride even if there is none. As a result, the listener may interpret innocent remarks and general statements as personal attacks and feel victimized, offended or hurt. People who are sensitive, angry, or distrustful, or those who suffer from low self-esteem or persecution complex may engage in this type of listening as they feel repeatedly victimized and offended for intrinsic reasons and faulty interpretation. People who resort to defensive listening do not listen well as they try to protect and defend themselves against perceived threats even if there are none.

3. Passive listening: Passive listening is mechanical listening in which the listener listens rather passively without any reaction from his side either because he is complete agreement with it or because he is simply uninterested or indifferent. In passive listening it is difficult to know whether the other person has listened and understood the message or how it is interpreted. People may resort to this listening style, for various reasons from complete apathy to submissiveness. Passive listening is one way listening, which is not necessarily bad unless a person is engaged in an important conversation. People may resort to passive listening in social situations, where they do not want to attract attention themselves or make themselves vulnerable to criticism and controversy.

4. Active listening: Active listening is also known as reflective listening or effective listening. In active listening one listens with active engagement and reflective thinking, facilitating the communication as a two way process. It is the best listening style, where the participants listen actively and attentively, remaining in the present, and engage in the communication objectively, listening and speaking according to the situation. Active listeners listen with interest, with an open mind, and without any hidden agendas. They focus not only upon what is being said, but also upon the feelings and the people who are involved in the conversation. They use both their minds and hearts in the listening process, and respond appropriately neither to dominate nor to defend, but to know, learn and understand.

Improving your listening skills

Of the four listening styles, active listening style is the best. It leads to increased awareness, participation and better rapport. We can cultivate active listening skills with effort and become an active and effective listener. The following suggestions are useful in this regard.

1. Improve your thinking and attitude. Your listening habits are a part of your personality and a reflection of your beliefs and attitude. If you have little respect for people, do not believe in them, or trust them, it reflects in your conversation and listening habits. If you are prone to speak rather than listen, you have to examine your beliefs and habitual thoughts. You have to pay attention to your own thoughts and attitudes when you speak to them. If you treat people as your equals, you earn their trust and confidence and facilitate a two way conversation. Many are conditioned by social and cultural beliefs to speak rather than listen in social situations. While sometimes it is necessary to make your pitch or defend your position, in case of general conversations you should spend more time listening rather than just speaking about yourself. People are easily repulsed by those who are selfish and self-centered, and can see it coming even before you speak to them. Therefore, you must control your natural urge to dominate a conversation and let others participate in it. You can become a natural listener by being attentive, curios, open-minded, inquisitive, patient and appreciative.

2. Improve your auditory memory. People differ with regard to how they store information in their minds. Some store it visually as images, some as sounds, some kinesthetically as feelings and emotions. Although, most information in the human mind is stored as images, some memory is also stored as sounds and feelings. You can improve your auditory memory through active listening, by paying attention to the sounds, voices and tonalities of the people who talk to you. It may also help you to notice subtle changes in people's voices and tones, and become intuitively aware of their feelings, emotions hidden intentions.

3. Control your mental noise and self-talk. A calm and composed mind facilitates good listening experience. It is difficult to pay attention or listen when you are distracted or disturbed. One of the best ways to overcome distractions and mental noise during conversations is to make a conscious effort to stay in the present and establish eye contact. You should also learn to relax and be yourself in the presence of others. Studies show that relaxation, meditation, adequate rest, concentration and mindfulness improve your emotional states and perceptual ability.

4. Cultivate an open mind. Many factors interfere with your listening. Prejudice, preconceived notions, selective perception, habitual thoughts, learned beliefs, acquired preferences and illogical thoughts act as mental barriers and prevent you not only from listening to others but also relating to the world and deal with it with maturity, understanding and objectivity. No one can enter a closed house. The same is true with the mind. With a closed mind, you cannot listen to others without imparting your own values and judgment. Therefore, having an open mind is important for active listening. Some of the ways in which you can keep your mind open are not to prejudge people, counter your self-talk and inner chatter, not to rush into judgment, and not to go by surface thoughts. You should also learn to ask questions and seek clarifications whenever you are in doubt rather than making assumptions and drawing faulty conclusions without supporting evidence.

5. Listen with rapport and empathy. Empathy means feeling the emotion behind the words you listen, and rapport means aligning yourself mentally and positively with the other person during communication. Both are important to active listening. With empathy, you can connect to the other person both at the mental and emotional level and improve your perception and understanding. With rapport, you can make your communication pleasant and harmonious. The two are like two invisible wires with which you can connect to others and establish a deeper communication that goes beyond words, gestures and social rituals. When you bring them into play, your become intuitively aware of the other person's hidden intentions. You can develop both by becoming genuinely interested in people and paying them attention with compassion and understanding.

6. Improve your verbal skills. Language is a powerful barrier to effective communication. You can improve your communication skills by developing proficiency in both spoken and written language. It is also important how you use your language skills to communicate with others according to their level of proficiency, maturity and understanding. For example, you cannot communicate effectively with a lay person in a technical language, unless you know how to express the technical jargon in simple words. Language also plays an important role in listening. You must possess, good vocabulary, idioms and native expressions, apart from familiarity with local and dialectical variations in accent and tonalities. Knowing more than one language increases your communication reach, while with larger vocabulary you can express as well as understand complex thoughts and concepts without ambiguity.

7. Practice active listening. Active listening means listening actively with attention, respect, empathy, curiosity, and interest, without the compulsion to dominate others or defend yourself. In it, you listen not only to words and their meaning but also to the emotions and intentions involved in the communication. Studies show that many people cannot not remember or recollect much of what they listen, because they do not listen actively. Actively listening can greatly improve the quality of your relationships and communication. You can practice active listening with the help of the following suggestions.

1. Stay in the present by maintaining eye contact and paying attention to the facial expressions of the other person.
2. Keep an open mind, without rushing to judgments, and stay calm as you listen.
3. Try to be pleasant and friendly to establish rapport and facilitate ease of conversation.
4. When you listen, do not focus on what to say next but what the other person is communicating.
5. Let the other person know that you are listening, with an appropriate response such a smile, gentle nod, or "uh huh."
6. Do not interrupt the other person in the middle. Wait until he stops speaking.
7. Improve the conversation and the level of understanding with questions, clarifications or rephrasing what you just heard.
8. Avoid making any critical response to what you listen, unless it is requested.
9. Pay attention to the body language and nonverbal communication.
10. Listen for the ideas and the general drift of the conversation.
11. Let the other person know through your gestures and responses that you are genuinely interested in the conversation.
12. Avoid any facial expressions or body movements that show impatience, irritability, anger, or frustration.
13. Do not act as if you already know what the other person is going to say, or try to supply words for him to finish his statements.
14. Do not change the subject of the conversation on your own, unless the other person is ready.
15. Convey clearly what you understood and thank for the opportunity to speak to him.

Active listening does not mean that you have to remain silent or passive in a conversation, or you have to be pretentious or tactful. Imagine you have spoken to someone for half an hour and the other person just listened without any response and left you wondering what happened. In active listening you listen as well as respond appropriately.

The purpose of active listening is not to listen merely or outdo the other person, but to improve the quality of your communication and remember much of what you listen. You may also engage in it to know and understand others and improve your relationship and rapport with them. Sometimes you may have to speak for yourself or even defend yourself, but it should be done selectively rather than habitually. Under normal circumstances, you should listen actively, restraining your urge to speak aggressively or unpleasantly.

Active listeners enjoy their conversation with others. They remember much of what they listen, and participate in the process of communication solely to improve their knowledge and understanding. They speak only when necessary and listen with both their hearts and minds, paying full attention. Therefore, you should aim to become a better communicator by developing active and effective listening skills.

Critical & Analytical Reading

An important lesson which students learn early in school is that they should organize their reading material according to the needs of their class tests and grade requirements. They find that some subjects and topics need greater attention because they are either important or difficult to understand. We follow a similar pattern later in life in choosing our reading material. We learn from experience what to read and what to ignore. Using commonsense, we read what is interesting, familiar, or relevant to our lives and professions. It is true that one has to be selective in reading since there are limitations to what one can read in a lifetime. For example, you do not have to read or know about the massive storm that has been raging for centuries on planet Jupiter unless you are an astrophysicist or a space scientist. You have to read a business agreement, or a legal contract with great care and attention while you can just browse through a newspaper or a magazine. As we grow older, we also tend to develop specific reading habits and rigid attitudes which may interfere with our learning and lead to faulty knowledge and misconceptions.

The importance of reading

Reading is an important part of self-development. It is difficult to achieve success in this age without the ability to read and write. It is true that in the past people who lacked literacy skills also often achieved greatness and entered history books purely on the strength of their birth or hereditary rights. Those days are now gone. Nowadays, you cannot secure a white-collar job or career success without literacy. Indeed, in some parts of the world having proficiency in more than one language is considered an added advantage and an additional qualification.

Reading is an important mental activity. It nourishes your mind and improves your knowledge and understanding. You acquire your knowledge mostly through reading only. You may acquire some through observation and listening, but they are not as effective. Studies show that children who learn to read and write early in their lives make better progress in schools. Some even suggest that people can enhance their reading and comprehension skills using their subconscious minds, and can learn even in sleep. There is not enough evidence to know how far such methods are useful or reliable. However, we know surely that simple reading stimulates the human brain and builds strong neural networks, which leads to improved memory, knowledge and intelligence. Good education may not guarantee better knowledge and skills, but those who regularly read books and information have better chances of knowing and doing well in their lives.

Reading nourishes the mind and prepares it well for problem solving, survival, and adaptability. It helps us to grow mentally and intellectually with increased knowledge and ability to make sense of the world and adapt to the environment. As stated earlier, regular reading improves brain functioning and leads to better analytical and problem solving skills. In this information age, reading gives you competitive edge and knowledge based power. To keep your knowledge current and relevant, you have to constantly read a lot of relevant information. Rapid changes in technology and the pace at which our world has been progressing, make reading even more important. Reading is an active mental exercise, which improves your self-awareness, confidence and self-esteem, and your chances of achieving success and happiness, by keeping your knowledge up-to-date and staying ahead of competition.

Cultivating reading skills

Today, because of the volume of information that we have to deal with every day in our personal and professional lives, good reading skills have become more important than at any time in history. Information is now coming to us in many forms as books, newspapers, eBooks, websites, e-mails, blogs tweets, newsletters, magazines, memos, pamphlets, news updates, phone messages, chat messages, letters, voice mails, spam, and junk mail. If we are not selective and discreet in our reading, we will be swamped with information overload and suffer from stress and mental fatigue.

Like many other skills, reading requires effort and the use of appropriate techniques. Because of several factors, not all can equally read or grasp what they read. In this regard many internal and external factors play an important role, such as education, knowledge, language skills, thinking, attitude, interest, and a favorable environment. You might have observed that your reading and comprehension improve when you are relaxed and free from disturbances and distractions. Discipline, health, exercise, education, focus, and intelligence also play an important role. The following suggestions are helpful to improve your reading skills both for casual and serious purposes, and manage various types of reading material that you have to deal with every day.

Serious reading

Serious reading is required in both academic and professional fields. You cannot acquire mastery of any subject without it. In this type of reading, you pay close attention to what you read and try to acquire depth of knowledge. Hence, you may also call it insightful reading. It helps you to know, think, understand, remember and practice what you learn. It is especially helpful in academic study, creative problem solving, research, specialization, fieldwork, professional presentations, negotiations, arguments, debates, and discussions. It is also useful for writing technical papers, and reports, and managing complex projects. You may use it not only to understand and remember but also to assimilate and integrate the knowledge you learn. When you integrate knowledge into your mind through serious reading, it becomes your own. Serious reading is a five step process. To gain complete mastery, you have to develop skills in each of them. They are explained below.

1. Overview: In the overview, you briefly survey what you want to read, paying attention to the headlines, salient points, and overall structure of the material, with an aim to establish reading objectives, and determine the level of complexity and effort involved. You may compare it to looking at a map or driving through a town, or a street, to familiarize yourself with the area for a more detailed exploration later. Once you know the general outline of the subject, you can then focus upon specific areas of study for more intensive reading. During this phase, to be more systematic you can keep a notebook and establish your reading goals, what you want to know, what answers you have to find for the questions you have in mind, and how much time you need to complete the reading. You may also determine your further reading requirements.

2. Reading: This is where you do the actual reading and apply your mind and senses to the act of reading, keeping your mind focused, paying attention to the major concepts and ideas, and capturing the essence of what you have read. Additionally, you may also compare and contrast what you read with what you already know. This will help you to connect and integrate your current knowledge with what you already know and remember. Studies show that your reading is effective, and your comprehension and memory improve, if you relate what you read to the knowledge that is already stored in your memory. To avoid mental fatigue and strain, you should divide your reading material into small parts and rest your mind in between. At the end of each reading session, try to summarize in your own words what you have read. If you are not sure of what you understood, you should go through the material again. It is equally important to choose the right time for your reading activity. Most people find it beneficial to read when they are relaxed and feeling fresh.

3. Analysis and assimilation: Reading is one part, and remembering is another. Many people read but do not remember what they have read because they do not analyze or understand it well. What is the use of reading any information, if you do not remember or understand it in the end? You might have seen many students, who cram their textbooks or reading material just before the tests to get through. They may manage to pass or even secure good grades, but it is doubtful whether they would really learn anything. Your reading must be followed by analysis, comprehension and assimilation. You must give a thought to what you read, and examine it from different perspectives to see how you can interpret it using your own experience and understanding. Otherwise, your learning would be incomplete and ineffective. It is also not necessary that you have to blindly agree with everything you read because you cannot rule out bias and logical errors in the interpretation of the authors. If you are analytical, with a mind of your own, you can avoid this problem. One way to consolidate your knowledge is restating what you read in your own words, or explaining it to yourself. When you explain, your mind becomes lucid and you become aware of the gaps in your understanding. Another technique is to see whether you can relate the information to your own experience or to some other subject. Moreover, you can explain what you have read to others. Lastly, you may also discuss it with others and see whether you can gain further insight into the subject from them.

4. Review and revision: In this step, you review what you have read and decide whether your reading goals have been met. If you are not satisfied with the progress, you have to decide whether to read the same material a few more times, read other books about the same subject, or talk to someone who knows the subject. Each textbook comes with a bibliography, which you can use to select further reading material. You may also do Internet search or consult another person who knows the subject. As for revision, you may choose revision time according to your study needs. If the subject is important, you have to do your first revision as early as possible. In other cases, you may give yourself some time before returning to it. Depending upon the need and importance, you may choose a proper strategy to do revision. The good thing is, with each revision you will be spending less and less time to read the same material. You have to use the review and revision process to consolidate the gains you have made from your reading effort and improve your memory and recall.

5. Application: The purpose of reading is mainly to acquire knowledge that has practical value, which you can put to use in real life situations. It is not necessary to test the validity of everything that you read or learn. However, you must know how far your knowledge can be applied to real life situations and related to your own experiences, and whether it has any relevance to reality and life at all. You may also think about its future implications and the possible consequences that may arise out of its use. Your understanding and insight into the subject are complete, only when you know the practical values of the theoretical knowledge you learn. Therefore, when you are reading anything as part of your study and self-growth, try to find out how that knowledge can be used in real life and how it can help you and others.

Light Reading

Most of the reading we do is light reading. We do it to gather information about people, products, events, and current news. You use it to read newspapers, magazines, office memos, e-mails, movie reviews, pamphlets, etc. In light reading, you do not tax your brain or spend too much time pouring over the details. You read a lot, but remember only what appeals to you or interests you. Much of the light reading is passive reading. You do it to keep yourself informed and entertained. Light reading is the main source of general information in the present day world. We use it to cope with the information overload and remain in touch with the happenings around. Since it is an important source of information, we cannot ignore its importance or consider it an inferior activity. You do not need great skills to do light reading. However, if you want to benefit from it, you can use the following suggestions to improve your light reading skills.

1. Choose your reading material carefully.
2. If the information is important, read it more than once.
3. Jot down the main points if you want to use the information for future reference.
4. Try to use the opportunity to practice speed reading, which is discussed below.

Speed reading

Speed reading means reading at a faster pace and reducing the time involved in reading the same material, without compromising the quality of your reading or the gains from it. You can increase your reading speed by learning a few techniques. Even if you succeed a little, it improves your efficiency and saves your time and effort. You may use speed reading both for serious study and light reading. However, in both cases you have to use discretion, since speed reading has some drawbacks such as the following.

1. You may miss important information as you focus on reading rather than grasping.
2. You may misread information as you do not pay adequate attention to details.
3. You may not remember the details, since you may spend less time reviewing and summarizing.
4. You may read information that is not important or relevant to your life or profession

Despite these drawbacks, light reading is still important, since you can use it to save time and cover a large information base. The following suggestions are useful in this regard.

1. Read as many words as possible in one glance. Speed readers use a wider eye span and cover more words at a time, compared to slow readers who focus upon one or two words at a time and read slowly. Therefore try to increase your eye span and read as many words at a time as possible.
2. Minimize your eye movements. Your reading speed depends upon how you move your eyes from one end to another as you read. If you move them from word to word, you will take more time. Instead, you have to move them from one group of words to another or from one line to another.
3. Avoid sub vocalization. Some people read aloud and do not understand much. Some move their lips while reading silently, which is called sub vocalization or auditory reading. Both practices slow down the reading speed and interfere with comprehension. Since these habits arise due to deeper psychological problems, in some cases, professional help may be required. In other cases, one may practice the two suggestions mentioned before and resolve the problem. When you use a wider eye span and read blocks of words rather than single words at a time, you are automatically forced to avoid reading each word mentally.

Know your limitations

Reading is an important, mental and intellectual activity, which determines the quality of your thinking, choices and success. Although there is no limit to what you can potentially learn, there are limits to how much you can read and learn in your lifetime. Even if you perfect your reading skills, certain factors influence your reading habits, comprehension and learning. Considering the constraints of time and resources, you should be selective in what you choose and how much you can read. Reading is a serious, mental activity, which requires effort, interest, and concentration. You also need a favorable environment that is conducive to reading. For example, you cannot read a book seriously when you drive a car, while playing a game, or speaking to someone. You cannot read regularly if your days are hectic and you get tired in doing your day job. In such situations, you should use your time wisely, and select your reading material carefully. You may also gather information through other means, such as observation, listening, problem solving, etc.

Develop Your Negotiation Skills

You may wonder how a chapter on negotiation is going to help you. True, this article is written mainly for professional use. However, do not assume that negotiation skills are not useful to you in your daily life. Whether you know it or not, you negotiate every day, with your friends, family members, colleagues, the people and the companies you deal with, and even God. Early in life, as you begin to negotiate with your parents and peers for certain favors and concessions. You learn the importance of negotiations, as you bargain for play time, television time, or some other gain to do your homework, eat your food, or keep your room clean. Later in life, you use that skill to negotiate with other people, including your teachers and friends. You also learn that if you are not careful, others will take advantage of you or may consider you weak. Therefore, although this chapter deals with advanced negotiation techniques used by professionals, you may still find it useful in some parts.

What is a negotiation?

Negotiation is a communication process, in which we try to resolve differences and conflicts by holding discussions. In the process, through the effective strategies of cooperation, compromise, and collaboration, we build or strengthen relationships, understanding and harmony. The result of a successful negotiation is an agreement or an amicable settlement. The Constitution of the USA is a negotiated document. The treaties signed by a county are negotiated agreements. So is the paper you sign when you accept an offer of employment or hire a technician for servicing and repairing your heating and cooling system. We all use negotiations to achieve our goals, meet our expectations, protect our interests, work out a compromise or simply to avoid trouble with others. Sometimes we negotiate for ourselves, and sometimes on behalf of others as mediators or representatives.

Negotiation is also a decision making or a problem solving process, involving two or more parties, who are in a conflict and unable to reach a compromise because of conflicting interests and opposing views. In simple terms, any negotiation between two opposing sides is a kind of conflict resolution or a settlement process, in which they aim to achieve their respective goals using various means. Both communication and strategy play an important role in the successful completion of a negotiation.

From a negotiator's perspective, each negotiation is a balancing act, in which emotions have to be managed, conflicting ideas and interests have to be prioritized, solutions have to be found, and expectations have to be adjusted, before the participating parties can arrive at an acceptable and amicable solution. People in a negotiation have to deal with one important task. It is how they can maximize gains and minimize losses for all the parties involved and avoid friction and rancor to the extent possible so that in the end everyone is comfortable with the outcome of the negotiation and feel satisfied.

Phases in a negotiation process

Just as not all conflicts are alike, not all negotiations are alike. Depending upon the situation and conditions, you have to use different strategies and approaches to conduct them. Most negotiations are conducted professionally and adhere to a specific pattern involving the following four main phases: perception, preparation, resolution and post resolution. Whether we negotiate with a salesman or more formally with a builder or an organization, this is the usual manner in which the negotiations proceed. The importance of these four phases is discussed below.

Perception: This phase beings when the parties realize the need to hold negotiations to resolve their problems, or fulfill their needs and expectations. To begin the process, each side may formally express their willingness to participate in negotiations to work out a settlement or explore the possibilities of a settlement. At the same time, they may also consider other options and alternatives to see whether they can manage without holding any negotiations or an agreement. In this phase, the future of the negotiation depends a lot upon how the parties to negotiation perceive each other and how they weigh the threats, opportunities, strengths and weaknesses of each side. Further, both sides must perceive clear advantages in coming to terms. Otherwise, there will be no incentive to hold the negotiations. If only one party is interested, they have to take the initiative and sweeten the offer to compel the other side to consider the option. In case of individuals, the perception phase begins when a person becomes aware of a problem or a need and approaches another for a solution or help. Alternatively, it may begin when a person or an organization makes an offer or suggests a solution.

Preparation: In this phase, the parties agree in principle to negotiate their terms or expectations as a way forward to address their differences and arrive at an understanding. Once an explicit understanding is reached, they begin preparations to present their side of the argument. In most cases preparation involves an organized effort to gather information about the problem, determine the formalities and procedures that are necessary for conducting the negotiations, weigh the pros and cons, and play out various scenarios and contingencies that may arise. Parties may also work out place and time, goals, resources, strategy, and backup plans to deal with the outcome of the talks. In more complicated negotiations, they may gather information about the participants, decision makers, and stakeholders, their vulnerabilities and personal strengths, where they may agree or disagree, and who may create problems and obstacles and requires special attention. In this phase, both parties try to let the other side know their concerns and expectations and how they want the negotiations to proceed. In individual negotiations also the process is practically the same, where each side may collect necessary information to strengthen their arguments or counter those of their opponents. In some cases, they may consult friends, family and experts for additional advice or inputs.

Resolution: In the resolution phase, the parties focus on how to protect their interests, stake their claims, defend their positions, and meet with the expectations of the other party, without sacrificing their own. They may also decide upon how to overcome the objections and demands of the other side, without disrupting the negotiation process. The duration of this phase depends upon the nature of negotiations, the terms of the agreement and extent of differences to be resolved, and how the negotiating parties view each other. The talks will continue if both are serious about the settlement and willing to make necessary sacrifices and adjustments. This is considered the most difficult and problematic phase of negotiations, because all emotions, past differences and animosities resurface as both sides come face to face to state their terms and protect their interests. If not handled properly with maturity and skill, the whole process may collapse, making any further reconciliation between them even more difficult.

During negotiations the parties have to manage not only facts and issues but also the impressions they may create through their words and actions. They have to ensure that they put on the best show, and are not perceived as weak, vacillating, or insincere. In the end, even if the terms are unfavorable and the negotiation was largely one-sided, the losing side does not want to look as if they have lost. Since negotiations involve egos and personality issues, one cannot take the outcome for granted. As the discussions proceed, people on both sides may use tactics, power plays, and strategies to secure their aims, or coerce the other side to gain advantage. Sometimes, this phase may prolong indefinitely, if the parties are not mentally prepared to reach an amicable settlement and finalize the matter.

Post resolution: This phase begins after a settlement has been reached and a formal agreement has been signed. When negotiations are complete and the terms are finalized, both parties have to implement their side of the agreement, and fulfill whatever legal, moral, and statutory obligations they have under the terms of the agreement. If the agreement was reached without conditions, they will focus upon the terms of the agreement. If there are preconditions, they arrange to meet them before they can move on to the next phase. Sometimes it may be necessary to appoint a mediator, or an arbitrator to supervise the settlement process to ensure that there will be no further consequences. Generally, after an agreement has been signed, companies tend to review their actions to see how they fared. This phase is crucial because, if not managed well, it may result in legal disputes, delays, problems and misunderstandings. An unpleasant situation may arise if any sensitive or secret information related to the agreement or the negotiation leaks out without the consent of the parties.

Negotiation and conflict resolution

Any negotiation is essentially a conflict resolution process. In both cases the goal is how to resolve the differences and reach an understanding or agreement. How conflicts are resolved through negotiations depends upon various factors. Every negotiator needs to understand them well to improve his or her chances of success. Conflict resolution depends upon various factors, which vary in each case. However, studies show that the conflict resolution approaches used by people fall into the following five basic patterns, namely avoidance, accommodation, compromise, collaboration and confrontation. Whether the conflicts involve individuals or big organizations, the basic approaches or strategies are the same. The importance of each in the context of negotiations is discussed below.

Avoidance: In this approach, the parties remain silent and show no desire or initiative to seek any agreement or participate in any negotiations. They may do it either for emotional or strategic reasons to complicate the dispute, gain advantage, create pressure, intensify the conflict, or cause deliberate harm. Parties may avoid negotiation, if they think the relationship is unimportant, see no apparent benefit in negotiating, or do not want to face the emotional and mental turmoil. When both sides are reluctant to break the impasse, a third party intervention or a legal injunction may be required to bring them to the negotiation table and resolve their differences. Unless the conflict is unimportant or the resolution has negative consequences for one or both sides, one should not use this approach to deal with any conflict. No conflict is ever truly resolved by avoiding it or ignoring it. Hence, avoidance is the least favored strategy in negotiations unless there are valid reasons. Misunderstandings and differences arising from confusion and miscommunication should be resolved immediately. Simple conflicts can lead to bigger problems, if they are not resolved in time. If parties to a conflict are reluctant to resolve their differences, it is the duty of the negotiators to make them aware of the consequences. Negative emotions such as fear, distrust, or anger prompt many people to avoid dealing with their problems or conflicts. Cultural factors also play an important role. Some people use conflicts to display their strength or aggression. If they are weak they avoid facing their opponents, until they gain strength. For them, avoidance is a temporary strategy.

Confrontation: This is a negative, hostile and difficult approach, in which one or more parties to a dispute aim to resolve it through a flagrant display of naked power, aggression and negative emotions. The one-sided approach and frequent use of threats and coercive methods make the whole approach rather unpleasant and emotionally disturbing. People who resort to confrontation do so mainly because they refuse to acknowledge the rights of the other side and treat them as equal. They want to be heard, but do not like to listen to the arguments of the other side. They want to give nothing, but take what they want. From a rational perspective it is the worst way to settle any dispute, since it brings into play many negative emotions and leads to many complications. Confrontation is a lose-lose approach. In a game of confrontation no one wins in the end, except perhaps the middlemen and third parties. Yet, sometimes confrontation may still be useful, without the aggression part, as a strategy to deal with unrealistic demands, delay the negotiations or soften the demands and expectations of the other side until they are ready for a negotiated settlement.

Accommodation: In this approach, one side agrees to accommodate the other either because the demands are genuine and acceptable or because there is a strategic need to establish and nurture the relationship. This approach is appropriate only if the demands are genuine and the relationship between both parties is important. It is good if the accommodation is done on merits and in the best interests of all, and the beneficent party does not make a political capital out of it. However, if onside is forced to accommodate the other, under fear of threat or law, or by the intervention of a coercive third party, there will be unhappy consequences for both as their relationship is damaged forever and any future reconciliation between them becomes utterly impossible. An unpleasant situation may also arise if both do not give due credit to each other for the sacrifices they made to reconcile their differences, but try to claim victory for themselves.

Compromise: In a compromise, as the name suggests, both parties resolve their conflict by making tradeoffs, sacrifices and adjustments to their needs, demands and expectations. It is a good way to reconcile differences and establish goodwill and mutual understanding. However, any compromise is a partial or a temporary solution. It is effective only when both sides have a strong case and have to be content with some gains and tradeoffs.

Strategically it is not the best solution, since as the term implies each side should be willing to accept less than what they originally want and content with both gains and losses. Depending upon how fair and equitable the terms are and how they perceive their gains and losses, a compromise can cause disappointment and dissatisfaction, and make the parties vulnerable to criticism. For example, if the circumstances change and new facts emerge people may view the whole deal in a negative light and question those who organized and facilitated the negotiations. They may eventually become the scapegoats of a failed deal.

Collaboration: When both parties willingly and actively work together to solve a problem, explore an opportunity, or resolve their differences, it is collaboration. It is effective when the collaborating parties respect each other and willingly trust and work together to fulfill their respective obligations and find a solution or consensus. It is ideal for situations where a solution is not readily available with either party and both need to work together and pool their resources to work it out, either directly with their active participation or indirectly by forming a task- force under their joint supervision. Collaboration is also useful when the goals and interests of the parties are interconnected and a solution resulting from their collaboration benefits both. Another situation where it can be used is when both have a stake in each other's success, and the success of one party contributes to the success of the other. Collaboration is a win-win approach, even in a competitive environment where both sides can complement each other's strengths and weaknesses and work together as a team. It minimizes friction and increases understanding and cooperation. It is better than other strategies because both parties gain from the collaboration and contribute to each other's success.

The components of a negotiation

Each negotiation has two main components: the substance and relationships. The substance is the information, which is material to the negotiations and forms the basis of the communication and terms of agreement. It is the totality of what you negotiate with the other side before you formalize an agreement. The relationship is about the dynamics of the communication and understanding that exist between the people and the parties in the negotiation, and the factors that influence their behavior and decision making. In negotiations you have to give due importance to both, since they are vital to your strategy and success. In addition, you may have to pay attention to the background or the history of the negotiations also, and the people who are involved in it and responsible for it. Negotiations become increasingly difficult, if the current situation is precipitated by a series of failed negotiations, unresolved conflicts, ego clashes, and misunderstandings.

Any negotiation is essentially a civilized means to repair relationships, resolve differences, and work out mutually acceptable agreements. When you negotiate, you have to consider the repercussions your actions and decisions may have upon the agreement and upon the people who are a party to it. If you are a hard negotiator you may win the argument, but lose the relationships. If you damage a relationship, you may find it hard next time to negotiate with the same people or entities. Even when you negotiate with people who have a lesser bargaining power than you, as in case of when you deal with a supplier who depends upon you, you have to treat them well and avoid using aggression and intimidation as yours strategies to force them into an agreement. A skillful negotiator balances both aspects of the negotiation, unless there is a valid reason to choose one over the other. For example, at times, you may have to focus upon the substance and ignore the relationship, if the relationship does not matter, but the terms are important. In an alternative scenario where the relationship also matters, you may have to think of using compromise or accommodation as your strategy to reach an agreement.

Qualities of a skillful negotiator

A successful negotiator knows how to negotiate objectively without giving in to emotions and personality issues. He knows beforehand what he wants to achieve and organizes his negotiations with cautious optimism. In negotiations, it is important to know your needs and expectations as well as those of the other side, to ascertain what you can expect in the end, and whether it is worth negotiating at all. If you are not clear about your goals and terms you cannot set your terms clearly, make your demands, or deal with the contingencies when they arise. As a negotiator, you must negotiate with clarity and purpose, and prepare for the occasion well, by gathering all the required information.

You must know not only how to deal with the objections of the other side but also how to present, defend and strengthen your case. Good communication skills and an open mind are very necessary. You do not have to promise anything in advance in any negotiation, except your willingness to participate in the discussions with an open mind and present your case.

There are no shortcuts to become a skillful negotiator. You have to cultivate the skills by using opportunities, which present themselves to you every day when you speak to a salesman about a product, or service when you sign up for a service contract when you visit a restaurant, or when you meet your supervisor or employer to negotiate the terms of your employment. A successful negotiator is open-minded, mature, objective, patient, and reasonable. He is focused, assertive, practical, proactive, and adaptive. He combines in himself the roles and responsibilities of a leader, communicator, risk taker, and learner. Although he is flexible and acts differently according each situation, he is not prone to make decisions to please others or win their approval. Setbacks and failure do not deter him, as he does not take his failures personally

Guidelines for effective negotiations

Negotiation skills play an important role in shaping your life and destiny. You can use them to protect your interests, claim your rights, reach your goals, or explore various opportunities to improve the quality of your life. Using them you can not only stay ahead of competition and secure success and happiness, but also protect yourself from the greed, envy and over exploitation of others. Your success in life depends upon how you negotiate with others to achieve your goals and protect your gains. Hence, whether you negotiate for professional or personal reasons, you need negotiations skills for a better life. The following suggestions help you to improve your negotiation skills, and use the power of negotiations to secure the best things in your life.

1. Know what you want and be clear about it. If necessary, write down your goals before you negotiate with others.
2. Ask questions and seek clarifications to know what the other side wants or expects from you, and

acknowledge their right to state their terms. Unless you ask, you will not know whether you should hold the negotiations or not.
3. Do not hesitate to state clearly what you want and what you expect from the other side.
4. Understand the rules, conditions and limitations that apply to the negotiations, and the framework in which you can set your terms.
5. Keep the alternatives in your mind, but do not reveal them in advance.
6. Do not offer anything in advance, unless you are sure that the other side is willing to respond to it favorably. Make your offers or reveal your terms incrementally. Alternatively, respond to each offer with a counter offer.
7. Do not let the other side know your entire strategy in advance. Use your knowledge to your advantage.
8. Be courteous, but assertive and do not hesitate to state your terms or expectations without being aggressive.
9. Keep your cool and do not let you emotions betray your thoughts. If you are calmer and more assertive your negotiations will be more effective.
10. Try the strategies of collaboration, accommodation or compromise, before deciding to avoid further negotiations.
11. Give equal importance to both the substance and the relationship aspects of your negotiations.
12. Practice good communication skills. Listen actively and mindfully, and pay attention to both verbal and nonverbal types of communication.
13. Keep your emotions firmly under control when you are provoked or when you have to respond to emotional and stressful situations.
14. Do not promise what you cannot deliver, or ask what the other side cannot give.
15. When an agreement is reached, make sure that you understand the terms clearly. If necessary ask questions and seek clarifications.
16. Do not negotiate in a hurry, or out of fear and anxiety. If you do not have time, request for rescheduling the meeting.
17. If other people's approval is necessary, discuss with them all details and take their consent before you

agree to any terms. Many negotiations fail because of ego problems and personality clashes. Therefore, keep everyone in the team informed and take nothing for granted.
18. Negotiation itself means a two way communication process, in which there must be tangible benefits for both sides when they reach an agreement. Therefore, facilitate that two-way communication, without trying to shut down the conversation, or impose your will. Even if you are the stronger party, it is better to be courteous and make the other side feel comfortable.

For a negotiator, building relationships is an ongoing and continuous process. In most negotiations, you have to deal with human emotions and learn to keep your cool and act professionally. You have to acknowledge those who help you, and respect those who disagree with you. When your interests are at stake, you should persist in keeping the communication open, until an agreement is reached or a solution is found, without succumbing to fear, pride, anger, egoism, aggression, or intimidation. Also, when you reach an agreement, you have to keep your promises and fulfill your obligations.

Accept Full Responsibility for Your Life

It is easy to dodge our responsibilities, but we cannot dodge the consequences of dodging our responsibilities. - Josiah Charles Stamp.

You must take personal responsibility. You cannot change the circumstances, the seasons, or the wind, but you can change yourself. That is something you have charge of. - Jim Rohn.

For the truth is, we control our life. We control how lucky we are. We create our fortune with our effort. We alone have the power. - Rick Pitino, Basketball Coach.

Larry, whom I knew from a friend of mine, weighed about 260 pounds. When he looked at himself in the mirror, he did not like what he saw. His weight affected his self-esteem and made him feel bad in the presence of others. For the last several years he neglected his health, and did not do enough to remain in shape. In the past, he used to exercise few times a week. However, as his responsibilities grew, he became accustomed to sedentary life and began spending more time in front of his laptop. He knew that his boss was not very happy with him because of how he looked and would not hesitate to fire him if he got an opportunity.

Four years of neglect and resentment against himself, his boss and his company took a toll on him. He found it difficult to relax or sleep well as he was assailed by negative thoughts and negative self-talk. He ate with a troubled and guilty mind thinking of some incident or problem that bothered him. He felt pain in his feet as he walked. When he climbed the stairs, walked briskly, or carried some weight, he struggled to breathe or stand straight. He had trouble finding the right chairs to sit, as they creaked and groaned under his weight, often prompting the people nearby to exchange meaningful glances and smirks.

He had trouble getting into his old clothes or wearing his old shoes. He felt uncomfortable when he had to park his car in a faraway lane and walk some distance to reach the departmental stores. His wife and daughter would tell him that he snored loudly whenever he fell asleep and made sounds when he rolled in the bed. They were concerned about his health as they watched him struggling to walk when they went for a walk or shopping. He loved his family but felt miserable, listening to their comments. Occasionally, when he mustered his will and tried to exercise at home his body ached for rest and would not let him continue for long.

Larry's problem was self-inflicted. By not taking care of his health and fitness, he let himself down in a self-destructive way. He allowed himself to gain excess weight by eating indiscriminately and leading a sedentary lifestyle. It as if he hated himself and acted upon a death wish. In the process, he even forgot his achievements and positive traits. Except for the weight, Larry had a brilliant mind. He was smart and intelligent, and met his work goals. His health made it difficult for him to find a new job. Therefore, he stuck to his current job, even though he did not like the working conditions and the way he was treated in the office.

Yet strangely, when I first met Larry, he did not seem to accept responsibility for his problems. He felt as if he was a victim of circumstances, genes and hormones, and the world owed him an apology. He was filled with resentment against people, who he thought made fun of him and made him feel miserable. He resented his boss, whom he believed was responsible for his weight gain as he drove him into depression and made him feel sad and guilty all the time. He blamed his colleagues for their patronizing ways when they met him but laughed at him on his back. He blamed the company for promoting incompetent people because they looked smart, and ignoring very smart people who had some weight issues.

Fortunately, Larry's self-induced illusions did not continue forever. One day, he sat down quietly in his house when no one was around, and began analyzing what was going on with his life and career. As he thought about it deeply, it became clear to him that he had lost control of his life and career. He realized that he had two choices. He could either live passively letting things happen to him as he was doing before or take control of his life actively and do something about the problems that were bothering him and dragging him down He felt that things would get worse if he remained passive and self-destructive, and decided to take control of his life and resolve his current problems by doing whatever were necessary.

Once he took the decision, he created an action plan and implemented it immediately. He worked on his resume, with the help of some books he borrowed from the local library, and sent copies of it to the local recruiters and hiring companies he knew. He contacted his close friends and asked them to help him to network with important peers and people they knew personally so that he could improve his chances of finding a better job. At the same time, he also decided to deal with his weight problem as it directly influenced his morale and self-image. He visited a nearby gym and signed for a two-year contract with them. He hired a trainer recommended by the manager of the gym and began working his body under her supervision. These initial efforts tremendously boosted his morale. As he took responsibility for his life and decided to change it, he experienced new energy and enthusiasm. Within a few weeks he began receiving calls from some of the companies to which he applied.

He also realized that his weight problem was partly caused by his thinking and attitude, and in turn it affected his relationship with others as he felt miserable about himself in their presence and indulged in self-pity and guilt. Hence, he did some study, and worked on his negative self-image, using positive affirmations to present himself positively before the recruiters and hiring managers. Finally, after a few initial setbacks, he succeeded in getting a good job in a large firm. His new boss not only matched his previous salary but also promised to promote him after a year if he exceeded her expectations. His former boss tried to stop him from leaving and offered him a higher salary and a week extra leave, but he politely declined, because he did not want to be haunted by old memories and vexing colleagues.

Larry changed his ways for good. He continued to go to the gym every day and workout for more than an hour. During weekends, he also went on long walks in a nearby park. He also made some important lifestyle changes, which helped him. He changed his diet and sleeping time, and reduced drastically his daily intake of coffee and soft drinks. Within a few months, he lost a lot of weight. He was happy to see himself getting into shape, as his body responded positively to the exercise he did at the gym and the calories he burned working on the machines. He also stopped eating fast-food during lunch hours and having dinners outside. Instead he began taking healthy homemade lunch to work, which helped him not only to lose weight but also save money.

I did not see Larry for a long time when he was busy trying to get into shape. When I met him later during a business meeting, I was pleasantly surprised to see him fit, happy and healthy, as if I met his younger brother or cousin. His drooping gait and depressing looks were gone, along with the scowl that often settled in his face when he spoke about his boss. He looked healthier and younger, brimming with enthusiasm. There was a glow in his eyes and certain lightness in his walk. During the recess when I found him alone, I asked him how he managed to lose all that weight. He told me what happened and how he decided to take control of his life and responsibility for his actions.

"Are you happy with what is going on now?" I asked him.

"Absolutely," he replied with a glowing face. "I realized that I could think differently, act differently and bring some changes in my life."

"I am glad you did it, but are you sure these changes are going to be permanent?"

"Oh, yes," he replied confidently. "I want to keep doing it as long as I can. I am confident about it, but you know in the end it all depends upon me. It's what matters and it's what I need to keep remembering."

I left him later, wishing him well.

I knew Larry for some time. I knew that he was going through difficulties because of his health and overweight. I was happy to know that he changed his thinking and took personal responsibility for his life. What he did was very exemplary. He made a life-changing decision and went with it. It is not easy for anyone to break out of old and habitual patterns of thinking and behavior, without building the resolve. He did it and won an internal battle. By taking control of his mind and body, he changed his thinking, habits, beliefs and responses to the problems he faced and the doubts he harbored. He took responsibility for his actions, health and happiness. Instead of indulging in self-pity and letting destructive forces consume him with negativity, responded positively and constructively to a serious situation in his life. He left behind what happened to him before, and chose a new alternative, accepting him as the source of his problems and well as solutions.

Larry was one of the few fortunate people, who chose not to become passive spectators of their own lives. He seized a negative condition in his life and used it to build himself. The truth is, we are mostly responsible for what happens to us in our lives. People may accuse others, or blame their fate and unseen forces when they face problems. The fact is we precipitate many situations in our lives through our actions, inactions, and choices, and even interfere with our destinies. We create our lives, with our thoughts, actions, aspirations and emotions.

You may blame others, God, or fate for your suffering and live in a state of denial. You may hold your parents, friends, spouse or family members responsible for your difficulties and blame them for the turn of events in your life, whereas, you and your life are largely in your hands. They are shaped by your thoughts, desires, decisions, actions, beliefs, and prejudices. Others may interfere with your life, only to the extent you allow them.

Much of your childhood is not under you control, since it happens largely according to the wishes of your parents and elders as they try to bring you up according to their values and beliefs. However, when you grow up, and assume responsibility for your life you become its author. You become the writer, producer, director and the main character of the tragedy and comedy that you create in your life. You write the screenplay. You invent the characters and the situations, and you act in it. Some people never grow up and do not assume that personal responsibility, as it happened in case of Larry before his transformation. Many problems arise when we give away the ownership of our lives to others and choose to live like passengers on an airplane run by others.

You are creating your life, right now at this very moment, as you think, sleep, or dream. Events that are seemingly beyond your control are in fact your own creations. If you analyze them and trace back their root cause, you will know the truth. Your current life is a culmination of your past actions. Knowingly or unknowingly you draw to yourself what you like or dislike, and if you are not careful you may accumulate enough negativity that you will find difficult to resolve. Circumstances may create problems for you, but your solutions must come from within and you must put them into action with resolve. Even to watch a game of professional football as a spectator in a large stadium, it costs money and effort. To live like a spectator of your own life, it costs even more, while the entertainment you get is much less.

If you want to realize your dreams, you must take responsibility for your life and actions. You must find your purpose in life, set up long term and short term goals, and work for them. When you make mistakes, you must correct them; when you damage relationships, you must rebuild them; when solutions do not work, you must find new ones; and when problems arise, you must show courage and initiative and take timely actions. This is the way forward to make things happen instead of letting them happen. When you realize this truth, you will not only succeed in reaching your goals and dreams taking control of your life but also stop blaming others for your problems and suffering. Whether you believe it or not, as far as your life is concerned the buck stops with you. Whether you like it or not, the government does not monitor your life or shape it. You are the controller of your life and the master of your mind. You may seek the help of God, or people in your life to resolve your problem and reach your goals, but ultimately the choices you make, actions you take and the problems you choose to solve, which largely determine the course of your life, are your responsibility. Even when others control your life, it happens because you let it happen.

You can participate in life and position yourself in the world in two ways: either actively and attentively creating your own life and destiny with your thoughts, actions and words or passively and carelessly as a spectator, letting things happen, not responding to problems and difficulties and holding others responsible for your life and problems. It is difficult to find people who fit exclusively into either of the categories. In most cases, people vacillate between these two models. Even in this regard the responsibility rests with individuals, since they decide about what they want to control about themselves and where they prefer letting others control them. There will be times when you can do nothing about what happens to you, like for example, when you are hospitalized and bedridden. Even there, you will have opportunities to control certain aspects of your treatment, recovery and recuperation.

When you accept responsibility for your life, you bring a paradigm shift in your thinking and attitude as you look to yourself for solutions and analyze your thoughts and actions to see how they are shaping it, rather than complaining and blaming others when you face difficulties. You may still blame others, but only in the context of how you let the problems arise. When you analyze and introspect your actions and decisions, you learn from your own experience, which in turn will help you to become better in what you do. This is the most important blessing of taking responsibility for your life and responding to your problem with a self-directed effort. There are other benefits also which stem directly from this effort. As you take charge of your life and act responsibly, you will see improvements in your leadership ability, decisiveness, timing, confidence, dynamism, attentiveness, responsiveness, self-esteem, mental clarity, purpose and self-awareness. You become more organized and effective in setting goals, using resources, correcting mistakes and persisting in your effort.

You can use these principles, as Larry did, and change your life for good. You can begin by taking up some aspect of your life, with which you are not happy, and analyze it to know how you let that happen and what solutions you can find on your own. If you cannot find solutions on your own, you may have to find help from others. However, in both cases the final decision should be yours. Living responsibly means you have to bring out your uniqueness, your individuality, and your best skills into play. In any case, your transformation has to begin from within, and the reigns of your life must be in your control. The motivation to do or not to do anything has to come from within. With faith in yourself and determination you can use the following suggestions to take control of your life and shape it according to your desires and expectations.

1. Understand that you alone can change your life. You cannot change others unless you have considerable control over them, but you can surely change yourself in many respects because your mind and body are within your control, while others are not. To think that you can change others is an illusion. By exercising your will, you can change your thoughts, your goals, your attitude, your actions and your behavior. You can do it through auto suggestions and by establishing concrete goals and quantitative standards to monitor your progress.

2. Stop blaming others. There is no point in blaming others. Even if they are at fault, recognize your role in letting them do it. Accusations and faultfinding will lead you to nowhere. If you think others have seriously wronged you, accept responsibility for your role in it and do whatever is necessary to prevent it from happening again.

3. Stop complaining about myriad things in your life, over which you have no control. Stop criticizing the social, political, or economic conditions, and institutions for your problems. Ignore the media-noise. You have no control over the world. No one has. However, you can control how you can relate to it and make a difference through your actions. Therefore, focus upon what role you can play in society as an individual within your limitations, and what difference you can make through your contribution.

4. Begin to pay attention to yourself and know how your thoughts, actions and decisions are shaping your life and leading you into future. Learn from your experiences. Learn from others by watching them or knowing about them. Improve your self-awareness by observing how you act or react in specific situations and what you can do to improve your knowledge, skills and your responsiveness.

5. Learn from your mistakes and failures. When things do go wrong, ask yourself questions like, "Why I made this happen? Why I attracted this situation? What thoughts and actions precipitated this reality?" From the introspection, you will learn about the causes of your mistakes and take corrective action. Your mistakes and failures should help you to know your imperfections and deficiencies, and the improvements you should bring in your thinking, attitude, and actions.

6. Minimize your expectations and dependence upon others about your personal matters. Instead, you should have an expectation from yourself. When you seek the help of others or expect any help from them, make sure that you communicate well and monitor the progress, since it is you who are getting the help, and your interests are at stake.

7. Establish positive and fulfilling relationships. You are responsible for the relationships in your life. You have to decide which relationships you want to strengthen and which you should ignore. Each relationship is a two way process. When you build relationships with others, recognize their rights and your responsibility in honoring them. Acknowledge their value and importance in your life. Relationships are like trees. If you nurture them, they grow. Otherwise, they will wilt and die.

8. Pay equal attention to your actions and goals because both are important to create the life you want to lead. You should set your goals according to your skills and abilities, and match your actions with the goals you want to achieve. To achieve anything in life, you should have clearly defined goals and action plans.

9. Do not make any excuses for your failures. When things go wrong, accept responsibility and work out better alternatives. Do not blame extrinsic factors when you do not reach your goals. Failure is an essential part of the progress. When you accept failure for what it is, it becomes a learning opportunity. Do not let any failure impair your ability to stay motivated and take corrective actions.

10. Focus upon how you respond and interpret your experiences. You may not have control over the situations in your life, but you can control your responses. When certain situations in your life trouble you, analyze your thoughts and emotions and examine whether they are triggered by irrational beliefs and habitual thought patterns. By learning to control your responses to external events and changing your perception of them, you can greatly control your behavior and responses.

11. Use positive affirmations to take responsibility for your life and keep yourself motivated. You may use the following affirmations every day, until they become part of your thinking and behavior.

- I take complete responsibility for my life.
- I can make things happen or not happen.
- I am in charge of my life.

- I am responsible for my life and destiny.
- I may not have control over every situation, but I can control my responses and perceptions.
- I create my future largely through my thoughts, words and actions. I therefore pay close attention to my thoughts and emotions.
- I recognize other people's right to be themselves and live their lives according to their expectations.
- I can change myself and my actions with resolve.
- I create my life with my thoughts, desires and beliefs. I attract things into my life according to my fears and expectations.
- I refuse to interact with negative people, and I will not let them control my life or destiny.
- I refuse to live my life passively. I take action to resolve my problems and reach my goals.
- I forgive others so that I can move forward and let the past bury itself.

This planet belongs to a multitude of living beings, not just humans. We come here as guests, enjoying the hospitality of the earth. We may own things. We may celebrate our victories or stand apart from others in what we do and how we think. However, but none of this matters, if we spend our lives here feeling miserable and depressed. Just as we share the environment, we also share many common problems the world faces today. However, not all react alike to them or live their lives alike. When there is a crisis, some panic and loose hope, while some remain calm and rise to the occasion. Some live in self-denial, while some acknowledge the situation and accept the reality. You can always do something about any problem or situation in your life. You may not have control over the world or people, but you do have control over your thoughts, actions and reactions. It is how you think, act, react or respond to external situations, which matters. It is where you can assume responsibility for your life and empower yourself to make things happen.

Therefore, take charge of your life today and accept responsibility for everything that happens to you. Make things happen, through your thoughts, dreams and actions. The sun may rise in the east without your permission, but you can decide when to wake up and how to spend your day. Do what is possible and what you can control. You are the lone warrior, who has to shape your own destiny and work out your own salvation. When you sit on a horse, you have to hold the saddle. You cannot let others hold it for you.

Coping With Fears

Fear is an adaptive, learned, and conditioned response to any perceived threat. The threat may be real or imaginary. Fears caused by real threats are normal, but those caused by imaginary ones are not. The latter are known as phobias or irrational fears, which leave a crippling and disabling effect upon people who experience them. To overcome them, professional help is required. This article is about ordinary fears, which people experience in normal situations, and which may interfere with their decisions and actions and prevent them from being who they are and what they can actually accomplish in their lives.

Our response to fear usually falls between the two extremes of avoidance and escape or confrontation. Simply speaking, they are the instinctive flight or fight responses, which both humans and animals use when they are threatened as their survival strategy. When we perceive a threat, depending upon the situation, we may act instinctively, emotionally, impulsively, rationally or irrationally. We may act with wisdom and knowledge, or with ignorance and delusion. Since we are prone to desires, expectations, beliefs, and values, we do not always respond to fearful situations in the same manner. When we are afraid, we may overreact, under react, ignore, suppress, strategize or just withdraw. Our response in each case depends upon how we perceive the threat and weigh the risks.

How fear manifests in our lives

Fear rules our minds and hearts, and affects the quality of our lives, success, thinking, and wellbeing, apart from how we deal with the problems we face in our lives. It is said that most of our emotions are variations of the same primal fear since they are produced by its presence or absence. In daily life, we experience fear in various forms as worry, insecurity, anxiety, insecurity, alarm, concern, fright, hesitation, apprehension, tension, nervousness, timidity, dread, horror, panic, breakdown, hysteria, palpitation, terror, and nightmare. We also experience it as lack of self-confidence, courage and conviction. When fear persists for long, we may experience stress and depression, but when it is resolved, we feel happy, relieved and relaxed. Thus, fear is the commonest, dominant and persistent feeling or emotion that we experience. Following are a few well-known fears we frequently experience in our lives.

- Fear of having what we do not want to have.
- Fear of not having what we want to have.
- Fear of losing what we love most.
- Fear of being stuck with what we hate.
- Fear of failure and fear of success.
- Fear of being lonely and fear of being in the company of difficult people.
- Fear of being caught doing something wrong.
- Fear of being criticized and ridiculed.
- Fear of hurting people or being hurt by them.
- Fear of pain and death.
- Fear of asking and fear of rejection.
- Fear of darkness, ghosts, demons, the unknown and the mysterious.
- Fear of losing control.
- Fear of conflicts and confrontation.
- Fear of losing one's money, honor, power, prestige, status, self-esteem and recognition.
- Fear of authority.
- Fear of wild animals, snakes and reptiles.
- Fear of intimacy and fear of being ignored and neglected.
- Fear of aging, sickness, injury and death

Our fears are conditioned or learned responses to external threats. Unless we know what caused them, we cannot deal with them effectively. Sometimes, we fear for no particular reason, even when commonsense suggests otherwise because the incidents connected to such fears many invoke in us negative memories and produce anxiety. Our fears are also aggravated by our thoughts, imagination, exaggeration, and pessimism, which makes our task of coping with them difficult. Some fears are caused by our subconscious minds. They are even more difficult to resolve, because we cannot easily ascertain their causes, as they remain hidden in our forgotten past.

How we experience fear

We experience fear as part of our survival instinct. Some fear is necessary and normal, because it keeps us within our bounds and alerts us to the threats present in our environment. It becomes a problem when we experience it without any real threat or when we experience it frequently and persistently insofar as it interferes with our health and wellbeing. We react to fears both physically and emotionally. When we are afraid, we experience several physical sensations in our bodies, including shaking and nervousness. The following are a few physical symptoms produced by the fears we experience.

- Sweating or perspiration
- Physical and mental tension
- Palpitation of the heart
- Shaking of the body and limbs
- Increased blood flow
- Dilation of the pupils
- Knots in the stomach
- Dryness in the mouth and throat
- Heaviness in the head
- Lack of hunger
- Indigestion
- increased blood pressure
- Sleeplessness
- Muscular and bodily tension
- Restlessness
- How fear influences our thinking

Fear regulates our lives in many ways. It is always present latently in our minds, even when we are safe, because a threat can surface anywhere and anytime without notice. During our lives, we become so accustomed to our surroundings that we may not even notice our fears when they are under a tolerable threshold. For example, when you walk down a staircase there is fear in the back of your mind, but you will not notice it because the threat is not serious enough. Fear limits our abilities, expectations, aspirations and hopes. Because of fears, we settle for less and compromise with many situations. When we are afraid, we do not negotiate well, feel empowered to protect our interests, defend out rights, or speak for ourselves. It is out of fear that we settle for less and submit to failure when we ought to be persevering to reach our goals. Thus, fear acts like the controller of our consciousness when we ought to be in control, and regulates the pace of our actions, the quality of our lives and state of our minds.

The following list contains a few important emotional and behavioral responses people are prone to show under fear. They indicate how fear shapes our lives and behavior and how it limits our abilities, opportunities and potentialities. When they are afraid, people show the following behavior.

- Stay within their comfort zone and refuse to take chances with new people, things and situations.
- Hide their true feelings, thoughts, and intentions in front of others, for fear of inviting their disapproval, anger and criticism.
- Remain stuck in their lives, doing the same job even when there is no satisfaction or opportunity to grow, following the same routine, even if it is boring, and clinging to relationships that are abusive.
- Do not defend their freedom and their rights.
- Easily give up.
- Are easily discouraged.
- Do not finish what they begin.
- Lack initiative.
- Do not take risks or try new methods and solutions.
- Constantly underestimate their skills and abilities.
- Negotiate poorly and settle for less, because of their low expectations and low self-esteem.
- Sabotage their own lives, by indulging in self-defeating and self-limiting acts.
- Are constantly haunted by their negative self-talk.
- Rarely trust others.
- Feel self-conscious in the presence of others.
- Think that they do not deserve a better life.
- Suffer from anxiety and depression

Coping with fear

Our response to fearful situations is conditioned by both intrinsic and extrinsic factors, and by both rational and irrational causes. Social norms, moral values, our own perceptions, beliefs and early childhood experiences play an important role. Recent studies indicate that even genetic factors may play a role. Prolonged neglect in early childhood, physical and mental abuse, natural calamities, accidents, unexpected injuries and financial losses, the death of near and dear, and similar traumatic experiences leave their lasting influence upon people and shape the way they respond to fear causing situations. However, since our fears are mostly learned responses, and since we can trace their causes, we can manage to control our fears by changing our thinking, attitude and responses. This seemingly simple approach however requires persistent effort before you can expect positive results. The following suggestions are helpful to deal with your fears.

1. Change your responses: You can control your fears, by thinking and responding differently to the situations that produce them. You can do it by paying attention to your habitual thoughts and knowing how you make yourself afraid with your thoughts so that you can think differently and respond differently to similar situations. It takes time, but once you know what thoughts create fear in you and how you make yourself vulnerable to it, you can dispute your own thinking and gain control over your emotions. This approach is based upon the principle that you cannot control external situations that induce fear in you, but you can control your responses to it and manage your fears as well as fearful situations. For example, you can train yourself to remain calm and thoughtful when you face a problem, instead of letting your mind picture the worst and produce negative emotions. You may also learn to dispute your irrational thoughts and beliefs that produce or aggravate fear and think about solutions to deal with it.

2. Practice visualization: While your fears may be produced by external situations, it is in the mind where you have to resolve them primarily and win your battles. You can do it by practicing visualization. It is the easiest and the best technique to prepare yourself mentally and emotionally to deal with your worst fears, since it helps you to change your thinking and responses and remain calm when they really happen. With visualization you can create in your mind the exact incidents that trigger your fears and use your imagination to visualize different ends using different responses and approaches. You can also replace your negative emotions with positive ones to build courage and confidence and empower yourself. For example, if you are afraid of speaking in public, visualize yourself speaking confidently in front of a large audience and hearing their appreciation and applause. If you are afraid of negotiating a pay rise, visualize yourself talking to your boss in a confident voice, and with a confident posture, stating the reasons why she should consider the raise. You can use visualization to change your response to any situation that habitually provokes fear in you, by visualizing the fear producing situation first, and visualizing a different response, which in our opinion is the best. Visualization is perhaps the easiest, safest and most effective technique to manage your fears in the very arena of your own mind where your fears are produced. In practicing it, you have the opportunity to bring out your fears into open and learn to deal with them rationally, apart from the freedom to experiment with various responses and outcomes without having to really experience them. For best results, you have to make your visualization as realistic as possible, visualizing all sensations and circumstances, including the feelings, and emotions associated with it.

3. Use positive affirmations: Your self-talk is both your friend and enemy: a friend when it motivates and inspires you, and an enemy when it makes you feel anxious and afraid. In fearful and vulnerable situations, you can potentially increase your negativity and weaken your resolve with self-criticism. One of the best ways to deal with the persistent thoughts that arise from negative self-talk in fearful situations is by using powerful positive affirmations that can boost your confidence and empower you to act rationally even in the face of fear. When you hold yourself responsible for any negative situation and keep feeling guilty and anxious about it, use affirmations to regain control over your emotions and stay in control. You can also use them to counter your self-deprecating thoughts that aggravate your fears and remain focused upon the solutions, instead of the problems.

4. Stay in the present: Many fears that we experience currently are produced by habitual thoughts and responses that we learned in the past. When we face situations that are similar to the ones that produced fear in the past, we may experience fear again, even if those conditions are not as serious. It is because certain memories remain deeply embedded in our minds and continue to influence our thinking and behavior ever after we become adults. When those memories are triggered by any current events, we tend to react as before and experience similar emotions. It is as if parts of our minds are frozen in the past and did not change with time. We can deal with this problem by analyzing our past, and knowing how we learned to act and react in certain ways. When we become aware of the hidden mental programs that guide our behavior, we can teach ourselves to act and react differently and break free from mental habits and conditioning. When your fears are caused by habitual thought patterns, you can remember that you are no more the person you used to be and the conditions and circumstances governing your life have changed. By affirming this truth repeatedly, you can break free from your past and deal with your current fears with maturity.

5. Practice detachment: When we are mentally attached to things and people, we experience fear and anxiety. The thought of losing them worries us. We react in this manner because of the attachments that we form in our lives. Life is uncertain. Change is the order of life. What we have today, we may lose tomorrow. In this world, no one can correctly predict the future. We cannot take anything for granted, except perhaps death. Regarding it also we are not sure how and when it may really happen. Therefore, unless you are ready for the uncertainties of life and your eventual separation from everything that you own and love dearly, you will be vulnerable to fear and anxiety. We can cultivate detachment by focusing upon the transient nature of the world in which we live and of the things to which we cling dearly. With the practice of detachment comes the inner freedom from the things that hold you in their grip and make you vulnerable to fear and anxiety. If you practice detachment, you will think clearly without prejudice and emotions, and you will see the world with awareness and understanding.

6. Practice yoga: If you have a problem practicing yoga because of your religious beliefs or convictions, you may skip this suggestion and go to the next. Yoga is the most ancient, but still a very useful and practical method to control your mind and body and experience peace and relaxation. The system of yoga, which was found in ancient India over three thousand years ago, helps you to get rid of the negativity, toxins and impurities present in your mind and body, which prevent you from seeing the world clearly and experiencing peace and happiness. With the practice of yoga, you can learn to stay in control of your thoughts and emotions and perceive the world with greater clarity and understanding. People from various social and religious backgrounds found yoga effective to control their thoughts and emotions and reduce their stress levels. Yoga is not just a traditional method of exercising your body. Its main purpose is to help you to achieve self-control so that you can see the world objectively, without the interference of your desires, beliefs, emotions, feelings, thoughts and memories. It is the tested method to cultivate stability.

The ancient classical yoga offers several techniques such as breath control, mind-control, body postures, concentration and meditation with which you can look into yourself and know more about yourself. By practicing yoga you can calm your nerves, and deal with situations that produce fear and anxiety. There is no magic here. For any problem the real solution is knowledge. As you gain a deeper knowledge of yourself through concentration and meditation, you learn about your fears and anxieties as well as their causes and remedies. When you find the root causes of your fears you will know what to do with them. Yoga gives you strength to withstand the uncertainties of life by controlling your own thoughts and attitudes. It does not promise to change the world for you, but your own perception and awareness of it, so that you can see the world and you with greater clarity, purpose and wisdom. You may learn more about yoga by reading books about it or practicing it under the guidance of an experienced yoga teacher.

7. Practice positive thinking: When we are afraid, we inflate our fears by expecting and imagining the worst. In some people it can happen even with mild fears. It can get worse in some because of negative self-talk. When things go wrong, people lose their sense of reality and mentally enact negative scenarios, expecting the worst to happen. Early childhood experiences can cause persistent negativity in people and induce them to imagine the worst. However, our negativity does not necessarily arise from imagination and exaggerated thinking only. It can also arise from real threats in life, which need to be resolved effectively. It is difficult to foresee positive outcomes when the threat is real and when you have seen and experienced negativity from many sides. You cannot easily convince people about the virtues of positive thinking if they have been hurt and harmed in the past by those whom they trusted. Therefore, negativity cannot be considered a problem of thinking and attitude only. It should be addressed appropriately when the threats are real with effective and rational solutions that can restore the balance and create a sense of security. The best antidote to a real fear is quick and timely action. If it is unreal, you have to dispute the irrational beliefs and underlying assumptions with facts and reason. Positive thinking can be cultivated by subjecting negative thoughts and irrational beliefs rational fact check, questioning your assumptions, and seeing possibilities and opportunities in problem situations instead of worst case scenarios. You can also use visualization techniques and positive affirmations to deal with your negative thoughts and imagination.

8. Learn to let go of things: Sometimes, it is very difficult to get rid of the feelings and thoughts associated with our fears. We keep returning mentally to the same thoughts and memories that trigger the fear and find it difficult to forget the whole experience. In most cases, this happens not because of the apparent causes that led to the fear, but deeply hidden attachments, which we form with certain beliefs and notions about ourselves. For example, if you are deeply attached to your own sense of self-importance or your own image in public, you may be unduly worried that the situation which produced the fear may also lower your image and prestige in public.

Thus, our attachments can aggravate our fears or lead to new fears. Fears that result from our attachments usually fall into two categories: fear that we may lose what we love dearly, and fear that we may come into contact with what we detest and dislike. Both create in us fear and anxiety, from mild to severe levels. For example, fear of loss, fear of failure, fear of aging, sickness and disease, fear of poverty and adversity, and fear of rejection are caused by our clinging and attachment. From a worldly perspective we cannot treat all types of clinging alike and simply let go of everything. We need certain things and relationships for our peace, happiness, success and fulfillment. However, at the same time, we cannot hold on to things that make us weak and vulnerable to suffering, anxiety and negativity. For example, many people carry the burden of their past and keep suffering for the situations that happened before. They cannot let go of the negative feelings and emotions associated with them or forgive those who caused them. By forgiving those who harmed us in the past and by accepting our past as a learning experience, we can let go of our unhappy past and get rid of the fears arising from them.

9. Keep yourself healthy and happy: Good health contributes to peace and happiness, while ill health can lead to depression, fear and anxiety. A healthy body contributes to a healthy mind and a healthy mind to a healthy body. Some of the fears people experience in their daily lives are directly related to their health. Presently, in many parts of the world life has become increasingly complex. For many people, prolonged ill health means loss of their jobs and a certain decline in their living standards. This is especially true in case of those who depend entirely upon their physical strength to earn their livelihood, since even a minor health problem can result in loss of income, fear and insecurity for them. The same holds true in case of many skilled workers who cannot survive without a regular job. In present day society, where competition is acute and companies are primarily focused upon profit, and where old family values have perished, people's livelihood and living standards very much depends upon their health and earning capacity. Thus, health problems are a major source of fear, worry and anxiety in the present day world. Old age also brings in its wake its own problems, as old people find it increasingly difficult to stay healthy and competitive and meet the expectations of their employers. None can escape from aging or the health problems resulting from aging. We cannot also completely avoid health problems or the prospects of ill health. However, we can minimize the health risks to which we are exposed by cultivating clean habits, eating healthy food, following a healthy lifestyle, keeping our minds active and healthy, and going for regular medical checkups.

10. Take action and resolve your problems in time: Ravi, a friend of mine kept complaining about pain in his left arm for several days, but did not go to the emergency until the problem became acute. He hesitated because he was afraid of going through the medical tests and facing the reality that might eventually emerge. A few days later, he had a massive heart attack and had to be admitted in emergency. The best antidote to any fear is facing it and taking timely action. Many fears, which arise from real problems in our lives need to be resolved in time. They cannot be neglected, postponed, or wished away, since the delay can lead to other problems. Take an inventory of the problems that you have either postponed or neglected so far because you do not want to deal with them or afraid of dealing with them, and see what you can do about them. It is the best way to deal with your fears and build confidence and self-esteem.

11. Accept yourself unconditionally: If you frequently suffer from self-doubt and negative self-talk and do not feel good about yourself or your abilities, you will not be able to deal with your fears confidently. Those who face a lot of criticism in their early lives become fearful by nature. They suffer from persistent doubts about their abilities and competence, and prefer avoiding situations that produce fear and anxiety rather than facing them. Low self-esteem puts a dent upon one's abilities and self-confidence. Those who suffer from it also indulge in self-sabotage, since they believe that they do not deserve success and happiness or they cannot manage success and happiness. Such people prefer living in their comfort zones rather than venture out and take a few risks to better their lives. Hence, it is necessary that you accept yourself unconditionally and not subject yourself to cruel self-criticism and negative self-talk even when you fail and falter. When you make mistakes you have to forgive yourself, while you may learn from them, and give yourself a chance to be happy and successful. If you are prone to low self-esteem, you have to keep affirming to yourself that you deserve a better life and you are good at whatever you do. Occasional failures and setbacks should not stop you from facing your fears and taking necessary action.

Fear is the most dominant emotion in our lives. It is part of our survival instinct. Many emotions that we experience are indeed variations of fear only. Therefore, accept your fear as a part of your identity and consciousness, without feeling guilty or inadequate. Know that you cannot eliminate fear from your mind, but can only proactively manage your fears by thinking about them and responding to them differently.

What You Can Learn From Successful People

Successful people are pathfinders. You can learn a lot from them by following their examples and techniques. They raise the standards of human achievement and show you what anyone can do with a given mindset, within the limitations to which you are subject. You can learn from them and even surpass them, writing your own stories of grandeur and excellence. Next time, when you read about successful people, pay attention to the exceptional qualities, which contributed to their success. See whether you can cultivate some of them and improve your chances of success.

The seven practices of successful people

The following principles and practices are gleaned from the lives of successful people. You can use them to boost your performance and realize your goals and dreams.

1. Successful people build their success around their strengths: Successful people rely upon the skills in which they are proficient. They make their best use, doing what they love and excel in it. They know clearly their strengths and weaknesses, and plan accordingly. They are realistic enough to accept their strengths as the foundation upon which they can build their success, while devising suitable strategies to work around their weaknesses. They know that as human beings they cannot do everything on their own and for certain tasks they have to depend upon others or use their knowledge and skills to compensate for our own weaknesses. By using such clever strategies, they focus on their strengths and maximize their chances of success.

Working upon your strengths and compensating for your weaknesses is perhaps the best strategy that you can learn from successful people and use it in any profession you pursue. Whether you are an employee or an entrepreneur, you can put this strategy to work for you. Besides maximizing your chances of success, it will help you to reduce overexertion, chances of failure and unnecessary stress. Therefore, to achieve success in your life, you should make a realistic assessment of your strengths and weaknesses, and what you can or cannot do on your own in a given situation. Using your strengths as your prime resources to reach your cherished goals, you can build your dreams around your goals. In this regard, you can use the suggestions mentioned in the following paragraphs.

Make a list of your strengths and weaknesses. Take professional surveys and personality tests to know what you are good at. Ask for comments from your friends and family members what they think about you. Grade your strengths and weaknesses on a scale of one to ten to know exactly where you stand regarding each of them. Now, find out your dominant desires and passions and see what you can do to satisfy them, using your strengths. It may be your communication skills. It may be your extroversion. It may be an artistic talent, intuitive ability or salesmanship. Identify your passions, connect them to your strengths and create your central goals and purpose to create the life you dream. Once your goals are in place, see what you need to do to reach them. See how far your strengths will help you and how far your weakness will hamper you. See what you can do to overcome them.

For example, you may be good at writing and want to start a writing career through a blog or a website. However, you may not know much about the technology or the programming skills needed to create the website. You may seek the help of either a web designing company or a professional webmaster to build one for you, or you can find a web hosting company, which can provide you with the necessary tools to build one by yourself without any programming knowledge. Internet and local chambers of commerce and association are the best sources to know where you can find professional people with necessary skills to complete your projects.

Sometimes, you may find it necessary to work upon your weaknesses and improve them. On such occasions, you have to see the costs, time, and effort involved. It is much better, if you can frame your goals in such a manner that you do not have to rely frequently upon your weaknesses. However, it may not be a right strategy to build your success solely based upon your strengths, since it may limit your opportunities for success. Hence, you need a strategy which will enable you to remain focused on your strengths and work around your weaknesses.

Not all are fortunate enough to get a job of their dreams. What would you do if you are stuck in a job that you do not like? If you are smart, you can still find ways and means to express your talents and use your skills to boost your career or professions. You can talk to your boss or your colleagues to see how best you can utilize your talents and make a name for yourself. If you are not willing to take major risks, you can use your talents to make extra income in spare time. If you are in a business or a profession, you can work around your weaknesses by finding a business partner who can take care of the areas where you are weak, or you may hire an independent professional or an employee who can do the work for you. You can also contract your work to another firm after negotiating the terms. When you choose any of these options, you have to make necessary inquiries to minimize your costs and the risks involved.

We do hire professionals to work for us where we do not have skills or knowledge, such as tax and legal consultants, but we do not follow the principle consistently or utilize our strengths adequately. Most people entertain such rigid beliefs and prejudices that they do not allow even their children to pursue their education according to their talents and passions. They want them to pursue their dreams according to their own expectations and failed ambition rather what their children really want to do in their lives, whereby the children may spend the rest of their lives in frustration blaming their parents and themselves for their unhappiness.

By answering questions such as the following, you can know whether you are building your success around your strengths or weakness.

- What are my strengths and weaknesses?
- Am I using my strengths adequately?
- How am I coping with my weaknesses?
- How can my strengths improve the quality of my life?
- What is my passion? Am I using my strengths to express it?
- Was there an occasion when I was happy because I was able to use my talents and skills well and win recognition and appreciation?

Your desires are the doors through which your heart speaks to you about your goals and dreams. Listen to your inner longing, what you want to do or achieve in your life, and what makes you happy and fulfilled. Pay attention to the level of comfort you experience in doing things and studying subjects. Find out what you can do easily, what comes to you naturally, and which goals according to you express your life's hidden purpose. Success does not necessarily come from a heroic struggle or pure hard work, unless you match your vision with your passions and try to build your life around it with well-defined goals and good strategies. Know what you are and what you can do easily, and pursue it with resolve and intelligence, until the doors of success open to you.

2. Successful people are goal oriented: Successful people employ their energies and attention in the direction of their goals, prioritizing their resources according to their needs and aspirations, and relying upon their strengths to establish their goals. They focus on using their strengths to their best advantage to reach their goals, without being limited or hampered by their weaknesses. They create goals that define their lives and aspirations, and provide them with a vision of future, which they can translate into reality with their thoughts and actions. They use their goals to remind themselves of what they need to do to be happy and successful. Success is a self-actualization process, in which you make the best use of your resources, talents and skills to give expression to your inmost aspirations and the highest ideals, which you identify to be an integral part of your life's purpose. In doing so, you either actualize your strengths or externalize them, in an attempt to become the best in what you chose to do. Simultaneously, you identify your weaknesses and make plans to prevent them from interfering with your goals or halting your progress.

When you align your goals with your strengths, you will find rhythm and harmony in your thinking and actions. You will feel inspired, energized and motivated to work for your goals, and as you rely upon your knowledge and skills in the area of your expertise, you will vastly improve the chances of your success, and your problems-solving and decision-making skills. You may also experience greater satisfaction and fulfillment, as your dreams begin to manifest. Your goals must speak for you and your life's aspirations. Therefore, create goals that are in harmony with your abilities to increase your chances of success. Work for them with single-minded determination, using your strengths and working around your deficiencies in smart and intelligent ways.

Goal setting is a tricky process, which demands precision and pragmatism. Many people do not realize that in setting your goals, your heart is as important as your mind, and your goals should match your aspirations and inner strengths. Here is what you can do to create powerful and awe inspiring goals that propel you towards success.

- Identify the central purpose of your life and build your goals around them.
- Write down your goals for clarity and consistency, and keep them handy for easy reference.
- Make your goals SMART (specific, measurable, attainable, realistic and timely).
- Make sure that your goals are in alignment with one another and do not create conflicts or slow your progress.
- Know what to do clearly to reach each goal, and to avoid setbacks and failures work out detailed action plans for of them.
- Ensure that your goals are in harmony with your values, your sense of morality and personal ethics, and use the same approach for your plans and actions.
- Keep ready alternative plans and strategies to deal with possible failures and setbacks, and subject your plans to reality check by questioning the assumptions and prejudices underlying your plans and decisions.

Whether you would like to disclose your goals to others, or not depends upon how you want to pursue your goals and whether you seek the help and cooperation of others, especially those who can work in harmony with you. If your goals are going to create competition for you or attract the envy or ridicule from others, it may be not in your best interest to disclose them to others. You should, however, always share them with your spouse or life-partner, whose cooperation is of utmost value for you and your success, (unless of course you prefer to live alone.)

3. Successful people are focused and committed to their goals: A goal well remembered is well achieved. After creating goals, successful people remain focused on them, never doubting their ability to accomplish them. They constantly review their goals against their accomplishments and remain committed to them. They organize their lives around their goals, making sure that they are not distracted by frivolous activities. Failure does not deter them, or distract them, from their goals. Since they are realistic people, they deal with their failures and move on.

Your commitment to the goals you choose is equally important. With commitment, you enhance the chances of your success and your effectiveness in achieving the desired results. Many people acknowledge the importance of having goals, but do not show enough grit to carry them through. Having established their goals, they go back to their routine and forget what they wanted to accomplish. If you want to realize your dreams and rise above mediocrity, you have to accept responsibility for your life and work for your goals persistently keeping them uppermost in your mind. Once you set your goals, you cannot relax. You cannot take a back seat and let go of your control over your life and actions. Your preparation must be complete and your effort must be sincere, drawing the right plans, making the right effort, cultivating the desired qualities and acquiring necessary knowledge and skills.

Goal oriented effort is very much like driving a vehicle towards a desired destination. Your journey does not end when you choose the destination. It actually begins with that. You will not find many differences in thinking and approach between the effort to reach a goal and drive to a specific destination. Both require a lot of effort, knowledge, skills, commitment, awareness and concentration. You have to know in advance or in time where to go, how to go, when to accelerate and when to use the breaks. You have to respect the rules of the road, watch the traffic and drive within the speed limits, as you remain focused on what you do and where you are going. Most importantly, you cannot fall asleep while driving. Successful people are self-motivators. They remember their goals frequently to remain inspired, accepting responsibility for both their successes and failures and willing to take necessary risks and make necessary sacrifices to reach them. The very prospects of achieving their goals keep them focused and committed. You can improve your focus and commitment to your goals, with the following guidelines.

- Write down your goals and frequently refer to them.
- Spend some time each day, thinking about your goals and performance.
- Monitor your progress constantly against the plans you have drawn.
- Visualize your success, the end you want to achieve.
- Use positive affirmations to remain committed and focused on your goals.
- Internalize your goals to let your subconscious mind know clearly what you want.
- Read books and watch programs that keep you motivated and improve your knowledge and skills.
- Minimize distractions and avoid wasting time on frivolous activities.
- Make a promise to yourself that you will succeed, whatever may be the difficulties.
- Associate yourself with right minded people, from whom you can learn.
- Whenever you are distracted or disturbed, divert your attention to your goals and to your current reality.

4. Successful people aim for excellence: Successful people are not merely interested in achieving success. They aim for excellence. To be different and distinguished for their performance, knowledge and ideas and to stand above the rest, they go the extra mile, pushing themselves and those who work for them against their limitations, focusing on the quality of their products and services, demanding the best from everyone and establishing higher standards of performance. For them excellence is the means to rise above their mediocrity and ordinariness, which plague many, by expressing what is the best in them. They seek excellence not to dominate others or neutralize their fears and insecurities, but for a genuine passion to excel, as the means to self-exploration, doing what they can in the best possible ways to test their limits, and stay ahead of others in both competition and achievement. Since they are not excessively concerned with self-esteem issues, they do not hesitate to admit their failures or learn from them.

When you aim for excellence, you set yourself higher standards of performance, constantly learn, and do not feel easily satisfied with your achievements. You invest energy and time in improving your knowledge and skills, paying close attention to the comments coming from others, and use it to evaluate your performance and motivate yourself to improve further. Successful people look for long term success, based on their true abilities and hard work. They want to be trend setters and leaders in whatever profession they choose. They also prefer building their success on a strong foundation of moral values and quality concerns, which stand the test of time. Here is what you can do to bring out the best in you and achieve excellence.

- Resolve to bring out the best in you.
- Do not settle for mediocrity.
- Put service ahead of the rewards you expect.
- Compete with the best of the best in the field where you want to excel.
- Bring out quality and excellence into every aspect of your life, not just those aspects which receive maximum attention.
- Do it for your satisfaction, not to impress others or prove your greatness to others.
- Do it as a matter of habit, even while performing normal and routine tasks.
- Do it for passion to set new standards and stand apart from others.
- Challenge yourself every day to improve your skills and exceed your own expectations.

5. Successful people use their subconscious minds effectively: The conscious mind is what is awake and aware. It is the observing, analyzing and thinking mind, which we use to make sense of the world and deal with it. We rely upon our conscious minds to regulate our lives. However, our conscious minds have many limitations. They are rather clumsy and do not manifest reality, without corresponding physical action. The subconscious minds are more powerful and reliable instruments to manifest our desires. They work silently in the background, listening to our thoughts and intentions, and create conditions for manifesting them. Consciously, unconsciously, or intuitively, successful people know how to use their subconscious minds to improve their actions and chances of success. Your subconscious mind has no will of its own. However, it is subject to the will of your conscious mind, and works like a genie, accepting your dominant thoughts as its ultimate commands, always agreeing with them and obeying them. It does not always necessarily manifest the reality you desire, because it works in mysterious ways, following your deepest thoughts, which your rational mind may not even know that they exist.

From the earliest times, people have been using their subconscious minds to achieve their goals. However, it remained a guarded secret, confined to a few wise people. It was only in recent times that we have begun to understand its real value and importance in cultivating skills, reaching goals and solving problems. Some people excel in using their subconscious minds to manifest their goals. They know how to resolve their inner doubts and conflicts and direct their conscious minds to envision their goals so that their subconscious minds know exactly what needs to be accomplished. Since the subconscious mind is an inseparable part of our consciousness, we can learn to use it effectively to reach our goals and manifest our desires. Here are some useful suggestions, which you can use to unleash its powers.

- Make your goals as clear and specific as possible to send clear signals to your subconscious mind and let it know what exactly you want. For better results, you may practice visualization.
- Keep images and pictures of what you want to manifest in your life. Refer to them regularly.
- Deal with your self-limiting and self-destructive thoughts and your negative self-talk to feel confident about the outcome of your actions.
- Believe in your skills and abilities to reach your goals.
- Believe in the power of your subconscious mind. This is important, because if you believe that it has no power, it will obey your conscious mind and act as if it has no power. The opposite is equally true.

- Practice meditation. Through meditation you can visualize your goals and leave their impressions in the deepest parts of your consciousness.
- If your subconscious mind does not produce the desired result, try again, without losing hope.

6. Successful people aim for quality relationships: We hear stories of people exploiting others for their own ends, and discarding them once their purpose is served. By such means one may become successful, but at what cost? Of what use is the means, which degrades human character and elevates self-interest to the point of veneration? How can anyone be successful and happy, by ignoring the very relationships, upon which one's success is built? People are intelligent enough to know when they are used or exploited by others and, unless there are compelling reasons, they would not let it happen repeatedly. People know instantly whether you are phony or genuine. They can read between the lines. They can know what you are up to. Once you leave an impression, it is difficult to erase or replace. You do not have to be a genius to spot opportunists and self-centered chameleons. Once you deal with them, you know. You may continue to talk to them and deal with them, but you no more respect them in your heart.

We find many successful people who are lonely with a limited circle of friends and family members. It happens because of the changes in thinking and attitude, and the problems and circumstances wealth create. However, we also find some who know the value of relationships and how to build them and keep them with honesty, respect and trust. They know the value of people who work for them or serve their interests and build relationships with them in mutually beneficent ways. They also know how to spot talent and encourage people to excel in their careers. Whatever limited relationships they may have, they maintain them well. Most of them also use their wealth, influence and connections for charitable and philanthropic purposes and pay back to society part of the gains they make as donations and grants.

To be successful, you do not have to be extremely outgoing. There are many successful people, who are introverts. What is important is the quality of the relationships you maintain and how you treat those who serve you interests and play an important role in your success and happiness. You must have the discretion to know who are trustworthy and who are not, and with whom to build relationships and whom to avoid.

With wealth and success arises a lot of responsibility, and as you become a role model to others, you may have to make some adjustments and personal sacrifices to live up to the image, which people expect from you. You must be dutiful and responsible towards those who depend upon you and to whom you owe a debt of gratitude, besides being honest and transparent with your family members and closest relationships, letting them know that you love them and care for them. Most importantly, you must build relationships with people, who matter to you according to the good values as stated before. The following suggestions are useful in this regard.

- Focus on quality relationships, by choosing your friends, mentors and well-wishers carefully. When you are successful, you will arouse the envy and enmity of many. Therefore, you have to be selective and careful in choosing and trusting your friends, business partners, associates and allies.
- Many problems arise from expectations when they are not clearly communicated. Let your partners and friends know what you expect from them and what they can expect from you.
- Trust builds when you keep your promises. Therefore, you should not make any promises, which you cannot keep.
- You should accept responsibility for your life and actions, and not blame others for the problems and failures you may face.
- You should be fair in rewarding people who work for you and contribute to your success and goals.
- Be fair and impartial in your attitude, judgment and opinions.
- Keep a written record of important decisions you make and the negotiations and agreements you reach to stay organized.
- When there are conflicts, avoid aggression and confrontation and see whether you can resolve them amicably before you try other methods.

- Treat others with dignity and respect, just as you would expect them to treat you.
- Nurture your relationships when you climb the ladder of success so that they can be with you when you start descending.
- Aim for win-win relationships, based on the principles of equality and mutual self-respect.
- When you hire professionals to help you, check their background and competence. After you hire them, give them freedom to express their opinions, whether you agree with them or not, since the final decision always rests with you.
- Help others, especially those you know, when they are in difficulties, or when they need help. Try to be generous with people who serve you.
- Respect the freedom and privacy of those who work for you. Do not meddle in their private affairs, unless they ask for help.

7. Successful people are adaptable: Successful people are growth oriented. They do not become stuck in their lives since they are dynamic, flexible and adaptable in their thinking, and approach to changing circumstances. They constantly innovate and improvise to keep pace with the world and stay ahead of others, updating their knowledge and skills and making necessary adjustments to their goals, plans and programs. However, at the same time certain aspect of their personalities do not change such as their character and integrity. They keep their core values, in which they firmly believe, and their primary goals, which they pursue relentlessly. They are realistic enough to know what they can or cannot change, where they can yield or compromise, and how important it is not to take anything for granted. Their flexibility and adaptability help them to resolve conflicts minimize mistakes, and take corrective action whenever necessary. It also helps them to prepare for the battles of life, and resolve their problems and challenges, with awareness and understanding.

If you want to achieve and manage success, you need to know when to be flexible and when to be firm when it is appropriate to change your goals or your plans, and when you should stay the course. For example, if you start a new business and if it does not work out as expected, at some stage you have to decide whether to persevere and keep investing your time and resources in it or accept your failure and move on. You have to be honest and rational in your assessment of situations, problems, and your progress to choose what works for you, and discard what does not. While it is true that successful people persevere in their effort and do not easily give up, it is also true that they are realistic and practical enough to use their discretion and know when to hold on and when to let go. It is their discretion and adaptability, which makes them successful. The following suggestions are useful to build flexibility in your thinking and attitude.

- Know that there is always more than one way to do anything, solve any problem or reach any goal. You have to find the best option in the context of your resources and your circumstances.
- Do not go by surface thoughts and first impressions in reaching your decisions or conclusions. To avoid making mistakes, you have to dig deep into your own thinking and challenge any assumptions and irrational beliefs that may be responsible for your decisions and opinions.
- Admit your mistakes, without letting your ego, pride and status come in between.
- Have backup plans for important goals and actions, and take nothing for granted.
- It is good to be an expert in any field, but you should not assume that you know everything, even if you have access to certain information, which is not readily available to others.
- Listen to others, and pay attention to the inputs and criticism coming from them.
- Learn from your failures and mistakes.
- Do not categorize people into stereotypes. Treat them as unique individuals and see what you can learn from each of them.
- Have an open mind and keep looking for opportunities to know, learn and improve yourself.
- Question your assumptions and constantly challenge your ideas and beliefs.

Conclusion

We all have the potential to be successful, irrespective of our age, gender, family or financial status. Your chances of success increase greatly when you have an opportunity to align your goals to the best of your abilities, and do what you naturally love to do. It gets even better, if you can bring your values into it. To be successful, you have to identify your strengths, and use them in creative and intelligent ways. You have to establish meaningful and well-defined goals that are in alignment with your personality, hopes and aspirations, and working for them with conviction, commitment, perseverance, integrity and faith. Since you cannot achieve success entirely on your own, you must look for people who can help you to achieve your goals, and participate in your success as your friends, allies, partners, well-wishers, associates, or independent professionals. You have to be consistent in what you do and keep doing it until you achieve your goals, minimizing your mistakes and distractions, improving your skills and knowledge, and learning from your setbacks and failures. You should know clearly what success actually means to you, and how relevant it is to your life's overall purpose. You should know what makes you happy, where your interests are, and what you should do to keep yourself happy and fulfilled. They should be part of your definition of success so that you can build it on a solid foundation of good values and principles, without subjecting yourself to moral conflicts and dilemmas. In short, you have to build your success according to your strengths and the basic values in which you strongly believe, with clear aims and a central purpose that defines you and sets you apart.

How to Improve your Memory

Some things we remember for years, and some we forget quickly. Some people leave a lasting impression on us, and we remember them for long. However, sometimes we do not even register mentally their names. Why is it that our memory does not always work uniformly? Why do some people have better memory than others? What makes our memory stick? We will examine these issues in this discussion.

Good memory is not a special gift, except very rarely. Some people are born with photographic memory, also known as eidetic memory, and recollect images and sounds with extreme accuracy. People born with certain mental disabilities are often endowed with exceptionally good memory. So also are those who can recollect perfectly what they read or listen just after one or two attempts. However, they are exceptions.

Good memory is the result of organized and conscious effort, which is motivated by the need to know and remember or to use it for specific purposes. The function of remembering is a natural, mental process, but the effort to recollect what is stored in the mind is both an art and science, which can yield wonderful results through persistent effort. An awareness of the factors that contribute to better memory and a little practice can vastly improve our ability to deal with the information that we have to process in our daily lives nowadays.

Long term and short term memory

There are two types of memory, short term and long term. Short term memory is what you remember for a brief time and forget. Every day, we gather a lot of information about people, objects and events, and forget most of it after a while. The person you saw while crossing the road, the car that went by, the salesman who knocked on your door and wanted to sell you a magazine subscription, or the birds that flew over your lawn while you were mending the fence, perceptions such as these that catch your attention but fail to register in your mind for long constitute your short term memory. Unless you frequently use them, they do not become part of your long term memory. You long term memory is what you are able to recall after several days, months or years. It is made up of strong impressions that have alternative associations and pathways in your neural network, which are difficult to erase. Your short term memory is limited, whereas your long term memory is almost unlimited. Your short term memory becomes long term, if it is retained for long and frequently used. There is nothing wrong with short term memory. It is the most convenient way for your brain to organize information. Your mind holds the information in short term memory and waits to decide whether it is worth moving it to long term. If the information is useless or not likely to be used, it will be forgotten or pushed into the subconscious.

Memory and recall

It is important to note the difference between memory and recall. They are not the same. Memory is what you store in your brain. Recall is what you remember out of it. All your experiences and perceptions are stored in your brain. They constitute your memory, some of which may be buried so deeply that it becomes subconscious and unavailable, while some remains in the active part of your brain and is easily accessible. Your ability to recall what you remember does not depend upon how much information you have stored in your brain, but upon how that information is interconnected in your mind, and how your brain has built the neural network to store that information. In other words, mental associations and neural networks play a vital role in your ability to remember and recall.

As mentioned earlier, you are able to recall only that part of your memory, which you frequently use or remember. People differ from one another not much in their capacity to store information in their brains, but in their ability to recall, which depends upon a number of individual factors and lifestyle choices. No one can tell accurately how much information an average human being can hold in his brain. The mind keeps expanding as long as a person is alive and mentally active, as perceptions keep flowing in, and knowledge and memories keep gathering. If you store more information in your brain and make use of it, you will have an increased capacity to build and accommodate a larger and more complex neural network. A brain with a large neural network facilitates the higher functions of thinking, reasoning and problems solving, called the executive functions. Therefore, to improve our mental efficiency, we have to remain mentally active and keep learning.

Factors that contribute to good memory

Presented below are the factors that contribute to good memory. With persistent effort, they can positively lead to improved memory in a perceptible way. This article is not about specific memory techniques that lead to improved capacity to remember or recollect long lists of information or numbers. It is about general factors, which contribute to good memory. If you want to know about memory techniques, you may read books that are available on the subject, some of which are listed in the last section of this book.

1. Interest. You remember what you love. If you are not interested in something, you will not think about it or try to remember it. Studies show that we remember well what interests us, inspires us, excites us, and motivates us. If you are enthusiastic or passionate about something, or if you can relate to something strongly, you will remember it well. Similarly, people remember whatever that invokes their curiosity or touches them emotionally. For example, people do not forget their religious icons or spiritual experiences that invoke their religious fervor. They also least likely forget unique and strange experiences that invoke in them strong emotions. Therefore, to improve memory in any subject, you should have interest in it. Since we cannot be interested in every subject we want to know, it becomes necessary to cultivate interest in those subjects that are vital to our success and competence. Some of the proven ways to cultivate interest in any subject are, increasing your knowledge of it, making use of it, becoming familiar with it, and finding in it useful information, which can be related or associated with what you already know.

2. Attention. You will not forget anything, in which your heart and mind are fully involved and when you are fully absorbed in it. Many first experiences are like that. We will not forget them easily. We remember them for long or recollect them easily because when they happen our senses and minds remain actively engaged with the experience or the perception. However, as situations become routine and repetitive, we begin to ignore them. This teaches us an important lesson that to remember anything we must pay full attention to the world outside and see things clearly, letting our senses and minds participate in it without distractions. Our minds are easily distracted. Therefore, we rarely pay attention to the happenings around us. Our brains are conditioned to filter a lot of perceptual information and store only what is necessary for our survival. They do it habitually to conserve energy and prevent information overload. Many factors facilitate it, such as your beliefs, prejudices, expectations, preferences, and preconceived notions. Our perception is also influenced by our states of mind. If you are unhappy, depressed, bored, or lost in your own thoughts, you will not pay attention to the life around you with the same interest and enthusiasm when you are happy. Therefore, to improve your memory through better attention you should not only engage your mind and senses fully but also remain in a positive state of mind.

The process of observation consists of four essential elements, namely concentration, focus, creative pause and conscious appreciation. Concentration and focus serve the same purpose but in different ways. In concentration you fix your mind upon a single object as if nothing else matters. In focus you may widen your attention to see not only the physical features of the object but also its related aspects such as its value, uniqueness, relationships, etc. In concentration your mind acts like a laser beam, whereas in focus it acts like a searchlight. The creative pause helps you to absorb the perception into your consciousness and let it settle down in your memory. In conscious appreciation, you evaluate your perceptions either consciously or habitually to know whether they are useful, meaningful, and relevant to you. You can improve the quality, intensity, span, and duration of your attention through mindfulness, in which you have to remain in the present and actively engage the mind and senses in the process of observation, without judgment, preference and desires. You have to pay attention to details and distinguishing features, using as many senses possible to have the experience stand out. For example, if you want to remember people look at their faces and remember the features that set them apart, with your mind in the present and fully focused.

3. Comprehension. You remember what you understand or comprehend easily, or what makes sense to you. If you read a subject for hours, but do not make sense of it, you will neither understand it nor remember it. You may remember the effort you made, the circumstances of it, and the accompanying emotions you experienced, but not what you tried to read, know, or understand. It is not because you lack the skills or intellectual ability, but because you cannot fit it into your current knowledge, thinking, and memory, and relate to it specifically. You may remember it mechanically, like some people who may memorize a poem or a whole passage from a foreign language without knowing its true meaning, but it will not stay in your memory for long.

To remember any subject deeply and imprint it firmly in your mind, you must grasp its essential meaning and significance, by knowing the basics, words, ideas, concepts, and technical terms associated with it, using your cognitive skills such as thinking, reasoning, creativity, and intuition. You can facilitate it further and gain insight, by relearning, reviewing, analyzing, summarizing, discussing, rephrasing and paraphrasing. When you master a subject, it becomes a part of your long term memory, and you will be able to recollect it easily. The following are a few general and useful means to improve your comprehension.

- Read different books about the same subject.
- Gather information about the views and opinions of different authors and scholars about the subject you want to know. Evaluate them objectively.
- Think deeply about any subject you want to remember.
- Ask questions and seek clarifications.
- Explain to someone or discuss with someone.
- Improve your vocabulary.
- If it is a technical subject, familiarize yourself with the technical language and the fundamentals.
- Integrate the knowledge deeply into your memory by relating it to what you already know or to your own experience.

4. Repetition. Repetition is the most popular and tested method used by many people to memorize any information. Many students regularly practice it to stick important information in their memories before taking tests. Professionals and politicians alike practice it before they give speeches or participate in debates and discussions. Until the invention of printing press, repetition was the trusted method used by people to remember important information. It was practiced in India until recent times by students to remember religious texts such as the Vedas. Without a written script, and proper writing materials, in those days it was the only way by which scriptural knowledge could be passed on from one person to another and from one generation to another. Even today, repetition is the trusted method to memorize anything and still used by many students to secure good grades. You can use it to prepare for your speeches and presentations, score well in tests, or just to impress others with your knowledge and erudition. The following techniques are useful to practice repetition and memorize long texts, poems, lists, and quotations.

- Use pictures and mental hooks, like acronyms to remember the sequence in which information is organized.
- Write and rewrite several times what you want to remember.
- Use index cards and frequently refer to them.
- Record the information you want to remember and frequently listen to it.

5. Review. Review means doing a mental survey of what you have read or perceived. In review you may take a second look or go through the same information several times to refresh your memory or strengthen it. Passive review is a mechanical process, like repetition, in which your aim is to remember the subject rather than integrate it. In the active review, you focus upon the ideas and concepts in the material and do a critical evaluation, reexamining it and reevaluating it.

In contrast to repetition, review is an intellectual process, in which you weigh the topic from different perspectives, study the pros and cons and develop an insight, which will connect it with what you already know. Review is useful to gain mastery of a subject, consolidate your memory, keep the neural network active, strengthen fading memories, convert short term memory into long term, exercise your brain, improve your recall, and integrate your knowledge. When you review any information thoroughly, it becomes part of your memory.

6. Application. We remember what we frequently and repeatedly use. We may forget the name of the author of a book, or the product we saw in an advertisement. However, if we met that person or used the product, we may not forget it easily. You may forget a recipe you saw on the Internet, but if you use it to cook a dish and do it several times, it will stay in your memory for long. However, you may have a hard time trying to remember the ingredients, if you try to cook the same dish after a long gap. It happens because we tend to forget what we do not frequently use.

Our knowledge and skills will deteriorate with time, unless we put them to regular use, since the mind tends to keep only useful information in the active memory and push the rest into the background. Therefore, another way to keep your memory intact is to frequently make use of your knowledge and skills. When you use information in real life repeatedly, it is integrated into your consciousness and becomes personalized. Hence, to retain your knowledge and mastery, you should keep using the knowledge in practical situations. For example, if you are learning a new language, try to speak and write in that language. If you are learning new words to improve your vocabulary, you should use them in your communication. Such practices strengthen your memory and improve your recall.

7. Recall. Review and recall serve the same purpose, but they are different. Review is an intellectual process, whereas recall is a mechanical process. For example if you read a book and speak about its contents and your impressions of it in a descriptive way, it is review. If you list its chapter titles in a correct sequence, it is recall. In review you examine one or more times comprehensively, analytically, or carefully what you want to remember by focusing on the main points. In recall you try to remember what you already know, by focusing on the details, the sequence or broad outlines, without doing any critical analysis or evaluation. Recall keeps your memories fresh, by repeatedly bringing them into your active memory. Frequent recall also helps you to retain the information in your long term memory and keep it within your easy reach. You can improve your ability to recall any information by repeatedly paying attention, reading and memorizing same subject repeatedly, and mentally reminiscing over it. You may also use specific techniques called mnemonics to strengthen your memory, in which you organize information in easy-to-remember sequences, using acronyms, rhyming words and sentences, images, symbols, shapes, colors, or humor. They are mechanical techniques, which help you to connect small pieces of information mentally or through visualization around a central idea or object and hold them together for easy recall.

8. Association. Studies show that we organize memories in our minds by forming associations, whereby the memory of something may invoke in us memories of something else. For example, when we remember a person, we may also recollect many events and experiences associated with the person, or we may remember another person or several people, who may be known to both. Similarly, certain words, place-names, images, smells, memories, sounds and other objects invoke in us several thoughts, memories, feelings and emotions that may be either related or even unrelated to them. When we visit some places, which we visited before, we may feel nostalgic, filled with memories, feelings and emotions. When we remember someone's birthday, we may remember the birthdays we celebrated or attended in the past.

We experience them because our minds store memories in a neural network, just as we organize information in a computer as files and folders, which can be accessed by other computers in the network having an access to it. When we recollect anything we activate a specific location in our minds, whereby not only that information but also all the related information stored there becomes active and accessible. We do not know exactly how the human brain manages all its memory and facilitates recall, but we know that it follows some sort of algorithm to facilitate both random search and sequential search so that one keyword or memory can invoke a number of memories as in case of a search engine. We can take advantage of this tendency of our minds to improve our memory, by actively linking the information we want to remember with the information that is already present in our memory. When you learn a new subject or topic, you can connect it with the knowledge you learned about it in the past. If the subject is new and you have never studied it before, you may connect it with something else by comparing and contrasting. For example, if you want to remember place names or people's names, associate them with familiar words or phrases that rhyme with them. When you meet people associate their names with their faces and physical features, so that you can remember their names and faces well. This technique is particularly useful if you are in the habit of remembering people's faces but forget their names.

Another technique that you can use to practice association is the free association method, which is similar to catharsis and mind-mapping techniques used by many to generate new ideas or unearth hidden patterns. You can practice it in the following manner. Start by keeping a pen and paper. Pick up any idea, word, concept, or object, and start thinking about it. Allow your mind to flow freely, as you jot down whatever thoughts, memories and ideas that surface in your mind. At the same time, ensure that you will not let any judgment, preference, prejudice, analysis, criticism, or control interfere with your thinking during this phase, and you will let your mind move freely with the idea or the concept, even if some of it does not make immediate sense. You should keep doing it until you exhaust all the ideas and thoughts associated with it. At the end of the exercise, you may review what you have noted down to see whether you can recognize in it any meaningful patterns, associations, or creative ideas on which you can work further. This technique is especially useful in breaking your habitual and routine thinking, and find fresh ideas and solutions.

9. Imagination. You can use imagination, or creative visualization techniques to improve your memory. A large part of our sensory input is stored visually as images. Our memory depends a lot upon how quickly we can retrieve the images and bring them into our wakeful consciousness. We remember experiences and events that are unique, vivid, colorful, unusual, disproportionate, humorous, odd, absurd, or exaggerated. We can use this habit of our minds to our advantage and improve our memory by practicing visualization. Here are a few ways in which you can do it.

- Use visualization to exaggerate what you want to remember, whether it is an object, person or situation. Try to make it vivid, colorful, odd, or even ridiculous by adding, deleting, increasing, or decreasing its shape, size, color, looks, or any other prominent feature.

- Visualize yourself walking through an aisle in a shop or through a street and seeing the things you want to remember arranged in a specific order. You have to remember the setting and the order in which you saw the things. Later, when you want to recall the information, you can invoke the whole sequence and see the things as they were placed.
- Create mental maps to organize key ideas, related words and concepts, mapping their associations and connections. To improve your memory, frequently refer to them.
- Recollect important events and experiences in your life vividly, as if you are dreaming or seeing a mental film.
- Certain subjects like history, art, literature, and science are suitable for learning by visualization. Visualize the information you read and animate the people, ideas, and events associated with it.
- Visualize yourself as standing in an auditorium in front of a large audience, showing them your ability to recall a large sequence of numbers, lists and information, and being applauded by them.

10. Physical health. Our health influences our memory. A healthy lifestyle keeps the mind in good shape and contributes to good memory. Studies show that about 20% of the total body energy is consumed by the brain, of which a major part goes to keep the nerve cells or neurons to fire signals. If the body does not get enough nutrients and proper rest, one may suffer from mental exhaustion, and in severe cases mental fatigue. The brain receives its energy as glucose through the blood vessels. It is used in the production of a particular chemical called adenosine triphosphate, which is the main source of energy for the nerve cells to perform their functions. The influence of proper diet, exercise, sleep and general health conditions upon the brain, and its energy consumption, is still under investigation. However, studies suggest that they improve brain efficiency and thereby contribute to active memory. Some findings indicate that a sugary diet may temporarily boost brain's energy levels and prevent mental exhaustion. Certain activities like listening to music or watching a good movie do not cause fatigue, whereas difficult tasks such as taking a test, doing an unpleasant routine, or keeping a night watch may.

Certain factors such as aging, illness, stress, cardio vascular diseases, and hormonal imbalance may have adverse effect upon the brain functions and impair its ability to perform at optimum levels. Therefore, for optimum brain function and good memory, we have to protect our health by taking preventive actions. Since our memory is consolidated in sleep, it is necessary to give our bodies adequate sleep and rest, and keep them free from stress and strain. Studies also suggest that certain chemicals which contain cholesterol, sugars, fats, salt, and toxins in large quantities are harmful to the brain, as they may interfere with its functions. However, foods that are rich in antioxidants (vitamins C and E, and beta carotene), foods that contain B-vitamins (niacin and folic acid), and foods having sufficient amounts of omega 3 fatty acids are likely to improve the activity of the brain and reduce the memory problems caused by aging. Protein rich foods are also beneficial to the brain, as they contain serotonin, which creates pleasant feelings in the mind and increases our ability to fight feelings of depression.

11. Mental health. By nature, the human mind is always active and subject to instability and frequent disturbances caused by both internal and external factors. Even in sleep, a part of our brain remains active and keeps functioning, either firing up the nerve cells or recording information and dream activity. Many genetic and environmental problems play a role in shaping our behavior, perception, cognition and mental health. A lot of what we see, think, experience, and remember, depends upon what mental states we experience in a given situation and how we interpret them. If we are not happy or preoccupied with any problem, we may not allow our minds to perform at their optimum levels, and we may miss a lot of information that is relevant to our lives. Negative emotions, such as fear, anxiety, anger, and depression, greatly reduce the brain's ability to process perceptions and retrieve memories. The various emotions we experience release chemicals into blood stream, which directly affect the memory functions of our brains. Negative thinking, pride, fear, anger, prejudice, critical nature, envy, carelessness, apathy and depression interfere with our ability to process

- Conflict with law or criminal involvement
- Living in a foreign country as a refugee
- Living in fear caused by frequent wars, communal strife, or violence.
- Some essential facts about adversity

How you respond to adversity depends upon how you perceive it and interpret it according to your values, beliefs, experience and understanding. When adversity strikes, most people initially suffer from negativity, fear, and depression, but quickly recover from it and try to deal with their problems. However, some continue to suffer and feel depressed and helpless. Some people emerge strongly from an adversity, with determination and courage to set things right as they learn from it, while some develop distrust and suspicion and remain depressed and discouraged. Factors that shape your life and thinking also shape your response to adversity, such as your upbringing, personal beliefs, and past events. Maintaining focus and objectivity in adverse situations is difficult, but it is what you need, for which you require a proper attitude and a philosophy of life that can accept and absorb failures and setbacks, without breaking your morale and faith in the beliefs and values you uphold. You need to know what adversity means, and what it can do to you both positively and negatively. The following are a few well-known facts about adversity, and what it can do.

- Adversity brings out the best and the worst in us. It may provoke us to do our best or leave us feeling discouraged and frustrated by circumstances.
- Not all of adversities are the same. Depending upon how severe and critical they are for our happiness and success, they may improve us or destroy us.
- Adverse situations are caused by many factors. You may broadly classify them into three categories: those arising from your own actions, those caused by others and those caused by acts of God.
- Adversity may strike anyone at anytime. One may take preventive measures to minimize the chances of its happening, but no one can entirely avoid it by just being right always.
- Adversity tests our ability to survive and prevail against difficult situations and teaches us valuable lessons, rather harshly and painfully, about life and the world in general, and people and situations in

particular. It also opens our eyes to the truths about ourselves, our lives and existence and prepares us mentally to expect future problems.
- Sometimes, adversities may prevent people from being truthful and honest about themselves or their problems. Since society adores success and dislikes failure, people keep their problems to themselves and live in denial, instead of dealing with them rationally and honestly, and seeking timely help.
- People differ in their ability to cope with adversity. Some thrive well in adversity seeing opportunities that others do not see, while some suffer from fear and anxiety and become defensive or resentful.
- Adversity opens our eyes to the truths of the world, the true nature of people, who our true friends and enemies are, and how the world may turn against us when we are in difficulties. It destroys the many illusions and assumptions we may entertain about the world, people and things.

Factors that influence coping behavior

Adversity strikes everyone and none can escape from the suffering that is inherent in our lives. As some traditions believe, perhaps rightly so, adversity is the continuous reality in which one may experience temporary relief as happiness, success and fulfillment. People's attitudes and responses to adversities range from purely emotional to highly rational or spiritual. The same factors which influence our thinking and adaptability also shape our attitude and approach to adversities, and our problem solving abilities. Personality factors such as knowledge, awareness, health, self-esteem, genetic factors, values, beliefs, education and experience influence our coping mechanisms. Society and environmental factors also play a role, such as social and economic status, family support, gender, age, and personal reputation. Some communities are particularly harsh towards those who fail in their lives or go through difficulties, while some show sympathy and support to them.

Religions also play an important role in shaping our beliefs, thinking and attitude towards adversity. Almost every religion without exception provides the best emotional and spiritual support to people to deal with not only adversity but also the suffering that arises from it. Every religion attributes human suffering to a personal or divine cause. The scriptures suggest that human beings suffer because either they made mistakes in their lives or God wants to teach them lessons in virtue and improve them. Those who believe in karma think beyond this life and attribute adversity to the actions they committed in their past lives. They either embrace their pain and suffering as part of their self-cleansing or take suitable actions to improve their karma. People who believe in fatalism resign themselves to their fate and wait for the right turn of events. While in a majority of cases, religions provide the best emotional and spiritual support for people in adversity, in some instances they may induce them to indulge in delusion and superstition.

Basic strategies to deal with adversity

Each of is inherently capable of dealing with adversity by either resolving the problem or bearing with it. You cannot solve every problem you face, but when you face a problem that defies all solutions you must have the courage, conviction, faith, and ability to take it in your stride and move on with your life. While problems try to hold you back, you must try to move forward either by changing your ways or the circumstances. Nature has endowed us with the will and the ability to survive and win against odds. In this vast universe we are undoubtedly unique beings.

In our struggle for survival we have learned to cope with challenging situations and transcend our own limitations to establish a great civilization. We have resolved many problems in the past, through inventions and innovations, and vastly improved our knowledge and ability to deal with the problems caused by Nature, circumstances or our own actions. We know how to establish order and stability in an otherwise chaotic world and work for the greater good of all. Although we are prone to make mistakes and wrong choices, we can still evaluate situations and deal with our problems, rationally, realistically and effectively.

Broadly speaking our strategies to deal with adverse situations and problems fall into fight or flight responses. Depending upon how we perceive the problem and evaluate the consequences we either deal with it actively or avoid it willfully. This is true with regard to not only individuals but also nations and communities. These two approaches are discussed below.

1. Active engagement. In active engagement you do not back out of a problem. You will face it and deal with it with appropriate solutions and strategies. You will use your intelligence and resources to identify the problems and try to solve them. For example, if you have suffered a business loss or failure in securing a promotion, you will analyze the reasons, ask others for their opinions, search for rational and effective solutions and deal with the problem. You will keep trying until you find a resolution. It is possible that our solutions may not always be effective. Our ignorance and irrational beliefs may interfere with our ability to find right solutions. However, as long as we keep trying and dealing with the problem, even if our methods are wrong, we are deemed to be fighting the issue and not avoiding it.

2. Willful avoidance. It is common sense that when problems arise they must be resolved in time. In real life, it does not always happen. People may willfully avoid dealing with adversities, if they are too difficult to resolve, the resources to deal with them are inadequate or unavailable, the circumstances surrounding them are unfavorable, or fear and other emotional factors are too strong to overcome. They may also intentionally do it because of anger, frustration, erroneous beliefs, status issues, social pressure, or ignorance. When they fall into such mental or emotional traps, it is very difficult to motivate them to take suitable action. Since time is also healer and a teacher, sometimes one may use avoidance as a good strategy to sleep on a problem or wait for the right time. However, one cannot let that happen always. If problems are not resolved in time, they may cause additional problems or make them even more difficult to solve.

How to deal with any adversity?

There is no one better way to deal with an adversity. Even if you find one, you cannot be sure that it is the best. If it works, you are lucky and move on. If it is not, you have to find another, and keep doing it, until you find one. Since each situation is unique and the causes and circumstances related to it are different, and since people respond differently in different situations according to their beliefs, limitations, and emotions, every adversity requires specific solutions. In the following discussion we will focus on a general approach or a step by step program to deal with any adversity. You may customize them according to your needs and circumstances.

1. Study the situation carefully: Becoming familiar with the problem is the first step. Once you know and define the problem, it is easier to find solutions. The best place to begin the process is your own mind. You have to pay attention to your feelings and memories associated with the problem and analyze how it all began, and how your own thoughts and actions precipitated it or responded to it. Then, you may think of the comments you heard from others and what they felt about it. Most of the time, a problem will be so striking that you may not have to do a lot of analysis to understand it. You know internally what troubles you or hampers your abilities and happiness. However, it may still be necessary to do the study and introspection to unearth hidden causes and problems, especially to ensure that you are not in denial of the problem or making light of it because of your own defensive attitude. For example if you have a chronic health problem, you need to know whether it is curable or bearable and what options you have to deal with it within your capacity.

2. Accept the reality: If you are not honest with yourself, your solutions will not be effective. Many times problems remain unresolved and difficulties continue because people are not willing to be honest with themselves and acknowledge their role and responsibility in causing the problem or solving it. You cannot avoid problems by disowning them or blaming others. When you are in difficulties you have to accept that it is your life and your problem, and you are the one who need to deal with it. You cannot let yourself become a victim of denial or your own sense of self-importance. Adversities are great levelers. They can bring down even kings to their knees. In testing conditions you have to bring out your gut instincts into play to defend your turf and protect your interests, knowing well that problems have a tendency to aggravate if they are neglected and when you have problems you cannot trust or depend upon anyone blindly, because when you are weak your enemies strike you with all their might.

For example if you have lost your job, you have to accept responsibility to find a new job and prepare for it. You have to acknowledge that after you left the previous job your old colleagues may have a different perception of you, and may not always be forthright with you or readily help you to network. You may also have to prepare mentally to answer any questions that may be asked by the recruiters about your previous employment, and decide what answers you need to give and how it may interfere with your prospects or opportunities. If your employer is one of those mean spirited and vindictive people or companies, they may speak negatively about you to the recruiters and prevent you from getting a job in the same town. This happens many times if you live in small places where news spreads quickly. If it is the case, you may have to consider the option of relocating to a new place. Thus, in difficulties you have to keep your feet firmly on the ground and deal with the problems as realistically and honestly as possible, keeping all your options open and your emotions under control. When we are in difficulties, we have to be doubly honest with ourselves and clear any illusions we may have about our abilities, self-worth or influence. In difficulties, you should accept reality as your best teacher and humility as your great virtue. You can believe in God, but it is wise not to expect miracle to happen.

3. Accept responsibility: You are the driver of your life. You may seek others' help to resolve your problems, but primarily they are your responsibility. Others may help you, but the initiative to resolve them must come from you. You should also accept responsibility for what happened, instead of blaming others or the circumstances, especially when it was caused not by acts of God, but by negligence or human errors. Blaming others does not help you much, except letting you feel light by venting your emotions. By accepting responsibility for your problems and analyzing their true causes, you can think of the measures you can take to control or prevent them from happening again. When you seek others' help, you have to ensure that you will not undermine their effort and involvement with self-destructive attitude. For example, some people cannot digest the fact that they have to depend upon others for help. Therefore, to prevent them from doing it, they push them away with aggressive or destructive behavior.

4. Take timely action: What sustains a person in difficult situations is the belief that he can do something about it and eventually emerge out of. When he loses that faith, he becomes heartbroken and may even lose the zest for living. Many people give up trying or even commit suicide when they lose that hope. People say that at the end of a dark long tunnel there will always be light. That light is the hope. When that light vanishes, only darkness remains. When miners become stuck several hundred or a thousand feet below the earth in dark mines, with no easy passage to come out, what keeps them alive until they are rescued? It is not only faith and hope but also the actions they take to survive until the rescue comes. When adversity strikes, you should not only cultivate the right mindset to bear with it, but also find solutions to eventually emerge out of it with minimum damage. By far, this is the best and realistic approach.

Sometimes you need a lot of mental courage and inner preparation to cope with the challenges in your life, but it is worth trying since the alternative of not doing anything may lead to very negative consequences. Most problems in our lives can be resolved by finding effective solutions, and implementing them with determination and perseverance. In rare cases when you are unable to find solutions, you must look for alternatives, consult others, or learn to bear with them. For example, there are no remedies for certain types of degenerative diseases such as diabetes or heart disease. In such cases you have to make lifestyle choices to minimize pain and further damage, and adapt yourself suitably to the new reality. Since in this case you are making an effort to deal with the problem and not avoiding it, it cannot be considered willful avoidance.

5. Take preventive measures: We can learn a great deal from adversity and use the knowledge to minimize our chances of facing similar situations in future. It may not completely secure us against unforeseen problems, but it is certainly helpful to minimize our chances of facing recurring problems. We can learn a lot from adversity and improve ourselves. If we have the right attitude, we can use failures and setbacks to deal with our imperfections and increase our knowledge, skills and expertise. It is not that we should want them to happen, but when they happen we must be willing to take them in our stride and learn from them. Indeed, someone rightly said that if we do not learn from our difficulties, we will be forced to deal repeatedly with the same situations, until we learn our lessons. None can achieve success in life without leaning from their mistakes. If you want to progress, you should make an honest assessment of your weaknesses and vulnerabilities and see what you can do about them. By knowing what happened and what factors led to a difficulty, you can take preventive measures to safeguard your life and interests against possible threats. For example if you have started a business and faced serious losses, because you misjudged the market or introduced a wrong product, you can use that knowledge to avoid repeating those mistakes, and improve your chances of success.

6. Stay positive: How we reference or view an adverse situation and how we respond to it are more important than how we eventually resolve it. Adverse situations produce negative emotions, which are difficult to control or manage. When adversity strikes, many of our assumptions and expectations about people and life in general take a big hit, and as the world around us collapses, we open our eyes to a new reality, which we have not seen before. Such experiences may make us cynical and distrustful of human nature. We may begin to resent people and society in general and may even develop distaste for life itself. While we cannot completely avoid the emotional upheavals caused by adversity, we can cope with them in better ways by staying positive and keeping our expectations on the brighter side.

7. Cultivate detachment: In extreme cases, where nothing can be done or nothing seems to work, detachment may be the right solution to cope with difficult problems or learn to live with them with a sense of resignation. Unless you are spiritually inclined to live the life of a saint or a monk, you should not use this except as the last resort or the ultimate solution. For the right minded person, detachment is a virtue. Its practice offers many advantages. It is useful even in worldly life to remain untouched by the disturbances in life or failures and setbacks. Detachment means to accept life as it happens and to treat all conditions equally without preference or choice. Extreme practice of detachment may disengage you from life altogether. Therefore, you have to know how you can use it in your life without losing your balance, and without inner conflicts.

8. Cultivate the right mindset: Certain qualities are helpful to remain focused in difficulties and face your problems with courage and confidence. In this regard the following factors are found useful.

- Ability to see positive outcomes
- Flexibility and adaptability
- Emotional resilience
- Staying in the present
- Knowledge and expertise
- Willingness to learn
- Rational problem solving skills
- Focus and attention to details
- Self-motivation
- Positive self-esteem

Ultimately, the only person you can control and transform in this world with greater ease and certainty is yourself. You can control and manage your thoughts, actions, responses, ideas, plans, attitude and approaches. It is where you should focus, when you have problems in life and when you are unable to make expected progress. See where you are going wrong, what mistakes you might have made and how you may overcome them. Honest self-evaluation is the best policy and approach in adverse situations. If you right yourself, many things about your life and destiny cannot go wrong. With self-control and discipline you can mend your life and establish a firm foundation for your success and happiness. Adversity toughens and teaches you valuable lessons. It lets you know your vulnerabilities so that you can address them and make yourself stronger. Therefore, take each adversity as an opportunity to become a better and more capable human being.

Success Principles Worth Following

A principle is any truth or assumption, which you can use to guide your thinking and actions. A number of principles put together become a philosophy or worldview. Principles are the essence of our knowledge, wisdom and experience. You may draw them from your own experience or learn from others by study and observation. Principles shape your character, thinking and behavior and help you to live your life according to your convictions. The world may change, but your principles do not, unless you find newer truths that change your thinking and perception. Some principles are worth remembering because they give you a direction in life and the strength to withstand problems and difficulties. The following seven principles serve the same purpose. They are drawn from my own experience and observation. Please see whether you agree with them.

1. Your life is unique and precious: Your life is as unique and precious as the life of any person. It does not matter whether you are successful or not. The very fact that you are alive and active in this world is a blessing in itself. Many people do not realize how precious their lives are and how lucky they are to be part of this vast humanity. Unfortunately, some people even ignore it and commit suicide or indulge in self-destructive habits and actions. Some indulge in wanton destruction of life upon earth. The moments that make up your life are also precious because they never return. You may experience the illusion of continuity amidst change and impermanence, but in reality life moves in a linear fashion in a forward direction only. You may even say that life is but just one moment that keeps changing continuously. Things may repeat, but never exactly in the same manner. From the time we are born until we die, we keep moving forward. Whether we accept it or not, it is towards one destination only, which is death. Therefore, recognize your uniqueness and the value of your life, even if it is not a great one according to the world standards. Treat it with utmost respect and manage your precious time here wisely, without indulging in bad habits and self-destructive behavior, or in violence and cruelty.

2. We all eventually die: In the excitement and the attractions of our lives, we do not remember this sad truth about our mortality. Many people think and act as if they are going to live here forever, seeking things that also do not last, and believing that somehow they can defy death. It is only in old age that the thoughts of death begin to dominate the minds of many. It is true that for our welfare and happiness, we have to focus upon living, rather than death. If we keep thinking about death, we will not be able to experience peace or happiness. However, it is also necessary to remember that life is transient, and we cannot indulge in excessive worldliness and trade our very souls to secure material comforts. It is important that we not only live peacefully but also die peacefully with minimum regrets. One of the common regrets expressed by people who are nearing their death is that they should have spent more time in recreation or with their families. Therefore, remember the transience of life and spend your time wisely, knowing its value. Live a holistic life, or a complete and balanced one, without pursuing only one or two goals at the expense of other important ones, such as your health, your family, and your own happiness. Most importantly, live in the present and find opportunities to enjoy your life.

3. Do what you love most: Job dissatisfaction is a major source of unhappiness in the world. It is also a major source of health problems. People feel depressed and frustrated when they have to spend their lives doing what they dislike. When you use your abilities and talents, your chances of success increase greatly. You will also derive a lot of mental satisfaction. If you want to achieve distinction or excellence in your life, you must follow your dominant desires and use your natural talents and potentials. There is safety in being part of a crowd, but it may also make you unhappy and frustrated. It is worthwhile to live the life you want to lead by doing what you love to do, or what you are naturally inclined to do. Everyone is born with some strengths, talents and skills. You have to find them and build your life around them. Consider them your God given gifts, and use them as your capital to create your goals and reach them. By doing what you love most and planning your success around your inherent strengths, you will experience inner harmony and positive self-esteem. If you cannot change your job or take risks, you should use them to help others by teaching them or training them. You should focus upon the positive aspects of your job and try to make it more interesting and satisfying.

4. Aim for excellence in whatever you do: If you know the value of your time, recognize your uniqueness, and pursue your passions and strengths, excellence will follow. Excellence means giving your best in whatever you do. It does not have to be the best of the best, but the best you can achieve according to your knowledge, skills, ability, and circumstances. True excellence comes from perfection in your thinking and actions, which again come from self-discipline and commitment. Whether it is a simple task such as polishing your shoes or a complicated one such as designing a computer game, you can practice excellence by setting the best standards of performance and meeting them with right action and attitude. In this regard, certain qualities are helpful such as enthusiasm, dedication, honesty, diligence, intelligence, focus, humility, patience, resolve, tolerance, perseverance, and courage.

5. You are responsible for your life: Whether you accept it or not, your life is your responsibility. You are responsible for your actions and reactions, and how they shape your life. It is true that the events in your life may not always happen according to your expectations or with your knowledge. It is also true that your life is influenced by not only your actions but also the actions of others and that of God, or Fate. However, it is not a sufficient excuse to avoid responsibility or blame others. If you examine your life carefully, you will realize that although some events happened due to external causes, you still had a role in their happening, since you had opportunities to avoid them by making a few choices. You are the hub as well as the mover of the wheel of your life. You can depend upon God and seek His help, but you cannot ignore your duties and responsibilities. You have to think about your life, and know whether you are moving in the right direction for a better life or need some changes and improvements.

6. In doubt listen to your heart: We cannot ignore the importance of reason in solving our problems, cultivating wisdom or gaining knowledge. However, we cannot always depend upon it only. Sometimes everyone has to listen to his heart and follow its direction, especially when the information is insufficient, and the results are uncertain. Human consciousness is a mixture of reason and emotions, and we have to use both in our decision making. When ambiguous or uncertain situations arise, whose outcome is difficult to predict, we should turn to our feelings, instincts and intuition to know their drift. For example, many times we have to make important decisions which will have a major influence upon our lives, such as where to study, or which job to choose, or whom to marry. In such cases when you are unsure, it is better to listen to your heart to see whether it validates the solutions suggested by your mind. It will be difficult for you to listen to your heart, if your mind is too noisy. You can calm your mind with rest, prayers, meditation and concentration.

7. Your life is shaped by your self-image: Whom do you listen to most in your life? Do you frequently listen to others or follow your own judgment? Do you suffer from the compulsion to seek others' approval or care more for your own opinions? A lot of people live according to the expectations of others, and in the process compromise their values, beliefs, goals and decisions. It is important to know what you think about yourself and how you feel when you deal with others or seek their help. If you suffer from low self-esteem and low self-confidence, you will prefer staying in your comfort zone and settle for a mediocre life. You will not take risks, or use opportunities that may lead to failure and criticism. Low self-esteem may also result in self-destructive behavior, withdrawal, depression, fear and such behavioral problems. You can improve your self-esteem and thereby your self-image. In this regard, the following suggestions are useful.

- Know more about yourself
- Improve your knowledge and skills
- Face and resolve problems
- Know your strengths
- Learn from your mistakes
- Learn from others
- Do difficult tasks
- Establish your own standards of performance
- Forgive yourself
- Learn from your failures and mistakes
- Learn to appreciate yourself and others

A Lesson in the Art of Appreciation

Some people have all the qualities of becoming successful, such as good education, intelligence, having goals, focus, energy and enthusiasm. Yet they suffer from self-limiting beliefs and doubts, which prevent them from using their full potential and experiencing fulfillment. They suffer from a nagging feeling that their success might be fortuitous, and they may not truly deserve it. If they are successful in life, they experience disbelief and even discomfort. When they are appreciated for their achievements, they may play it down, or attribute it to external causes. Humility is no doubt a virtue. However, here what they show is not humility, but self-deprecation. If people cannot appreciate their own achievements and talents and if they do not willingly take credit for their success, it is likely that they are victims of their self-sabotaging behavior, which is a common problem, and which prevents many from being what they are and proving their true worth. There are some, who are talented, but find it difficult to speak to others to seek their help. They would achieve success and prosperity, if they venture out of their comfort zones, build working relationships and find people who can help them to reach their goals. Some people are wealthy and successful, but do not feel good about others. They usually end up being distrustful, alone and miserable.

Thus, the world is full of people who can neither appreciate themselves nor others. This article is about how we can learn to appreciate ourselves and others, and live with a sense of gratitude and respect for the blessings and the help we receive from others and the world in general. It is about how by appreciating ourselves, others, and the world, we can transcend our pettiness and selfishness, and experience unity and affinity with others and the universe. In the context of this article, appreciation means focusing on the positives, expressing gratitude, and learning from your negatives to improve yourself rather than to vent anger and frustration.

Appreciating yourself

Logically speaking, although appreciating one's own abilities, talents, and achievements should be easier than appreciating others, in reality many people do not feel good about themselves or their accomplishments. They suffer from self-doubt, low self-esteem and negative self-talk. When others criticize them, they even become defensive and rationalize their actions because of fear rather than conviction. True self-appreciation comes from self-awareness and self-acceptance, which gives you the strength to believe in yourself, to be yourself, and accept both your strengths and weaknesses as part of your identity. As your self-awareness increases through introspection and observation, you learn to use your strengths and work around your weaknesses to reach your goals. Self-appreciation can be very healing as you learn to forgive yourself and your mistakes, without letting them unduly interfere with your life. It gives you the courage and conviction to pursue your goals according to your values and principles and accept setbacks and failures without feeling small. Some people will have exaggerated sense of self-importance. It is not the same as self-appreciation, but vanity and conceit. Appreciation, which arises from of self-awareness, and which does not lead to pride and vanity, is authentic, balanced and accurate. It helps you to accept yourself, forgive yourself, heal yourself, and respect yourself as an individual.

Self-awareness, therefore, is the key to self-appreciation and even success and happiness. We all possess some degree of self-awareness. However, it is mostly based upon assumptions and irrational beliefs. If you want to know yourself better, you should dig deep into your thoughts, desires, beliefs, emotions, and actions with utmost honesty and objectivity, and know what motivates you or hinders you. With increased self-awareness, you will have a better knowledge of what you can or cannot do and how you can overcome your limitations and constraints. Self-awareness leads to the following.

1. Maturity in thinking and actions.
2. A deeper insight into your behavior based upon your own experience.
3. Increased self-esteem, self-confidence, and self-acceptance.
4. Realistic and achievable goals and plans based upon your strengths and weaknesses.
5. Compassion and forgiveness towards others.

6. Increased ability to take calculated risks and accept failures and setbacks as learning opportunities.
7. Increased awareness of how your thoughts and actions influence you for better or worse.

You can feel good about yourself by meeting your own expectations, reaching your goals, and by cultivating a non-judgmental attitude towards yourself. The first two help you to achieve success and progress in life using your talents and strengths, while the third one ensures that failures and setbacks do not undermine your self-esteem, weaken your resolve or halt your progress. It also prepares you to face the uncertainties of life without negativity. You can learn to appreciate yourself by practicing the following.

- Appreciate what you are, and the knowledge, skills, talents and potential with which you are endowed.
- Appreciate the talents and resources you have with which you can reach your goals and dreams.
- Appreciate the opportunities you have as a human being to live with self-awareness and intelligence.
- Appreciate the beauty and grandeur, which you can experience through your senses, and the gifts, which Nature sends your way all the time.
- Appreciate the life you have lived so far, the obstacles you have overcome and the experiences you have gone through, however pleasant or unpleasant they may be, for they have shaped you and groomed you to be who you are today.
- Appreciate the serenity of the current moment and your deep connection with the world around you.
- Appreciate those who love you as well as those who criticize you, for the opportunity they give you to know your weaknesses and imperfections and improve yourself.
- Dispute your negative self-talk and any doubts and anxieties you may have about your future, using positive affirmations and taking necessary action.
- Forgive yourself for your past mistakes and your current weaknesses.
- Be yourself and respect your uniqueness.

If there is some unhappiness in you about you, or if you are suffering from self-doubt or feelings of inadequacy, just do not sit there wishfully, drowning yourself in self-pity. Take action right now to address the problem, identifying its causes and finding the best possible solutions. Have goals that will increase your feelings of self-worth and work for them by taking responsibility for your actions. This is the best way to overcome your poor self-image and feel good about yourself. Whether you are successful or not, if you want to be truly at peace with yourself, you have to accept yourself fully and unconditionally, appreciating what you are and what you have, without victimizing yourself with feelings of guilt, inadequacy, fear or criticism. You cannot be successful and feel fulfilled, if a part of you refuses to agree with you and keeps fueling your feelings of self-doubt and disbelief. You have to align your thinking and actions around your core dreams and goals, and navigate your way through the uncertainties of life, using your skills and resources to manifest your vision and your life's central purpose. You have to let go of things that hold you back or prevent you from being your best, and free yourself from your fears, prejudices and irrational beliefs to appreciate things as they are with increased awareness and wisdom.

Appreciating others

People who are unhappy with themselves readily find fault with others. Since most people in this world are dissatisfied with some aspects of themselves, they extend the same attitude towards others and appreciate them rarely and conditionally. In a majority of cases, people appreciate those who mirror their own qualities and attributes, such as the color of their skin, language, nationality, education, religion and values. In many places, minorities suffer from social and economic disabilities for this very reason and find comfort in the laws that protect them from public discrimination. It is unfortunate but true that our beliefs, habits, prejudices, expectations, likes, dislikes, and values greatly influence our attitude towards others and our sense of appreciation. It is also true that we have many people amidst us who harm others and show little compassion.

Beneath the diversity and the differences that exists among us, we must remember that we are humans and our survival, success, and happiness depend a lot upon others. Every day, several people cross our paths. In our eagerness to pursue our goals and interests, we do not give them much thought or feel any connection with them. It is not necessary that you should be friendly with everyone, but you must have compassion for the people and respect them as individuals having the same right to live upon earth and pursue their goals. Yes, you cannot trust everyone. There are still many people in this world, who do not feel any remorse or fear when they hurt others. Yet, it is important that your attitude towards others should not be shaped by them, but your own values and personal beliefs.

Although you may not be aware of it or acknowledge it, the world plays an important role in your personal happiness and survival. Whether you know it or not, you are helped by millions of people every day, who ensure that you will have food, transport, gadgets, water, electricity, television, security, and many such facilities to lead a comfortable life. Imagine what happens, if the roads are not built or maintained properly, if farming is stopped, and if all the public services come to a grinding halt. You may pay for the goods and services, and you may be paying taxes, but you must also remember that you are able to have them because millions of people are willing to do their work and make them available. We are the end beneficiaries of the work done by a vast network of humanity who do their part in keeping the wheels of the world moving, and help us to have basic facilities and creature comforts.

Thus, it is important to know that we cannot take full credit for the happiness we secure in this world, and how other people influence our lives. We must appreciate how our lives and destinies are intertwined in imperceptible ways with those of others. By knowing it and paying attention to it, we can acknowledge our interdependence and the role others play in our lives, accepting that while we may take pride in our own success we must be humble enough to acknowledge the invisible help we receive from others. It is easier to appreciate those who appreciate you or who are good to you. While doing it, you display an ordinary human trait, which even some animals display. However, the challenge and the test of your character lie in how you respond to those who do not appreciate your or who are indifferent to you. You can succeed in it only when you learn to appreciate others naturally without expectations, as a general expression of your character and integrity, rather your than vested interest.

True appreciation arises from compassion, tolerance, understanding, and forgiveness, while envy, pride, anger, and fear reduce it. Appreciation degenerates into mere sycophancy when it is laced with self-interest or hidden agendas. Your appreciation must be genuine and a natural expression of your higher nature. Everyone deserves our sympathy, even the animals. Whether they are successful or not, share some physical features or not, and agree with you or not, they have to be treated with consideration and respect.

Next time when you feel frustrated or angered by the people around you, think of how many people contributed to your success and happiness, starting from your parents, the people who took care of you, the teachers who taught you and educated you and the people who helped you to reach where you are today. Express your gratitude to them, appreciating the help you received from them. In this regard, the following suggestions are useful.

- Extend to others the benefit of doubt, compassion and consideration which you extend to yourself.
- Cultivate a general attitude of gratitude and a positive state of mind that appreciates life without expectations, conditions and hidden agendas, as an expression of your higher nature.
- Appreciate the help you receive from others.
- Appreciate people for their uniqueness and achievements, not for their looks, or appearance.
- Appreciate that everyone is just like you, having the same concerns and anxieties.
- Appreciate that everyone comes into your life to teach you lessons. Know what their message is and what you can do about it.
- Appreciate people for the good they possess, without any expectations.
- Appreciate the help you do not receive and the harm someone intends to do.
- Appreciate the help and support you receive from others, both directly and indirectly.
- Appreciate people habitually, even if you do not like them or their actions.
- Appreciate those who are giving you a tough time, because they are teaching you valuable lessons.

- Help others in whatever way you can, without any conditions and expectations.
- Do not harm anyone, even if you have compelling reasons to do so.
- Accept those who annoy you, anger you or irritate you as opportunities to express compassion, tolerance, and understanding.

Appreciating the world

The world is a physical manifestation of our collective will and consciousness. It is a living organism made up of diverse individuals and living beings. Silently and imperceptibly, it makes things possible for us, amidst chaos and uncertainty. When we appreciate the world in a very general and nonspecific way, without any expectation, and send out our silent prayers and blessings into the universe, wishing for its welfare, peace and harmony, unknowingly we begin to experience friendliness towards everything and peace and gratitude. The Vedic scriptures are a great example of how people can tune into the higher powers of the universe through prayers and powerful wishes and seek its blessings. The Vedic people appreciated all life as sacred, all divinities as sacred and the universe itself as a physical manifestation of the universal supreme God.

The world is always with you. Whether you are asleep or awake or rich or poor, it provides you with a place to live, air to breath and water to drink. Wherever you go and whatever you do, it is always there with you. As long as you are alive upon earth, like your own world which lives in you, it is an integral and inseparable part of your life. Whether we are willing to believe it or not, we are part of an incredible story of creative intelligence that manifested in the universe for reasons unknown to us. Even though we do not know clearly why we are here, we are presented with a unique opportunity to appreciate all that we experience here with our limited abilities, knowledge and awareness, and our inseparable connection with the universe in which we live.

We are like worlds within worlds. What we do or do not do creates ripples in the consciousness of the world. We have a sacred responsibility to align ourselves with the world and appreciate its value and importance in our lives. We cannot be truly successful or happy if we reach our goals by robbing others of their happiness and success. There is dignity and hope in knowing our boundaries of influence and appreciating the rights of others. There is moral and mental satisfaction in achieving success through self-righteous ways. Success devoid of virtue, social responsibility and right vision, may make one rich but not happy or loved. The world is not just you and others. There are innumerable things, invisible forces, manmade objects and everything that you can grasp through your mind or the senses, which deserve our love, gratitude, attention and appreciation. Being an essential part of our existence, they play an important role in our survival and the continuity of the universe. They do not exist in isolation, although superficially they may present such an illusion.

Appreciating everything

Appreciating everything wholeheartedly and accepting oneself and others unconditionally, is the sure path to individual happiness, peace and prosperity. It is also the sacred path chosen by the enlightened masters to experience oneness with the entire existence through loving kindness. Their sense of appreciation reaches glorious heights as they love one and all without distinction, preference and prejudice. It is also reflected in some people, whose love for the humanity and the world in general knows no bounds and who sacrifice their whole lives and personal comforts for the service of others. In the business world, it manifests itself as concern for quality and customer service.

The whole world is interconnected. Our success and happiness depend upon others, and so is everyone's. We do not live in isolation. What we do and think leave ripples in the collective consciousness of the world. Even if you escape from the world into a Himalayan cave, certain aspects of it will accompany you and stay with you. Right now we are connected with everything else. Think about it deeply. No one is ever truly successful all by oneself. From the teacher who taught you the alphabet to the person who first interviewed you for a job, and the unknown one who ironed or stitched your suit for that occasion, everyone plays a role in your success, or failure. Countless things, people, situations come together to make possible the dreams of one person who wants to taste the sweetness of life. Nature may seem to favor the survival of the fittest, but if you think deeply, you will realize that it does not actually favor fit individuals, but groups and communities of fit individuals. The primitive people could not have survived alone against adverse forces of nature, without the help of their tribe members. In life, as in games, there is a value and importance for teamwork and belongingness.

We have to be constantly aware of the interconnectedness of life and the good things that happen to us because of it, appreciating their value and importance in our lives. We have to be grateful for the things that help us and even those that seem to oppose and challenge us, because they too in the end help us only by providing us with many opportunities to learn, improve and progress. As you develop appreciation of everything as your natural state of mind, your opportunities to grow, prosper, and experience peace and happiness increase. In this regard, the following suggestions are helpful.

- Send out loving thoughts into the universe for no particular reason. Let your peaceful thoughts create their own ripples everywhere.
- Fill your heart with a sense of appreciation for everything that happened to you so far and let that feeling stay.
- Make a list of important events that happened in your life, including the negative ones, and analyze what lessons you learned from them and how they shaped it.
- Appreciate the role nature plays in your life, and how it is an integral part of your mind and body. When you go out into Nature, appreciate its beauty and grandeur, and your connection with it.
- Appreciate your connection with the world, how you are benefited by it, and what you have done so far to repay its debt, and express your gratitude.
- Appreciate the energy that you exchange with the world for the benefits you derive from it.
- Appreciate that you are alive and breathing in an uncertain and transient world, and you have many opportunities to enjoy life and experience its value and uniqueness.
- Whenever you pray, pray not only for yourself or your welfare but also for the welfare of others and

the world in general, wishing them the best. The Buddhists practice it and it gives them peace, besides elevating their consciousness.
- Wish for peace and happiness wherever you go and leave there the vibrations of your silent blessings.
- Spread good thoughts and good words through your actions and interactions.
- Ask for forgiveness from the universe for the inconvenience you cause to others through your actions, and the damage and destruction you may cause knowingly or unknowingly in your survival for the actions you perform.

It is not easy to appreciate everything in life, especially when you see a lot of injustice, cruelty and evil in the world. It is also difficult to maintain balance when you are subject to likes and dislikes. Unconditional appreciation of life arises from the highest nature in us, which requires a lot of inner preparation and cultivation of qualities such as detachment, sameness, equanimity, compassion, tolerance, humility, empathy, harmlessness, etc. It may take years before you reach anywhere near such an ideal. However, you should not set it aside as mere wishful thinking or pure idealism, especially if you have spiritual aims. In the initial stages you may try to cultivate an attitude of appreciation, or feeling positive and good about yourself and your experiences in life. You can gradually extend those feelings to others and the world in general. You may also begin the practice with those whom you dislike most, analyze your feelings and see whether you can replace them with positive ones. You do not have to seek their friendship. You have to just stop thinking negatively about them. Most importantly, you have to feel gratitude for all the good that happens and the blessing you have in your life.

The Art and Science of Relaxation

What is your general state of mind during the day? Do you feel relaxed most of the time, or do you suffer from money, health or family related worries that wear you down? Do you suffer from frequent headaches, indigestion, muscle pain, or other physical ailments due to worry and anxiety? If your answers to these questions are in affirmative, perhaps you are suffering from stress and need to relax. Some stress is normal and even necessary to stay healthy and active. Many common tasks and situations, such as walking in a crowded place, meeting strangers, driving through a busy lane, or giving a public speech can increase your stress. You also experience it when your desires are thwarted, when you step out of your comfort zone, or when you suffer from negative feelings and emotions, such as fear, anger and guilt. Nowadays stressful situations are so common and frequent that many people do not even know that they are stressed. Most people come to know about it during medical checkups, or when they experience other related symptoms such as indigestion, headaches, back pain, heartburn or sleeplessness, and seek medical help.

Long term strategies to deal with stress

When stress becomes unmanageable and persistent, one should take the problem seriously and look for immediate solutions. Stress is a silent killer. It may cause considerable damage before you even realize it, since it induces in the body the release of harmful chemicals into the blood stream, which interfere with its normal functions and overtime may damage the organs, including the heart, the kidneys, the liver, the eyes and the digestive system. Therefore, one should take the problem of stress seriously and seek timely treatment, before it causes grievous damage to the mind and body.

If you are prone to stress, and even if you think that it is not a major health issue, you should still consult your doctor and seek medical advice, because it can often result from hidden health causes, which can be diagnosed only after detailed medical tests. Normal stress can be reduced or managed within tolerable limits by healthy lifestyle choices, self-discipline, relaxation techniques, and clean habits. The following suggestions are meant to help you on a long term basis to deal with stressful situations and keep your stress within limits. They are not a substitute for medical advice. If you suspect that you suffer from chronic stress, or stress related problems, you should consult your physicians and seek immediate medical advice.

1. Make your health a top priority item in your list of tasks: A healthy body copes with normal stress better than an unhealthy one. Many people continue to overwork and overexert themselves, even if they are not physically or mentally well. If you are one of those who ignore their health for any reason, you have to decide what is important in your life and whether you can afford to do it habitually. If you are not in good health, professional or career success is not going to compensate you for it. For your happiness and wellbeing, you should give priority to your health and take preventive measures. You should stay physically and mentally fit by doing whatever that is within your control.

2. Give your body adequate rest: Your body is vulnerable to wear and tear. When you are engaged in serious physical and mental work, you need to rest in between and give yourself time to relax and recuperate. Prolonged strenuous work can increase your stress and reduce your immunity levels, and thereby expose you to several physical ailments. Since in a work environment you are bound to rules and cannot take frequent breaks, you have to learn to relax naturally while doing your job. You can do it by staying in the present, paying attention to your surroundings, and taking deep breaths. It is also important to sleep at least eight hours every day to let your body heal and recharge.

3. Stay with the moment: During weekends, sometimes a friend of mine goes on a long drive into the country side. One day his car GPS failed and he lost his way in a desolate place where he could not see even a single human being. He said that he was really exhausted, confused, worried, and hungry. Then he came across an old, rusted, iron bridge with a river flowing beneath. He stopped the car and stepped out of it to watch the river and the scenery on either side. The desolate road, green hills in a distance, the gently flowing water, corn fields, cool breeze, and calm surroundings filled him with indescribable peace, and he felt instantly uplifted and relaxed as if his tiredness had flown away with the flowing river and the passing breeze.

What happened to him on that bridge was that he transported himself from his mental daze to the present moment and found a connection with the reality. It is a simple technique which many people use to stay in control.

For a busy person the present moment can be very healing if he knows how to return to it in tense moments and become aware of it. Whenever you feel tensed up, just take a few deep breaths and look around or stretch your body. You will feel immediate relief. It is like lifting a pot of boiling water from the stove for a short time and putting it back. If used intelligently, it can work for you like a thermostat to keep your stress under control. Your mind is fickle by nature and becomes easily distracted by one thing or the other. In normal circumstances you can live with it. However, if you have problems and worries or if you are anxious about the outcome of certain situations that are troubling you, it may increase your stress and make you restless, as you keep thinking about them or your future. You can address this problem by training your mind to stay with the moment and become mindful of your immediate surroundings. You can practice present moment awareness by listening to sounds, observing the objects around you, focusing upon your breath or the tasks you perform, or feeling the sensations in your body.

4. Organize your work and your life: Some people are very meticulous and try to organize everything they deal with, while some are not so serious. When CD's and DVD's were newly introduced, I used them to back up a lot of information, but forgot to label the discs or keep a list of all the files I stored in each disc. It resulted in a lot of problems, as each time I had to spend considerable time looking for specific information. In a few cases, the files I thought I backed up were not found while some I backed up twice. Finally, I had to spend a whole day to reorganize them.

Life can get very stressful if you are not in the habit of organizing your information and resources. Organizing is an important aspect of life which many do not realize until they grow up. If you are a disciplined person, you know its value in your personal and professional life. Planning and organization go together. By organizing your life and activities, you can avoid many problems and mistakes. Organizing means you should have a place for everything, and keep everything in its place, and planning means you should know in advance what to do and when by making the best use of your resources. Both provide order and structure to your thinking and actions, and bring predictability, peace, and regularity into your life, besides saving you from a lot of avoidable stress caused by confusion, negligence, and frequent delays in completing your tasks.

5. Stay realistic and rational: You should not underestimate the problems that you may face in the long journey of your life. You have to be ready for the unexpected twists and turns. In recent times we have seen that in countries like Japan and Russia, people who thought that they would have a comfortable retirement life had to return to work when they had lost their savings in economic downturns. I heard of a person who went on a hike in a desert and lost his way. He thought that he would return to his camp in a few hours, but had to be rescued by others after a few days of search. Unrealistic and irrational beliefs and improper planning can lead to unforeseen problems, which in turn can cause severe stress. You must plan for contingencies, without assuming that there will be no problems and obstacles in completing your tasks. If you do not keep backup plans, things can get nasty. When you make decisions, set goals, draw plans or use your resources, you must be realistic and balanced. If you have a problem, you should not live in denial or deceive yourself with the hope that it will just go away without any action or response from your side. You should think clearly, without any illusions, and find solutions that can work. Imagine what happens when you have a health issue, and instead going to the doctor you decide to go to an astrologer and act according to his advice.

6. Practice traditional relaxation techniques: A young lady, who was an investment broker lost in succession first her dear mother to cancer, her boyfriend to her own friend, and her dog in an accident. She was in severe pain and wanted to commit suicide. A colleague of her advised her to go on vacation to India, and visit an ashram she knew. She went to India planning to stay there for two weeks, but she stayed back for about six months and learned yoga under the guidance of an expert teacher. The practice of yoga and meditation and changes in her food habits helped her to cope with her sorrow and recover fully. With renewed enthusiasm she returned to her home town to continue her journey and appreciate the opportunities life had given to her to learn lessons from the joys and sorrows of life. Many people vouch that traditional methods of healing such as mindfulness, yoga postures, acupuncture, meditation, regulated breathing, visualization, etc., can be effective to calm the mind and body and reduce stress. You do not have to go to India, or China to practice them. You can learn about them by reading books, searching the Internet, or joining a training class. They are inexpensive, easy to practice, and can be easily incorporated into your daily schedule.

7. Flow with the life: One of the techniques survival specialists recommend for situations when a person is lost in a forest or a difficult terrain is to try to find a river or a stream and follow its course. It is because somewhere along the course you will most likely find a human settlement, fishermen, or a boat, and you will have greater chances of survival. If you do not find them, at least you will have a better supply of food and water. In life also you can follow a similar principle. Your chances of survival and success increase greatly if you learn to flow with life. Instead of fighting and resisting what life has to offer you, sometimes it is better to surrender and let life happen, letting go of things and relaxing, with the conviction that you can deal with situations as they arise. This approach is especially helpful when nothing in your life seems to be working, and you face a lot of uncertainty about the outcome of your actions or the next turn of events.

It is not that you should be passive or indifferent. You must do everything possible to control your life and pursue your goals to the best of your ability. However, when you have done everything you could and yet could not achieve much progress, you must allow life to unfold itself and show you its hidden intent. Spiritual people will tell you that difficulties and problems in life arise to teach you important lessons and prepare you for inner perfection. Therefore, when you are unable to change your life or circumstances, or when everything seems to be going against you, you let your destiny unfold itself. You cannot change the world, but you can change your thinking or your methods to align with it. If you are pushing yourself too much but accomplishing little, it means you are out of tune with yourself or your destiny. In such circumstances, you must pause for some time and see how you can change the situation to your advantage.

8. Manage your expectations: I have a friend who is exceptionally talented and intelligent, but he is never happy because he thinks that he has not achieved even half of what his father had achieved. The reason for my friend's perennial unhappiness is his expectations to exceed his father's achievements, without realizing that his father achieved it over a span of nearly fifty years in a less competitive world while my friend is not even 30 years of age and has to live in a tougher world. There is a saying that expectations reduce joy. Your expectations influence the quality, course and the direction of your life. They also influence your thinking and attitude, and your health. You feel empowered when you achieve them, but experience a range of negative emotions when you do not, which may persist and cause you stress, depending upon how you interpret your failure and absorb the shocks.

You do not have control over all situations in your life. Hence, you always the run the risk of not meeting your expectations and suffering from the disturbances they cause, unless you develop coping strategies and a healthy mental attitude. Your life is shaped by not only your own expectations but also the expectations of others, such as your family, friends, society, government, the institutions you join or work for, and even God. Managing the expectations of others is even more difficult, and it is where most people experience stress and unhappiness, since they have to manage the emotions and expectations of others, apart from their own. You can address this problem partially by having clarity about what others can expect from you and what you can expect from them by having discussions and negotiations, and by asking questions and seeking clarifications.

9. Change your circumstances: Do you know why so many people are eager to migrate to the USA, sometimes risking their own lives? Many outside the USA do not know that for a first generation immigrant life in the USA can get very tough. Yet, many people want to migrate, by even illegal means, because they have no control over the conditions that exist in the countries from where they come. One cannot say whether they are making the right choice, because when you leave a country you also leave half of your soul and heart there. However, sometimes it is wiser to change your life and circumstances by leaving or avoiding the conditions over which you do not have much control. For example, if you live far away from your workplace and travel long hours every day, you can plan to relocate to a new location, which is closer to it or find a job near your home. If you live in a noisy neighborhood and unable to sleep properly, you can shift to a quieter area. If your job is creating a lot of stress, you can either negotiate with your employer for suitable changes in your working conditions or explore any alternatives. Such actions give you a sense of control and relief from causes which produce stress and unhappiness.

10. Practice Detachment: If you are an emotional person, who is prone to develop attachments you may not like the idea of detachment. When my daughter wanted a dog in the house, I was reluctant because I thought I would form an attachment with him, and someday we all would have to feel the pain of separation. The dog is now so much part of our lives that whenever we plan to go on vacation, or away from home, we find it hard to leave him in the dog-care. This is just a simple example of the various attachments we develop in our lives, as we repeatedly interact with things and people. Every attachment you form weighs you down with duties and responsibilities, and limits your freedom and choices. Every attachment is like the baggage that you carry in a journey. Having many attachments means you have to carry more weight, which ultimately wears you down. Hence, most religions put emphasis on the practice of detachment to teach you moderation and self-control and prepare you for peace and inner freedom.

Detachment does not mean that you should abandon your duties and responsibilities, and become a monk. It means that you should remain mentally free from the things you desire or seek, or when you enjoy them. With detachment you can control your mental and emotional dependence upon things and the need for fulfillment, which are responsible for many mental and emotional problems. It also means you should not be unduly worried about the results of your actions, but focus upon your tasks and duties, and do your best without anxiety and expectations. When you are mentally detached, you will have peace, equanimity, stability, and clarity in your thinking and purpose.

11. Avoid using drugs or medicines for relaxation: Studies show that using drugs, alcohol, and medicines for sleep and relaxation prove to be very harmful in the long run. It is like hiding behind a tiger to find protection from a wolf. After the tiger is done with the wolf, you will end up facing a very disturbed and aggressive tiger. Unless you are in severe and chronic pain with no better alternative, you should try to avoid it. Drugs, alcohol, and sleep inducing medicines do not address the real problems, but only provide a temporary escape from them. They give you an illusion of rest and relaxation, while they keep harming your mind and body, and create mental dependence. The best way to get a good night sleep any day is by doing hard physical labor or exercise. You can also practice yoga and meditation, instead of using drugs and sleep medicines.

12. Find time for recreation: The world would be a better place if we shut down all the radio and television channels in the world. People will then use their time for more productive work, and you will find more time for yourself. However, on the flip side it may also make the world a dull place to live and people unhappy. The ultimate purpose of life is the pursuit of happiness. One of the best ways to do it is to indulge in recreation and entertainment. In today's world, you have ample opportunities to enjoy life and keep yourself busy. However, since some forms of entertainment can be addictive, costly, and harmful you have to make wise choices. Recreation helps you to relax and find temporary relief from stress, but if you have major worries in life which you cannot easily forget, it may not be effective in reducing your stress. Instead of reducing, some recreations like dangerous sports also increase stress and anxiety. If you suffer from stress, you should avoid them.

13. Have realistic goals in life: To achieve success in life, it is necessary to set difficult, but achievable goals, and push your limits. However, your goals must be realistic. Unrealistic goals and overambitious targets may cause a lot of stress and strain and lead to overexertion, restlessness, loss of sleep and self-esteem. Your plans and targets must be according to your strengths and weaknesses and you must be realistic in your thinking, attitude, and approach. It is better to achieve them through honest and persistent hard work, rather than through deception and shortcuts in your anxiety to achieve too much in too short a time.

14. Control your perceptions and responses: Most of the time it is not what happens to you, which causes the stress, but how you perceive and interpret the experience. In this regard, our beliefs, thinking and attitude play an important role. For example, when an angry customer walks into your office, you may react one way and your supervisor may react in another way. You may think that the customer is there to create trouble and your supervisor may think she has a genuine problem, which needs to be resolved. Here the situation is the same, but you and your supervisor interpreted it and responded to it differently. In most cases our perceptions, actions and responses are influenced by our thoughts, values, beliefs, and judgment. So is the case with the stress. If by nature you are sensitive, distrustful and defensive, you may see threat even in ordinary situations and experience negative emotions. On the other hand, if you are confident and open minded, you may react positively to the same situations. Therefore, analyze situations that cause stress to see whether they are caused by your perceptions, thinking and attitude rather than the external events.

15. Have a positive mental attitude: Imagine you just entered your office, and you were about to switch on your laptop to begin your day's work when your boss rings you on the intercom and asks you to come into his room. You know he would not usually call you at such an early hour, unless there is a serious problem. You are aware that the company is doing restructuring and of late many people are being laid off. After hearing his anxious voice on the intercom, you may start worrying that you are going to be laid off and your boss called you to deliver the bad news. Anxiously you walk into his office and greet him with a nervous smile. He asks you to sit, and inquires calmly how your day was. Then without waiting for your reply, he informs you that he had a bad day. His car broke down on the way, and he had to arrange for its towing and take a taxi to reach the office. After a pause, he asks you politely whether it would be convenient for you to drop him at his home in the evening since it was located on your way to your home. You feel greatly relieved as you listen to him and happily agree to drop him wherever he wanted to go. What happened here? You aggravated your thoughts by exaggerating your fear and anxiety, expecting the worst to happen. Without any connection to reality, you envisioned a negative outcome. Stress is often caused by our negative thoughts, exaggerated fears, lack of confidence, and low self-esteem. It may also increase when you assume that the situation is beyond your control. When stress is aggravated thus, you can counter it by realistically analyzing the problem situation, challenging your negative thoughts, and find rational solutions.

16. Stay proactive: If your house is on a lakefront or a river front, you should better insure it against floods. The insurance companies will be reluctant to give you that cover, but you need to get it even if it costs extra because the risk is high. If you go on vacation, put all the valuables in a locker and let your neighbor know that you will be on vacation so that she can keep a watch on your house and take care of the junk mail placed near the mailbox. By proactive actions you can minimize risks and thereby stress. Some people do not like to be in crowded places for long. Some are stressed by excess noise, while some feel uncomfortable because of sight problems when they have to drive in the middle of the night. If you know in advance what makes you anxious or uncomfortable, you can proactively avoid those situations, or when it is not possible, you can mentally prepare to bear with them. By identifying problems in advance, and taking timely actions, you can save yourself from a lot of trouble, worry, and anxiety.

17. Have faith in yourself: One of the chief sources of anxiety is the lack of self-confidence. When you are not sure of the outcome of your actions, you feel anxious and insecure. Self-confidence does not develop overnight, since it is directly related to your self-esteem and experience. To regain your confidence, you have to face your fears and undertake tasks that help you to build trust in yourself. You also have to examine your assumptions and irrational beliefs, which you might have acquired in your childhood from your parents and peers, and validate them rationally against your experience and observation. There is no better cure for low self-esteem and lack of self-confidence than achieving success. Therefore, you should routinely set goals and keep achieving them. When you face failures and setbacks, instead of personalizing them, you should take them in your stride as learning experiences and move on.

18. Practice visualization: Since the primary source of your stress is your mind, with the help of visualization you can change your habitual thought patterns that produce stress and anxiety. Another advantage of visualization is you can image positive outcomes to difficult situations, without the need to go through them in real life, and learn to respond to them in empowering and effective ways to regain your confidence and optimism. You can also use it to visualize images, and scenery that soothe your mind and make you peaceful.

19. Practice moderation in whatever you do: The middle path of moderation is always the best path. We cannot withstand extreme conditions. Anything in excess is harmful to us. Two thousand and five hundred years ago the Buddha suggested the Noble Middle Path as the best way to live in the world and overcome vice and suffering. Moderation in life is still the best way to remain balanced and poised. Nature has created us in such a way that we cannot withstand extreme conditions of life. Therefore, enjoy all the good things in life with moderation, and avoid the stress and the suffering that arise from the extreme conditions of life.

20. Live a wholesome, balanced and holistic life: Do you have any regrets in life? Do you believe that you could have lived a different life? Dissatisfaction with your life or achievements, and sense of inadequacy, or purposelessness can lead to frustration and unhappiness. You can offset such feelings by planning your life properly and leading a holistic and balanced life in which you can accommodate both your material and spiritual goals, and secure peace and happiness without losing your inner poise. For example, you may regard your job or profession as important to you, but you cannot let it control your life or consume your energies. Everything in your life is a means, not an end in itself, and you cannot let anything enslave you or control you.

21. Manage your relationships: Relationships are a major source of stress and unhappiness in life, and unless you are careful they can cause a lot of mental trauma and leave you feeling disturbed or even devastated. You cannot control other people's behavior and responses. Therefore, you cannot easily predict how your relationships turn out in the long run. People may speak to you nicely in your presence and do the opposite on your back. They may betray your trust, or scheme against you. You should therefore regard your relationships with practical or philosophical attitude, with detachment, tolerance and understanding, toning down your expectations and controlling your emotions and responses. You may also choose your close relationships carefully, and avoid frequent interaction with negative and envious people, who are difficult to please or trust.

22. Have a philosophy of your own: Cultivate a personal philosophy or a belief system, which can shield you from the shocks and disappointments in life and provide you with a strong purpose and motive to continue in the face of adversity. For many people their personal philosophy is shaped by their religious and cultural beliefs, and in some cases by their experience. You can create it from any number of sources, including your experience or perceptions. It is better to have a broad based philosophy derived from various sources, since it will effectively protect you from difficult and stressful situations.

23. Share your problems: Sometimes it is better to let out your feelings and thoughts and lighten up your heart. However, you can do it only with people you trust or those who can give you sane advice. Even with them, perhaps, it is not prudent to reveal certain sensitive information, which may hurt you later. As a stress buster, it may not be a sure solution that will always work, but sometimes it can help you, at least temporarily, to lighten up and find solace. If you do not want to speak to others about your problems, you can write them down and let go of your thoughts and worries.

Manage your stress in healthy ways

Stress is a common problem in today's world. According to a survey conducted in 2013 by American Psychological Association, about 77% people regularly experience physical symptoms caused by stress and 73% experience psychological symptom caused by it. Of them a majority held that money, work, economy, relationships, and family responsibilities were the major causes of stress, which they experienced as fatigue, headache, muscle tension, etc. No one can avoid stress in this world because of our limitations, vulnerabilities and the impermanence of the world itself. Studies show that while about 60% of the people try to reduce their stress by some means, only about 35%-40% feel that they are doing a good job of it. Normal stress can be managed by practicing relaxation and visualization techniques we have stated before. However, chronic stress requires a more serious approach, which can be resolved only by disciplined and organized effort involving healthy behavior, and good habits.

Becoming Aware of Yourself

Self-realization is a difficult goal, which only a few can ever achieve. In a spiritual sense, Self-realization means going beyond your knowing and finding your essence. In the following discussion, we will not focus on self-realization, but self-awareness, or knowing the parts of you that make up your personality, and how you can shape it to realize your goals and dreams. The advantages of knowing your conscious self are many. It helps you to know your behavior and thinking so that you can decide which aspects to improve or strengthen, and which to ignore. With the insights you gain into your behavior and motives, you can mold your life according to your goals, abilities and values. Whether you change yourself or not, the knowledge itself gives you a better control over your thoughts and actions.

In every system, there are movable and immovable parts. Together they give stability to the system. The human personality is not different. There are certain basic aspects, such as your color, gender, body type, or intelligence, which stay with you for life. You cannot change them or remove them, without hurting yourself or doing damage to your mind and body. How you feel about them and what you do with them influences your self-esteem, your world-view and way of life. Whether you like them or not, you have to accept them and learn to live with them for the rest of your life, with some adjustments and coping behavior. You may regard them as your inherited karma. Problems arise when you struggle to change them. Imagine a celebrity in her eighties who want to look like a sixteen year old and compete with her for attention. There are limitations which you cannot defy, and which you should respect for your own mental peace. Our happiness lies in accepting them and adapting to them.

Then you have qualities and features, which you acquire not from birth, but from your experience and perceptions, starting from an early age until the very end. It is your experiential self, the edifice that you raise on the foundation of your God-given personality. It becomes integrated into natural self and influences your thinking and attitude for the rest of your life. Whether you will become an extrovert or an introvert, sensitive or intuitive, and trustful or distrustful, depend upon your circumstances and what you learn from them. Since it is deeply embedded in both your conscious and subconscious minds, you cannot change it easily without struggle and inner resistance. However, it is not impossible to change. With right knowledge and right techniques you can become a better person than what Nature intends you to be by changing the factors that influence your thinking and behavior and adapt yourself better to the growing demands of the world around you. You can not only change your current behavior but also acquire new behavior through learning and practice to reach your goals or ideals. In this discussion we focus upon the barriers that interfere with your perception and awareness, and how you may deal with them

Understanding your mental filters

Put ten people in a room and give them a topic to discuss. See how they differ in their thinking and approach. Everyone in that room believes that he or she is speaking the truth and what is right. They may be totally wrong about their facts and beliefs, but in their minds they are convinced that they are speaking the truth. Why is it so? Why do we have so much diversity among people about their thinking, beliefs, and attitude, while they all live in the same world? People belonging to the same family, living under the same roof, hold different opinions and beliefs and grow up to become unique individuals. How does it happen?

Modern psychology probed into these issues to find out the truths about perception and cognition. We now have some answers, though not all. It is now clear that the truths held by each individual are relative and may have partial or no connection with the universal truths that define the world. Rene Descartes declared that your self-concept arises from your thoughts. It is very true. Your self-image is created by not only your thoughts but also how you think. In receiving and processing perceptions, your mind acts more like a tube or a sieve, rather than an open system. Understanding the way it works and regulates your thinking and behavior is in itself a great challenge which you have to overcome in your search for truths about yourself.

Your mind protects you from the external world, filtering information and letting you know what you need to know to make you feel happy and comfortable. It creates its own myths and truths to validate your beliefs and prejudices. It colors your thoughts and opinions to help you to adapt to the world and find security and acceptance. It also filters information to save you from the trouble of dealing with a lot of information that may not be necessary for your survival and problem solving.

Thus, our minds rarely serve us as reliable instruments of truth. What you see and experience may not necessarily be the reality, but what you choose to believe as the reality. Because of its selective perceptions you see the world not as it is, but according to your values, beliefs, desires and expectations. It is a kind of self-deception, in which we engage rather unknowingly or habitually to manage and simplify our lives. Recent studies prove beyond doubt that your mind creates distortions and delusions out of your perceptions to validate and reinforce your beliefs and attitudes and your self-image. People entertain many illusions about how they look, think and act. They tend to overestimate their good qualities and achievements, and internalize their successes, while they attribute their failures and setbacks to external causes. They also spin their memories and rewrite them, or overwrite them to create their own narratives of what happened to them or to others. Many people may also suffer a nagging feeling that they may have been overrated by others and eventually people would find out.

This is the reality. Your mind stands between you and the external world and filters the incoming information according to your convictions, whereby you do not perceive truth, but what your mind presents you as truth. It actively selects, distorts, predicts and constructs your perceptions to create the illusion of continuity, reality, immediacy, and stability. It stands between you and the world like a prism or a convex lens rather than a plain glass. Hence, you rarely see things as they are.

Therefore, you cannot totally rely upon what you think is the truth or believe that only you are privy to it. Different people perceive the world differently and draw different conclusions and they all may be right partially or relatively, but not absolutely. The perceptions of the CEO of a company may be entirely different from those of the employees and customers, and unless there is an openness by all, the truth about the company and its operations may never be known. The same also holds true about each individual. If you want to know truths about yourself, you must know how to look beyond the illusions and the commotion of your mind to see the truth as it is. It is not possible unless you transform your mind into a clean and transparent glass. The classical yoga realized this principle thousands of years ago. Hence, it suggested that a yogi should suppress the modifications of his mind to know the truth about his true and hidden identity. When the mind is silent, you become truly self-aware. You see with great clarity. You become the seer or the pure witness.

Separating your true and mythical selves

Some psychologists believe that each individual is a compound self, made up of several selves or self-images. The person that you were with last night in the party may not be the same person you will see performing a task in the garden the next day, although she looks the same and bears the same name. Whatever may be the truth, we know that the identity or the individuality of each person is a mixture of both facts and fiction. You have in you the reality of who you are and the idea or the notion of who you should be or should have been. One reflects your real self and the other your idealized self, which is made up of your beliefs and mental constructs. Both coexist in the same consciousness, and you use them according to your needs and convenience to relate to the world.

Most of the time you present your idealized self to the world and hide significant truths about you to get along with others or present yourself in a positive light. You may reveal them to the world only rarely, or unintentionally, in weak moments when you lose control over your conscious mind. Otherwise, you manage to wear your mask in public or hide behind the games and rituals you usually play with others to avoid intimacy or closeness. If there is too much disparity between the two selves, you may suffer from feelings of guilt and shame, which in turn may impair your thinking and reasoning.

As both these identities become mixed up or overlap, you may not even know which part of you is active in you at a given moment. With these two identities coexisting it is almost impossible to know yourself truthfully and objectively, because to do it you have to depend entirely upon your mind, and use it not only as the subject and the object, but also as the presiding judge. Imagine what happens if in a particular case you are the judge, the public prosecutor, the defense lawyer, the witnesses and the audience. Even if that case is decided, it is difficult to know whether justice was delivered. To know yourself correctly, your mind has to play these roles simultaneously and sincerely, apart from acting as both a facilitator and obstructer. You must become your own mirror and reflect truth with integrity, honesty and transparency.

Understanding your behavior

How do you know whether your behavior is caused by internal factors or by external factors? How do you know whether you are short-tempered by nature or your anger is caused by circumstances? Just because you failed to make an impression upon the audience during a speech, should you consider that you lack presentation or public speaking skills? Your self-esteem and self-image depend upon how you interpret your actions and reactions and feel about them. Before you want to take any corrective action, you need to know which factors are responsible for your actions or behavior. If they are internal, you must change your thinking and attitude. If they are external, either you may adapt to the circumstances or avoid them or change them.

We have a tendency to attribute our successes to our abilities and effort, and our failures to circumstances or to others. If you won a trophy or an award, you may believe that you worked for it and take pride in it, but if you failed you may think that the judges were dishonest or your mother, teacher or friend did not let you prepare well. We do it so habitually that, unless we are extremely honest with ourselves, we will not know which causes are truly responsible for our actions and behavior. It is also true that we generally tend to attribute other people's actions to internal causes and our own actions to external causes.

The true test of whether your actions arise from internal causes or external causes is to know how frequently they happen and whether they happen consistently under dissimilar circumstances. For example, if you are unhappy most of the time in different situations, irrespective of where you have been or with whom you have been, it is an indication that the source of your unhappiness is internal rather than external. If you are angry most of the time, even with people who are good to you, it means that you have to resolve your anger issues. You can use this approach not only to know your strengths and weaknesses, but also to evaluate other people and your relationship with them. If there are people in your life who habitually lie, cheat, and deceive, irrespective of circumstances, you have to decide whether you can trust them and rely upon them or maintain a safe distance. If a person is by nature angry and abusive, you have to consider your relationship with that person and how far you can risk your own peace and happiness to keep that relationship.

Knowing your personality type

You might have noticed that you come across different types of people in your life. Some are extroverted, some are introverted, some are friendly, some are hostile, and, so on. Although people are by nature unpredictable and respond differently under different circumstances, we can tell from our observation that they possess certain behavioral tendencies and tend to act repetitively and predictably in most circumstances. This creates the assumption that we can categorize them into different personality types. Before we discuss this further, let us be clear that your individuality, self-image and personality are not the same. Your individuality is what separates you as an individual from others. Your self-image is what you hold as your true identity or self-concept, and your personality is the set of attitudes, responses, and behavioral tendencies, known as personality factors, which make you predictable to other people. While individual traits and behavioral patterns are many, psychologists have reduced them into five basic categories or types, called extroversion, neuroticism, conscientiousness, agreeableness and openness.

The scope of this work does not permit a detailed description of each of these personality types. Extroverts are doers and seekers, who are motivated by the prospect of a reward or gain. They socialize more. Neurotics are emotionally sensitive and prone to negative emotions. They are vulnerable to depression and anxiety, and prefer being alone. Conscientious people work for long term goals and resist short term gains for future rewards. They are organized and disciplined, and prefer leading predictable and routine lives. Agreeable people empathize and care for others. They are good listeners, friendly and pleasant to be around and relate well to others. They socialize, but unlike extroverts they do it out of genuine interest in people, not to seek attention. Open type people are highly creative, artistic, talented and intelligent. They may be interested in spirituality and parapsychology.

The personality types are not rigid categories and not mutually exclusive. A person may have a predominant personality but also possess traits of other types also. For example a conscientious person may also respond to the prospect of a reward, but she may not as readily respond as an extrovert. An agreeable person may also experience fear and depression, but not as frequently or as intensely as a neurotic type. It is also possible that due to circumstances a person may transition from one personality type to another. Awareness of the personality types may help you to determine your predominant behavioral tendencies and use the knowledge either to set your goals or to choose your profession or work for your improvement.

Understanding your rationality

Although we have the reasoning power to think rationally and it is supposed to help us to deal with our problems, we do not always use it or use it correctly to make decisions, or solve our problems. Just as our perceptions are filtered by our minds, our thinking and judgment are also clouded by logical fallacies, irrational thinking, and defensive attitude. They are responsible for our perceptual and cognitive distortions and irrational beliefs. In his book, Feeling Good: the new mood therapy, the author, Dr. David Burns, identified 12 cognitive distortions to explain how people view the world through them and experience recurring pessimism and negative view of the world. They are explained below.

1. **All or nothing thinking**: You see the world strictly as black or white. For example, if you are not with us, you are against us.
2. **Overgeneralization**: You over generalize a person or a situation based upon a single negative event or trait. If your boss does not approve your proposal means your career is doomed forever.
3. **Mental filter**: You let one small negative incident or detail cloud your judgment of the whole

experience. After giving a beautiful presentation and being appreciated by all the participants, you begin to worry about the one person who sat in the corner and kept looking at you questioningly without saying anything.
4. **Disqualifying the positive**: You undermine positive information by finding reasons. Your colleagues like you because you entertain them generously.
5. **Jumping to conclusions**: Without proper evidence you make quick conclusions. Your friend must be having an affair because you saw her twice in the same restaurant having lunch with a person.
6. **Mind reading**: You make assumptions about other people's feelings and emotions or attribute motives without any evidence.
7. **Predicting the future**: You anticipate negative outcomes and act as if it is a certainty.
8. **Catastrophizing or minimizing**: You either greatly exaggerate the severity of negative events or severely minimize the importance of positive events.
9. **Emotional Reasoning**: You reason that because you are emotionally feeling it must be true.
10. **Shoulding**: Due to guilt or distrust in yourself you believe that you must or should force yourself to perform certain actions because otherwise, you cannot be motivated to perform them.
11. **Labeling**: You extend a negative quality or behavior to a person's entire character. Your friend is an idiot. Your colleague is a racist.
12. **Personalizing**: You assume that you are personally responsible for the negative behavior of someone, even if it has nothing to do with it. You boss is looking upset because he may be mad at you.

Thus, we can see that our rationality does not necessarily help us to see the reality, deal with our negative emotions or solve our problems. Instead, we may use it to perpetuate our negativity, depression and delusion. By recognizing and evaluating our perceptions and understanding, and analyzing our thinking and reasoning, we can correct, at least partially, our negative and erroneous behavior.

Become aware of your physical self

Your body is your physical and tangible self. It is the bridge between you and the world. In Hinduism, it is called the food body because it is made up of the food you eat. Since it is your visible self, people know you and recognize you by it. Since you also communicate with the world through it, it plays a significant role in your relationship with it. There are many aspects about your body which you cannot change, such as your height, color and looks. Sometimes it can create problems and influence your self-esteem, health choices and relationships. Your body is a natural machine. Since it is subject to the laws of Nature and vulnerable to threats, it needs both your support and your protection. Your body is your moving vehicle, the seat of your existence and your resting place. You live in it and depend upon it. If it suffers, you will suffer too. You can take care of it by respecting its limitations, responding to its messages and warnings, following preventive measures, and nursing it well during sickness and disease. The following factors contribute to health and happiness.

1. Good habits and healthy lifestyle choices protect your body from wear and tear and disease.
2. As you grow older, your body needs more care and attention.
3. Your body has a threshold limit in tolerating and responding to pain and physical abuse.
4. Knowing the illusions you may have about your appearance helps you to come to grips with reality.
5. Seeing yourself clearly

We have seen that your mind is both a facilitator and an obstacle to self-awareness. Unless you suppress the mental noise, and transcend the logical fallacies, perceptual errors, cognitive distortions, and defensive mechanisms, you will not be able to see yourself clearly and understand your behavior. One of the effective methods taught in eastern spirituality to develop mental clarity is to silence your mind through meditation and concentration and become a passive but conscious observer of your thoughts, emotions, and actions. As you become your own witness, cultivating detachment and dispassion, you can perceive the reality of the world around you and inside you, without distortions and delusions. To maintain objectivity, you have to observe yourself as if you are observing another person. If you persist in your practice, at some stage, your mind suddenly opens up and you develop an insight into your thinking and behavior. You become aware of your irrational beliefs and undesirable behavior, and see yourself clearly and mindfully without the usual mental distortions. It leads to self-awareness and sensitivity towards yourself and others.

The Building Blocks of Your Life

Arun and Amrit are both brothers in their late fifties. They were brought up in the same house, educated in the same institutions, learned practically under the same teachers, and they both majored in medicine. However, after completing their education, Arun married the daughter of a rich local businessman and settled in the USA. He is now a renowned surgeon with huge investments in the U.S. and India. Amrit, the other brother went to Uganda, after the fall of Idi Amin, inspired by the vision of Gandhi, and remained there. He married a British nurse and settled in a town in northern Uganda, where he found an increasing incidence of AIDS. He set up a local clinic to help the poor. His father was not very pleased with him, but his mother was proud of her son. Last time when I met Arun he told me that his brother's wife, the nurse, left him for good and settled in London with her teenage son.

Now, what happened in case of the two brothers? What motivated them to follow different paths and live different lives? Their parents imparted them the same values, but somehow one saw a great value in wealth and prosperity and the other in philanthropy and humanitarian service. It is difficult, or even incorrect, to judge them based upon their actions and decisions, or compare and contrast them to determine which of them is a better human being. The one who went to the USA also helps the poor. He built a hospital in his native town in India and gave a large donation to the school where he studied. After he left for Uganda, his brother did not maintain much contact with India. He visits India occasionally to see his mother. The two brothers probably developed their own vision and values according to their perceptions and went their individual ways.

Different people pursue different goals in their lives and hold different values and beliefs. How they build their lives depend upon their aims and motives, which in turn depend upon their values and beliefs which may be shaped by both internal and external factors. While many factors contribute to the success and happiness of people and lead them on different paths, we can discern in them some factors, which are common and universal and help people in different circumstances to cope with their problems and pursue their goals, even though they lead dissimilar lives. The following are a few such factors, which help people to achieve success and happiness, irrespective of their age, place, or gender. They are, aptitude, attitude, acceptance, direction, diligence, discipline, learning and values. You may even call them the building blocks of life.

Aptitude

Imagine in your school days you had a friend who was a mathematical genius, who could crunch the numbers easily or solve difficult theorems, but his parents forced him to become an IT professional because they wanted him to marry a girl from a rich family who could afford a huge dowry and help him to settle in the USA. This is an imaginary story, but if you are from India, you would be familiar with the theme. Many youngsters pursue their education and careers according to the instructions of their parents or the demands of society, rather than their natural talents. Aptitude means what comes to you naturally, or what you are inclined to do or spend the rest of your life without much inner resistance. Some people have an aptitude for science, some for mathematics, some for some artistic activity and some for business.

Your aptitude may arise from your early influences or by your beliefs and interests. It is a combination of your skills, abilities, interest, and natural disposition. The earlier you discover your aptitude, the better it is for you. Many people become confused about their basic aptitudes because of parental expectations, desires, and social conditioning. You have better chances of achieving success, fulfillment and happiness if you pursue a career according to your basic aptitude rather than what others tell you or expect from you. If you set your goals according to the demands and expectations of your parents, or society, you may still achieve success. However, you may not be happy as you suffer from conflicts and dissatisfaction with your choices and find it difficult to come to terms with yourself. It may even affect your marriage, and relationships as you vent your negative feelings upon others.

Attitude

Attitude is how you feel and think about a thing, a person, a process, an action, a goal, a value system, a belief, or an ideology. If you are inclined to feel positively about it, your attitude is positive, and if you are inclined to feel negatively it is negative. Since both your heart and mind shape your attitude, it greatly influences your choices, goals, desires, and decisions, and how you react and respond to various situations in your life. If you do not feel positive about yourself, you will be unhappy and depressed. If you do not feel positive about others, you may avoid their company and prefer staying alone. If you do not feel positive about your career or goals, you may not put your heart and soul in performing your tasks.

Therefore, you should know your feelings and thoughts, before you choose your goals, make decisions about your education, career, marriage, and other milestones in your life. If you think that you do not have positive attitude about certain things in your life which are vital to your success and happiness, you must cultivate them by changing your thinking and beliefs or by reexamining your perceptions. You should also examine your attitude towards success itself. If you think negatively about wealth, money, success, or successful people, you may probably sabotage your own success and avoid those conditions subconsciously. In such cases you have to reset your thinking and values.

Acceptance

Acceptance means how far you are comfortable with your self-image, your relationship with the world, your goals, your circumstances, and the general direction of your life. If you are comfortable with your self-image, you will not be guided by the opinions of others to set your goals or to pursue them, and you will not be easily daunted by others' criticism. You evaluate situations according to your best judgment and act accordingly. Acceptance also means whether you accept your circumstances, relationships, the nature of the world in which you live and the uncertainties of life. When you set goals, you should know whether you accept not only the goals but also the conditions they may manifest. Acceptance also means how far you are willing to change, sacrifice your values and beliefs, or accept what you cannot change. Acceptance denotes your level of comfort with the things you seek or pursue and accept what you cannot achieve. For example, you cannot sustain your success, if you are unwilling to accept the challenges your success may manifest or the failures that you may have to experience while pursuing it. Your happiness does not depend upon your success as much as it depends upon your acceptance of it and the circumstances and conditions related to it. If you are successful, but not happy about it, it means that you have not accepted your success or the life it manifested.

Your self-image consists of both your strengths or weaknesses. It is necessary that you accept them both as part of your reality and deal with them according to your best judgment and goals. If you are uncomfortable with yourself you will undervalue your abilities, lower your expectations and underachieve, or you may overestimate your weakness and expect failures and disappointments. You must also accept the ever changing reality and the uncertainty, to which you are subject because what you consider your strength or an asset may become a weakness or a liability in some situations. For example, if you are knowledgeable and intelligent and find yourself working in a team of mediocre and apathetic people, they may intentionally subject you to group-think and undermine your strengths or discount your value to the team. In such cases, your strengths become your weaknesses.

Direction

The direction is the course of progress that you achieve in your life. How do you know that you are progressing in the right direction? If you are lost in a desert or a forest, you may walk for days or hours and finally without your knowing may end up walking in the exact opposite direction of the place from where you began. It may happen when are not familiar with the terrain, and do not know in which direction you are moving. Sometimes, you may keep moving forward, but if you face a major obstacle such as a deep gorge or a steep hill, you may have to backtrack and return to the spot from where you began. Experiences such as these prove that neither time nor action ensures progress unless you know where you are headed to.

John Dike, a baker, spent nearly six years running a bakery shop owned by his friend who lived abroad. His friend paid him a monthly salary and an annual bonus if the shop made profit. John did not save enough money during the six years. He toiled in the bakery, thinking that when his friend returned he would make him a business partner, and they both could continue the business. When recession hit, his friend decided to sell his shop, unable to pay for the mortgage. The new owners did not want to run a bakery, but open a jewelry shop. John ultimately managed to find a job as a baker in another bakery, but his dream of opening a business was dashed to the ground. For six years he kept working, but made little progress in securing his future, as he paid little attention to the direction in which he progressed. He was stuck in the routine and happy with it hoping that at some point in future things would change.

Like John, many people move in circles. They toil their whole lives, but hardly make any progress in the right direction. To know whether you are moving in the right direction, you have to fix goals and milestones and monitor your progress. You must verify your feelings against the values you cherish and know whether you are in alignment with them. You must know intuitively what to do when you are stuck in the same routine or feel that you are not able to fulfill the purpose of your life. You may change your plans, methods and strategies, but to remain motivated your direction must be aligned with your goals and your values.

Diligence

I knew a couple in India who were poor and had little education. However, both were good cooks and enjoyed cooking. They had a dream to own a restaurant. When they got married, they decided to make it happen. They borrowed money from a relation and started an eatery in a makeshift house in the outskirts of the town where they lived. Every day they would wake up around 3 o' clock in the morning and work until late in the night. In the daytime they would take rest alternatively for two or three hours so that they could stay awake in the night and do the preparation for the next day. They followed the routine for two years until they were able to hire additional hands and find time for their children and themselves. Last time I met them few years ago they owned three restaurants in the same town and employed about twenty people. They were also planning to start an upscale restaurant in the heart of the town. They told me that every weekend they served free food to the poor at a local temple, and once in a month they fed the children of a nearby orphanage. They have earned a good name and respect for the quality they maintain and the service they give. They are hired as caterers for most of the marriages and functions held in the town. Theirs is a fine example of how hard work pays off and contributes to success, even if you have some limitations such as poor education or lack of money.

Successful people share one common feature. They are hard working. There is no substitute for hard work. For success in any field you need persistent effort, even if it means pain and discomfort, so that when opportunities come into your way you can readily make use of them. You can put your talents and skills to right use only through hard work. Whether you are born in a poor family or a rich family, without hard work, you cannot achieve success. All successful people begin their career by working for hours in the pursuit of their goals, improving their skills, or looking for the one big break that would change their lives. They work even more after they achieve success to sustain it, perfect their methods, maintain quality, achieve excellence, improve their performance, or stay ahead in competition.

However, hard work alone does not guarantee success or happiness. Your goals, methods, decisions, and values are also important. Fraudsters and scam artists also work overtime to achieve their ends, but in the end pay dearly for their nefarious actions. Behind every true success you will find the contribution of hard working people. Hard work is the hub of the wheel of success and progress. It is the only way we can make miracles happen or invite luck into our lives.

Discipline

Discipline does not mean that you have to wake up early in the morning, do meditation and stick to your daily routine. Many successful people are disciplined this way, with rigid daily programs of their own, such as waking up early, doing yoga or exercise, eating certain types of food at specific times and focusing on the demands of their profession. However, there are also some successful people, who wake up late, but manage to live well and achieve success. A lot depends upon the nature of your job, and what you intend to do in your life. If you work for an overseas company on the other side of the planet, you may have to keep yourself awake in the night and work until morning hours. Therefore, your sleeping habits depend upon your circumstances or your personal choices.

Discipline truly means controlling and regulating your thoughts and actions and sticking to an action plan or a specific path until the end to produce desired results. A disciplined person leads a structured, systematic, and orderly life performing actions according to plans and rules, staying focused, and adhering to values and principles, whether he is watched by others or not. Discipline gives you the strength to match your thoughts and goals with your actions and persevere in your effort despite problems and challenges. You can practice discipline either personally to improve your wellbeing or professionally to improve the chances of your success and happiness.

Learning

As Dolly Parton wrote in her book, Dream More: celebrate the dreamer in you, learning is easier if you can read, but real learning is all about experience, how you look at your actions and circumstances and draw lessons from them. You can learn a lot by reading and a lot more by observing your actions and others' actions, and the world in general. The inferences you draw from your daily experiences can give you an insight into yourself and others, and improve both your common sense and wisdom. Your learning never stops. You keep learning your whole life. Even after you achieve mastery in any field, you still have a lot of scope to learn.

In the present day world, the importance of learning cannot be undermined. Progress in science and technology is happening at an astounding pace. Companies all over the world are forced to introduce new designs and products to satisfy their loyal, but demanding, and over expectant customers. Thousands of books and research papers are published every day. Thousands of articles are posted on blogs and websites every hour. Whether you are a doctor, lawyer, engineer, tax consultant, accountant, or employee, you cannot survive the competition and succeed in the overcrowded markets, without learning continuously to keep your knowledge and skills up-to-date. Learning improves you as a person by improving your knowledge, expertise, skills, productivity, and creativity. By learning from your failures and mistakes, you can also avoid making the same mistakes. You learn better when you cultivate openness, humility, and interest, and apply what you learn to the situations in your life.

Values

Your values are your heart's deepest desires. They let you know what you want to be, what the purpose of your life should be, what you should cherish dearly, where you should be going and how you should regard your successes and failures, or interpret your feelings and experiences. Values help you to find direction and keep you motivated in reaching your goals. Your values are different from your goals. Your goals are the end points of your actions or their end results, whereas values provide you with the impetus and the direction to reach there. Your goals have limited scope in the sense that once you achieve them you can forget them, whereas you keep following your values for the rest of your life. Your values give you the strength and purpose to continue even if you fail to achieve your goals. They help you to keep you going when the going gets tough.

John Chris had a passion for sports goods and opened a retail shop to sell sports memorabilia to the local fans. Unfortunately, his business did not pick up as he had to compete with major retailers, local museums, and internet websites that operated on minimum profit margins. John was not disheartened. He analyzed his failure and learned from his mistakes. He took personal responsibility for what happened as he did not foresee competition from the internet retailers and did not anticipate that in a recession people would not like to spend money on sports memorabilia. His failure did not deter him. He talked to a lot of people and explored various options before he decided to open a gym, which he thought was immune to both the internet and the recession. After careful planning and with the help of a few partners, he opened the gym choosing a location where there was no competition from other gyms within the radius of a few miles. Soon the new business picked up as customers in the area signed up taking advantage of the attractive deals he offered. John was able to absorb his business failure and emerge successfully because he believed in the value of perseverance and learning from his mistakes. He did not feel crushed by his failure but challenged by it. He learned from his experience and moved on. He opened a new business with due diligence, learning from his mistakes without blaming others or end up feeling resentful.

Your values thus help you when you need direction or regain your balance. They are an integral part of your character and personality. Since they reflect your heart's deepest desires, they influence your emotions and feelings. They are also important to your peace and happiness, because you experience them not only when you achieve your goals but also when you are connected to your values. In addition, in adversity and difficulties they provide you with reasons and a purpose to continue and persevere. Thus, your chances of survival and success under any circumstances depend upon your values.

Career Development

The dictionary meaning of career is any job, profession or occupation taken up as a lifelong activity. It also means progress made in a chosen profession for the duration of a person's working life. A career, therefore, is not a job, but what you can accomplish through it in your lifetime. For most people, work is central to their careers and lives. Many become so involved with their careers that they ignore their other goals and personal comforts. It invariably creates an imbalance in their lives and leads to unhappy consequences. The same jobs or professions, which make people happy when they are successful, also make them unhappy, frustrated and angry when they make wrong career choices, resort to unethical methods, develop too much attachment to their professions, or pursue wrong goals. The following suggestions are important to career planning and boosting anyone's career without losing focus and balance.

Understand group dynamics: What many people do not realize about their careers is that a person's success in any organization depends not only upon individual qualities and merits but also upon group dynamics and the culture of the organization. Your organization is a person in itself having a distinct character and personality of its own. It exists long before you join it, as it develops an enduring identity of its own, amidst change and growth, and outlasts you. So is the case with the group, or the team you work for. Once you join a group or company, your decisions and actions are influenced by your perception of the group, the power structure within the group and the norms the group follows.

Therefore, unless you understand the dynamics of group norms, group identity and conformity, and how the groups within the organization deal with individual members, you may not fit well into the organization or the teams you work for. Sometimes, your group may not appreciate your strengths and may even secretly want you to fail or expose your weaknesses rather than strengths. Your success within the organization depends a lot upon your alliances and political skills rather than your true talent. In many companies what matters in the end is not how much work you do but how you socialize and build your network.

Successful people learn quickly how power flows in their organizations, who the power players and game changers are, and build relationships with them. Through them, they extend their influence, power and authority, in addition to proving their own worth and establishing their authority. It is equally important that you let the stakeholders know your achievements and contribution, because if you are not careful others may take credit for your work..

Choose the right career: In choosing your career you can follow two criteria. One is that it should rank well in public esteem in terms of benefits and rewards, and the other is it should offer you a chance to use your skills and excel. The former gives you financial security and social status, while the latter contributes to your success, peace and happiness. You should consider yourself lucky, if your job offers you an opportunity to enjoy both. Ideally, you should choose a career where you can use your strengths and talents and excel. It is desirable to find such a job from the beginning of your career, so that your chances of success increase greatly as you gain experience and polish your skills. Many people do not think about their careers until they complete their education. Then, they find some job and try to fit into it. This is a haphazard approach. Your career planning should start from your school days. You should choose those subjects where you are comfortable and specialize in them. Once you complete your education, you should opt for a career where you can put your academic and professional knowledge to good use. It is also important to specialize in a specific field. If you just get a degree without specializing in any subject, you may still achieve success by hard work, but you may not get the same recognition as the specialists.

Adapt to your job: In life we do not always get what we want. Many people end up in professions they dislike. If you are one of them, you have to decide whether to adapt to the demands of your career or find the one you like. In a competitive world or in difficult times, you may not always find a job of your dreams. Many people arrive at it through trial and error. They do many odd jobs or low paying ones before finding the one that suits them best. Your career choices diminish with age, as you settle down and become entangled in your family responsibilities. Once you decide to stick to a job or a profession, you should adapt to it fully and do whatever is necessary to fit into it and excel in it. The worst thing that can happen to anyone in a career is to feel trapped and helpless. If you are chronically unhappy about your career or working conditions, you should examine whether it is caused by your career or your own negativity. Sometimes your dissatisfaction with your career may arise from comparison with others, when you feel that your friends or relations are enjoying better positions than you. You may also feel unhappy if you missed many good opportunities in the past. If you are the problem, you have to change your attitude and adapt to the demands of your career. Otherwise, you have to weigh the options and make an appropriate decision.

Take responsibility: Your success or failure in your job or career depends primarily upon your effort. Sometimes external factors may play a role, but if it happens, you can respond to them properly and minimize the damage. In a job situation you have different responsibilities towards the company you work for, customers or stakeholders, colleagues, and yourself. Your responsibility begins from the time you choose your job and continues until you leave. You are responsible for both decisions, and what happens to your knowledge and consent in between.

Responsibility means doing your duties diligently, taking accountability for your actions and accepting their consequences with courage and honesty. It means that you should know your duties, possess knowledge and skills, perform your tasks according to the best standards, and take responsibility for your own growth and career. You cannot take credit for the success of another, unless you genuinely contributed to it, nor can you allow others to exploit you for their own ends. You should also give credit where it is due. If you properly use the communication channels available to you, you can avoid most of these problems.

Keep learning continuously: To remain competitive in this fast changing world, you have to constantly improve your skills and job knowledge. In fact, for career growth, it is imperative. Years ago, I participated in a course about database design and development. The faculty member who trained us in SQL programming was particular about how efficiently we wrote the code but also how nicely we presented it with comments and indentation. In the class, he would keep reminding us that technical people who worked in big organizations for a long time would lose their competitive edge as they would be mechanically doing the same repetitive tasks for years without learning anything new. The might move from technical positions to become managers and generalists, but their technical skills would get rusted as they would have fewer opportunities to keep pace with the progress made in their field.

It is true that many big companies take time to adapt to current technologies because of the costs, risks, and other factors and allow inefficiencies to creep into their systems. Those who work for them will have to learn on their own to keep their knowledge current and remain competitive. Alternatively, in a small business you may not get enough opportunities to learn and improve. It means that you face the risk of obsolescence when you join an organization, unless you take care of your learning and career. It is not wise to ignore your career goals and skill development when you work for others and not let them influence your learning choices. Instead, you should constantly improve your knowledge and skills and keep challenging yourself by setting new learning goals, whether your job or profession is using them currently or not.

Have career goals and plans: An important part of career planning is that you must have a clear idea of where you want to go in five years or ten years hence. It is better if you can write down your goals clearly and specifically because it helps you to work for your success with definitive aims. If you cannot do it (which may mean your ambition has waned), at least you should have an idea in which direction you want to progress and where you want to see yourself in future. Having goals in itself may not help you much, but it helps you to plan your future and prepare yourself mentally.

Having mentors within and outside your field of interest, socializing and expanding your network through regular contacts are an important part of your career planning. They help you to prepare for managing higher responsibilities, and expand your zone of influence. Your mentors help you to learn from their knowledge and experience, while planning helps you to organize your resources and activities around your future goals and use them effectively. Both are essential for achieving excellence in any field.

The challenges you face in the early part of your career are much different from those you face later. In the early stages as you begin your career, job knowledge, job skills, team work and relationships matter. However, as you progress, leadership, social and business skills, and executive functions such as decisions making, planning, etc., become important. During this stage, if you work in an organization, you have to know the politics of management and leadership. You have to learn to form alliances with your peers and colleagues who are the decisions makers, and avoid making enemies. The higher you go, the chances of making mistakes and suffering from them increase, since you will be under the radar of many people, some of whom may be competing with you for the same space and attention. Learning in a career is thus a continuous process. You have to learn not only to perform your job better but also to survive and succeed.

Be proactive: In simple terms to be proactive means to stay ahead of a problem. In mechanical terms it means replacing a weak part before it breaks down and causes a systemic failure. In organizational terms it means creating backup plains, maintain checks and balances, planning for breakdowns and catastrophes, identifying and reporting problems in time, establishing and maintaining a line of command to deal with problems and complaints, resolving grievances before they become conflicts, taking measures to prevent security breaches, and anticipating the market trends to remain competitive. A few years ago a company's email system completely broke down because someone forgot to delete a test module from the code before moving it into the company's main servers. No one proactively monitored the installation process, or foresaw the problem and tested the code before uploading it. Many such problems can be prevented by being proactive. In personal terms, proactive means to avoid delays and procrastination, preventing health problems, keeping the costs down, saving for the rainy day, and planning for contingencies. Proactive thinking is a state of mind. It is a leadership quality and part of a pragmatic and positive approach, in which you take the initiative and assume ownership for your role and responsibility. Since they are forward looking and risk-averse, they are the most sought after people in every organization.

Improve your communication skills: In today's context communication not only means the traditional communication skills, but also knowing how to send and manage e-mails, deal with media, publicity, public relations, customer complaints and grievances, online communication, social networks, Internet marketing, etc. It also includes how you communicate with your colleagues and peers and influence them. Nowadays, many employers regularly monitor Internet communication, and social network activity of their employees, during working hours and during work from home. Hence, you should be careful about what information and messages you leave online or what information you store in your office phone, laptop or computer. In today's world, you should know how to speak for yourself, defend your decisions, actions, and opinions, communicate your achievements, and stay current with the happenings in your organization. You should also know how to set standards in speaking, listening and observing, when you lead and organize teams or manage people.

Do more than expected: Your success depends upon your effort and dedication. By doing more than what you are expected to do, you will earn recognition and good will. You will set in motion the law of compensation, which will bring you rich rewards. Years ago I was asked to prepare a report on a small African country where the company I worked for wanted to open on office and expand the business. They wanted to know whether the operation would be viable. I spent a few days gathering information about the country and its market conditions, and prepared a detailed report. I submitted the report with additional information, which the company did not expect me to cover since they did not give me much time. The committee to which I submitted the report was impressed by the details and the relevance of information and sent me a letter or appreciation signed by all the members. I did not get an immediate reward for my effort, but it left a good impression upon the stakeholders. It is better if you learn early in your career about the importance of going an extra mile or doing more than necessary. Successful companies, employees, and professionals practice this principle to stay ahead in competition. They give you more than you expect from them. Every assignment that you get in your job is an opportunity to improve your skills, and prove your worth, commitment and dedication. Some people whine when they are asked to do extra work. You should look for those opportunities even if it means some inconvenience. To succeed in any career, you must do more than what is expected. It sends a clear message to your peers, customers and everyone that you are serious about your job and you can be trusted and entrusted with higher responsibilities.

Pay attention to details: How many times you might have sent e-mails or posted messages on the Internet and realized that you did it without checking the grammar or spelling? Simple mistakes can prove costly and cause you embarrassment. If you work for a long time in the same job or in the same team you may become comfortable with the routine and ignore the details. It can cause you problems. For example, a friend of mine was supposed to make a product presentation in a nearby town. He drove there for two hours only realize that he left behind the most important file that was crucial for his presentation. Someone else had to drive all the way to give him the file. The golden rule is that you must be diligent in your work, as if you are self-employed and no one is supervising you. It is how people develop trust in you and look to you when they need help. If you are in a leadership or managerial positions you have to be even more careful because you depend upon others to complete your tasks. You may make mistakes if you do not monitor their work properly or pay attention to details. If you want to be successful in your career, you must pay attention to detail. The same rule applies when you perform simple tasks such as making presentations, preparing reports, writing programs, planning projects, or sending e-mails. You cannot ignore the importance of quality in your work even if it is a routine task.

Maintain ethical conduct: In a professional sense, ethical conduct refers to the practice of values, morals, and recognized standards of ethical behavior in performing one's duty. It means in performing your duties you should be consistent and truthful, maintain the highest standards, comply with rules and regulations applicable to your work, undertake your duties with due diligence and care, do your work lawfully, keep confidential information confidential, and provide accurate and correct information when you are asked to. It also means that you should be truthful, honest, sincere, transparent, objective, fair, impartial, respectful and lawful in your thinking, attitude and actions as you undertake your professional responsibilities and duties. At a purely personal level, ethical conduct refers to the means you adapt to pursue your career goals and perform your professional duties.

Aim for long term rewards: Stress is so common in call centers that people easily burn out and leave. To motive the employees who work there, floor supervisors organize competitive events to reward those who make maximum calls or collect the highest amount during the peak hours. Prizes are given instantly in front of everyone after the contest is over, amidst claps and cheers. The winners are given small gifts or monetary rewards for their effort, which include movie tickets, bags of candy, T-shirts, coffee mugs, etc. Sometimes a team supervisor organizes a pizza party during the lunch hour and invite all the team members. Life in a call center is very hectic and result driven, and those who work there are seldom promoted to higher positions. At the most they manage to become floor supervisors, which adds to their woes since it makes them responsible for the team effort also. Therefore, most of the them stay there temporarily until they find a better job.

The point is, unless they are desperate, people do not prefer doing any job or pursuing any career that do not offer long term rewards or opportunities for career growth. Short term gains may give you temporary happiness, but do not contribute much to your motivation. If you are looking for a successful career on an enduring basis, you must look for jobs where you can aim for long term rewards rather than short term. Long term rewards are qualitatively more satisfying and morale boosting. They also change your life substantially and financially. Sometimes you may have to sacrifice short term goals for long term rewards. For example, by working for long hours you may not get immediate rewards, but eventually you will succeed in earning recognition. Besides, it adds to your stature and reputation as a conscientious and reliable person.

Organize and prioritize: Several years ago, a friend of mine who worked for a government organization told me that he was posted as the manager of a remote rural office in a southern state of India. When he went there to report for duty, his predecessor received him and introduced him to the staff. After exchanging a few pleasantries, they sat down to complete the formalities. My friend told me that after acquainting him with the daily administration and the major problems that needed his immediate attention his predecessor took out a small pile of papers and office keys from his table drawer and put them on the table. With his hands upon them, he told him that the papers needed his immediate attention as they were most recent papers he received from the regional office. The rest, he said, were routine documents or official circulars, which he either kept in the cupboards in the manager's office or sent to the staff. He did not open the cupboards to show the papers and my friend did not ask for it as he trusted his words and did not foresee any problems.

Later, after he took leave, my friend opened the cupboard out of curiosity and found a pile of loose papers stacked inside. The files were neither indexed nor named. The person who handed him the charge and managed the office for the previous three years followed no filing system as he solely relied upon his memory to trace the papers from the pile. He sent the routine documents to the staff for filing while he put important ones and confidential information in the cupboards inside his office under lock and key. My friend had to spend several days to index and organize all the information and train the staff to follow a similar system at their level. He said that it was clearly the worst case of disorganization in his experience and he learned many lessons from it. What happened in case of my friend is not uncommon in many parts of the world, especially in government and bureaucratic institutions, where people run their offices without any accountability. They often do it deliberately to cover up irregularities and loopholes, and avoid paper trail.

Proper organization in any aspect of life is important for success, peace and happiness. Whether you work for yourself or others, you must be organized and systematic. Your organization skills begin with your immediate surroundings and the discipline you follow in your life. Without organizing and prioritizing your work, you will suffer from problems and stressful situations as you make mistakes or do not find the required information when you need it. After you reach a certain stage in your career you may use the services of an assistant or a secretary to do it, but until then you have to organize your life and work to improve your productivity and efficiency.

Do not neglect your personal life or your family: Your personal life and happiness are more important than your job or career. Your success has no value unless it is shared by your family members. In the ups and down of your life, they share your joys and sorrows and provide you with a sanctuary to recover and recuperate when you are down and beaten. None would be happier to see you succeed in life than your immediate family. If success and your preoccupation with the demands of your job keep you away from them, none would be unhappier about it than them. Even if you are very keen about achieving success in your life at all costs, you should not ignore their needs and expectations. They are the shareholders of your success and your cheerleaders. Any success that you achieve should improve their lives and happiness. Otherwise, your success would be without any meaning to them. Perhaps in the end when you retire from your career, it may not also mean much to you. The purpose of having a career is not an end in itself. It is the means to a complete life in which there is a place for your success as well as your relationships. In pursing your career goals, you should never lose sight of the truth that your life is not a part of your job, but your job is just a part of your life. Therefore, why not make your family the stakeholders in your success?

Plan for the contingencies: When I received the news of my father's unexpected death, my wife and I had to rush immediately. My father lived in another state, about 600 miles from where we lived. Since it was a long drive, a friend of mine volunteered to accompany us and give us company and support. During the journey, we had to drive about 100 miles through a dacoit infested area, which was largely made up of hills and forests. People usually drove through it in caravans with police escort in the front and back. When we reached that place in the middle of the night, we decided not to wait until the caravan was formed and the police escort was ready. We took a chance and drove through it alone in pitch darkness. After we traveled alone for a few miles, when we were negotiating a hill, the back tire of the car punctured. We had no clue what punctured the tire and whether anyone deliberately did it to stop the car. We had no option but to stop on that desolate road to change the tire. We were too afraid to switch on the torch light we had with us, since we were on the top of the hill and the light could be seen from far by anyone. In that eerie silence and darkness we changed the tire quietly and started again. We drove nonstop until we reached a safe town where we stopped briefly to get the damaged tire repaired and sealed.

We were lucky by all means, considering the stories one heard about the incidents that happened in the area. Kidnappings for ransom were very common. Part of the luck was because I took proper care to maintain the car in good condition and check the condition of the spare tire each time I left the town and went on a long drive. Imagine the situation if I did not keep my car in good condition or check the spare tire before leaving. In life and work, many times problems arise unexpectedly. Since you never know how things will turn out, you have to always plan for contingencies and keep backup plans. The same holds true for your career. Nowadays, when recession and economic downturns are frequent, you should prepare for unexpected developments in your life and career.

Know how to handle power: Power is the ability to take decisions, perform actions, or control and influence your actions and of others. Power arises from positions of authority, knowledge, skills and relationships. Whether you are an employee, businessman, or a professional, you have to know when to use it and when to obey it. One of the problems many midlevel managers face in their careers is that they do not know how to handle the power they are vested with or respond to the power others hold over them. A friend of mine, who was a performance driven executive used his power excessively and caused a lot of suffering to the people who worked directly for him. He took pride in his leadership to keep people under coercive control. At the same time, he acted very submissively before his superiors and tried to please them. His subordinates disliked him, while his superiors did not respect him as they knew what was going on. If you are a career driven and task oriented person, you may hurt others by your actions and decisions even if you do not intend to hurt anyone. It is difficult not to make errors when you have the power to make important decisions and deal with people from a position of authority. If you use too much power, people may not trust you, or express their true opinions before you. If you do not use it, they may not listen to you or respect you. Even if you are good to people, you may still displease a few who may not like your style. Therefore, you should know how to use power and lead others with minimum negative consequences.

Power is always a means, not an end. You have to use it to perform tasks and control processes, but not to make yourself important, settle scores, or make personal gains. True power comes from inside when you believe in yourself and when you are comfortable with being yourself. When you occupy a position of authority, you should know how to radiate power, without using threats or fear, or showing off your importance with rhetoric. Many times when you negotiate with others, or when you have to resolve tough problems, you may have to act as if you do not have any power. In an organization your power is always limited. For example even if you hold the highest office, you cannot set your salary or decide your retirement benefits. That power rests with others. Therefore, however powerful you may be, you still need the help, support and goodwill of others. It means you must be kind and a good person.

Learn from failures: Failure is relative to your hopes and expectations. What you think is failure may be success to others. Many people remain so focused upon their success or their goals that they do not really feel elated when they reach their goals. You will feel more excitement in the idea of achieving something or reaching somewhere rather than when you actually achieve it. Success is not an end in itself because there is no guarantee that with success you will live happily forever. Your success may create circumstances that may lead to suffering. For example, you may earn a lot of wealth, but may create many enemies for yourself or suffer from tax problems and bad reputation. Therefore, you should learn from both your failure and success, without losing your balance and focus.

Help others: Mr. Venkat Sharma retired as a senior engineer after working for nearly 35 years in heavy equipment manufacturing company in India. A year after his retirement, I attended his 60th birthday party and 35th marriage anniversary organized by his friends and family members. Nearly three hundred people, other than his relations, joined the celebrations. Most of them were his students whom he trained and coached when he worked as a faculty member in the corporate training college. There were some whom he helped with his money or advice. He never missed an opportunity to call people and inquire about their welfare. When people fell sick or lost their relations, he went to see them and console them. He helped many people to get jobs or join as interns. The love and affection he received from the people who came to see him was very visible. Venkat Sharma used his career not only to achieve personal success but also to practice his humanity and kindness. In my opinion, it is true success. Your success must radiate its own fragrance and touch the heart of others. It must help them to realize their goals. Helping others should be the career goal of every professional including you, so that in the end you can have the satisfaction that you helped many people, without any expectations and contributed to their growth and happiness.

Witnessing Your Own Fears

To know yourself better, you need to know your dominant thoughts, desires and emotions. Even they do not reveal much about you unless you overcome your internal barriers to self-awareness. We have already touched this aspect in a previous article when we discussed the mental filters we use in making sense of the world. One of the truths about our emotions is that except for a few primary ones, such as fear or anger, we cannot distinguish most of them, because in most situations we experience mixed emotions of different intensities rather than one pure emotion. Thus, one may experience fear and sadness at the same time, or anger and fear, or fear and guilt, and so on. Studies show that emotions disrupt our thinking and temporarily block our active memory whereby we can neither think nor act rationally until the blockage is cleared. Our knowledge and perception of situations also influence our emotions strongly. For example, in the middle of a group or in a familiar place you may not experience fear as much as when you are alone or in an unknown place. You may also experience more fear or insecurity, when you already know that the place or the situation in which you are is unsafe.

The mental dimension of fear

Emotions play an important role in our survival. Indeed, despite our rationality, we cannot resolve our problems or identify threats without feeling emotions. Emotions teach us a lot about our environment and impart meaning to the situations we face. Hence, emotional intelligence is considered an important aspect of human intelligence, which helps us to respond and adapt to situations. Of the emotions, fear is the most frequent one we experience. The following are a few well-known facts about human fear.

- **Fear is a universal and natural response**: Fear is part of the self-preservation instinct, which is common to both humans and animals. Everyone experiences fear.
- **Fear is a conditioned or learned response**: We are conditioned to respond to certain situations with fear. Examples are, fear of authority, fear of

law, fear of conventions and customs, fear of disapproval and criticism, fear of the unknown, etc.
- **Fear is caused by various factors**: Both internal and external factors are responsible for our fears. For example, fear may be caused by our thoughts, irrational beliefs, or by situations that are unknown, unfamiliar, or extreme.
- **Fear has many forms**: Fear arises in us variously from mild to intense levels as anxiety, distrust, worry, phobia, etc. Since, fear is situational and experienced at various levels physically, mentally, and emotionally, some even say that there are as many fears as there are situations.
- **We can change our response to fear**: While it is difficult to suppress fears, it is possible to change our conditioning, thinking and our response to fear.
- **Fear has a subconscious presence**: Fear dominates our minds most of the time. Even when we are asleep we are not free from it, as we experience mild to extreme fear in our dreams also. Fear is also responsible for many defensive mechanisms we use in our daily lives to protect ourselves rather unconsciously from threatening, painful, and stressful situations.
- **Our bodies can affect our fears**: Studies show that our fears can affect our bodies and our bodies in turn can affect our fears.
- **Some fears are persistent**: However you may try, certain fears cannot be simply overcome with simple measures.

Fear is also the most dominant emotion we experience, followed by greed, anger and envy. It is also the dominant emotion in the animals. Fear is responsible for our flight response and anger for our fight response. Using both the responses according to situations and perceptions, we prepare our minds and bodies to reach our goals and fulfill our desires. One may argue that fear is not an emotion or a feeling but an impulse or an instinct because it is closely aligned to our survival instinct. There is even an argument that most of the emotions we experience, such as guilt, worry, or anxiety are different forms of fear only because they mostly arise in association with fear or in response to fear, while many positive emotions such as happiness, joy or elation appear in its absence.

Beneath the surface of our lives, consciousness, activities, achievements, hopes, and desires, fear resides like a coiled serpent and rears its head whenever we are weak and vulnerable. Fear makes us aware of the threats present in our environment, but at the same time reminds us of the need to act courageously when it is necessary. On the negative side, fear is destructive and self-effacing. It can prevent us from being who we are, and from using our talents, resources, and skills or pursue our goals. Whether we are happy, unhappy, angry or envious, fear is always present somewhere deeply in our consciousness, regardless of what is happening in our lives.

Positively speaking, fear keeps us within our limits and comfort zones and prevents us from taking undue risks and harming ourselves or our interests. Fear influences our risk taking habits, and extreme lifestyle choices that may harm our minds and bodies. Fear also plays an important role in keeping the world and society in order, and a majority of people bound to certain norms of behavior. While fear is healthy and essential in some situations, excessive and abnormal fears interfere with our thinking and ability to deal rationally with the problems we face. Fear influences the following four important functions of your mind.

- **Perception**: Your fears filter what you perceive, and how you perceive.
- **Cognition**: Your fears determine how you perceive and understand situations and threats.
- **Expectation**: Your fears shape your expectations about yourself, others and your relationships.
- **Performance**: Your fears affect your motivation, goal setting, commitment to goals, and motivation to achieve them.

Fear is both physical and mental. It is felt at various levels physically, perceptually, cognitively, and memorially. It is experienced by both humans and animals. Irrespective of their nature, it can be induced artificially in people through conditioning and repeated exposure to stressful situations. There are three stages in the experience of fear. They are, perception , reaction, and expression. The reaction is both physical and mental, and so also the expression.

The spiritual dimension of fear

Long time ago, the Buddha declared that desire was the root cause of human suffering. Many eastern traditions, including classical yoga, recognize desire and attachments as the main cause of our emotions. As we become involved with the material world, fulfilling our needs and desires, accumulating things and acting selfishly, we experience various types of fear, such as fear of loss, fear of failure, fear of rejection, fear of criticism, fear of the unknown, fear of future, and so on. As a result, we spend a lot of time trying to deal with our fears, manage them, suppress them or forget them. From a spiritual perspective our fears are caused by the following factors, impermanence, judgment, expectations, attraction and aversion, irrational beliefs, and conflicts with our morals and values. Let us examine them one by one.

Impermanence: We live in a transient world, where we can hardly take anything for granted. We grow up seeing people, the world, situations and ourselves changing constantly. As we deal with the uncertainty arising from change, we suffer from fear, insecurity, worry and anxiety.

Judgment: Many times people avoid taking action or initiative because they are afraid of the criticism, ridicule or disapproval they may face from others. They also experience fear, self-doubt, negativity and anxiety because of their own negative self-talk and self-criticism. Therefore, they prefer to avoid situations rather than engage in them. Avoidance, withdrawal, submission, shame, guilt, worries, distrust are our typical responses to fear, which are caused by the judgments we pass against ourselves.

Expectations: You may experience fear when you expect negative outcomes from your actions; when you have over expectations about the actions, talents and skills of the people with whom you compete; when you expect to achieve goals that are either unrealistic or exaggerated; and when you have negative expectations from the people you deal with.

Attraction and aversion: We are afraid of coming into contact with the things that produce pain and discomfort, and of losing things that make us happy. Fear of failure, fear of loss, fear of adversity, fear of diseases, fear of separation from the near and dear, fear of the unknown and the unfamiliar, and fear of aging, are some examples of attraction and aversion which we experience.

Irrational beliefs: Several years ago I had a fear of elevators. I would worry that I would be accidentally crushed between the doors while entering the elevators or going out. I am not sure what was responsible for that. My dog is afraid of vacuum cleaners. When he hears its sound in the house, he runs away and watches it from a distance with suspicion. I tried to make him realize that it was not an animal, but he could not be convinced. By nature he is friendly and playful and likes human company. Many people experience such irrational fears, like fear of ghosts, spirits, psychic attacks, animals, heights, strangers, crowded places, etc. Some suffer from persecution complex, or the nagging belief that they are being criticized by everyone. Some become delusional and begin to worry that they are being constantly watched and monitored by an agency or by a real or imaginary person who intends to harm them.

Conflicts with our values: People experience fear when they are in conflict with their values and believe that their actions might bring them spiritual or physical harm. Fear of sin, negative karma, immorality, destructive habits and evil actions arise when we are in conflict with our highest values and ideals and the religious beliefs we practice and uphold. They create in us feelings of remorse and guilt.

Understanding and controlling fear

Identifying your specific fears is the first important step in controlling them, and limiting the damage they do to your wellbeing. Since fear is the most dominant emotion of your life, you can learn a lot by paying attention to it and knowing how it influences your thinking and actions. Following are some useful suggestions to understand and deal with your dominant fears.

- **Embrace your fears**: Fear is a natural, human response. There is nothing shameful or guilty about it. Everyone fears. Society may worship courageous people, but courage actually means the ability to act in the face of fear.

- **Understand and identify your fears**: Your fear arises variously. Each time you experience it, pay attention to the feelings and sensations it creates, and see whether you can identify its causes and label it clearly under a specific category.
- **Listen to your fears**: You can learn a lot about yourself from your fears, by knowing why you fear and what thought processes create them, aggravate them, or sustain them.
- **Resolve your fears**: If your fear is genuine or caused by really threatening situations, you must resolve them by taking appropriate action.
- **Analyze your fears**: Examine the irrational beliefs and habitual thought patterns that aggravate your fears and perpetuate them.
- **Change your thinking and responses**: Since fears are conditioned responses, you can change your thinking and attitude, by changing your beliefs and expectations, and your habitual responses to fearful or threatening situations.
- **Practice visualization**: Recreate in your mind situations that produce fear in you, and visualize different responses and approaches to deal with them.
- **Use positive affirmations**: You can use positive affirmations to ground yourself in reality and deal with your negativity, irrational beliefs and tendency to exaggerate your fears and their outcomes.

Many people prefer to ignore their fears or bury them deep in their minds to avoid the disturbing feelings associated with them. Let us admit, fear serves a useful purpose in our lives and we cannot impose upon it our own value system. We should break free from the traditional mindset that regards all fears as unwanted or shameful or a sign of cowardice. Fear is a natural human response. They serve the same purpose as messengers and spies who keep a tab on the enemies and report about their activities. You should not silence them. Our fears will not just go away if we ignore them or avoid them. Since we are vulnerable to many threats, we are bound to experience them. Let us not delude ourselves with false notions of courage and suppress our fears. We should deal with them only if they are seriously interfering with our normal lives. If our fears are valid and have a rational basis, we should respond to them realistically and rationally and resolve them as part of our self-preservation and survival. However, we should be concerned about those fears, which arise from irrational beliefs, delusional thinking, or hyper active reactions, and produce self-limiting thoughts, negative expectations, and low self-esteem.

Coping With Failure

Nothing hurts us more than failure and loss. The pain and fear associated with failure can be serious and crippling. It hurts even more those who suffer from poor self-esteem and low self-confidence. Repeated failure contributes to low morale and expectations, while fear of failure prevents many from using their skills and potentials fully to reach their goals. Since we live in a competitive world, where your social status and public image depend upon your financial success, people from all wakes of life react negatively to failure and experience despair and unhappiness. Unless you have a tough mindset, it is difficult to recover from failure and refocus upon your goals and tasks; and unless you develop positive attitude, with each failure a part of your hopes and dreams begin to die. Since it is not possible to predict the outcome of our actions and we cannot be sure that we will always succeed in our actions, we must learn to cope with failure in healthy ways and learn to keep our morale and confidence high. The following suggestions are helpful in this regard.

Know that you can deal with failure: A friend mine started an Indian restaurant in a small town in the USA. He suffered heavy losses and had to sell his house to repay the debt when the chef and the manager whom he recruited to look after the business betrayed him and ruined his reputation. Yet, within two years he recovered from the failure and started another restaurant. He is now doing fine as his business picked up. He told me that he learned from his father never to give up. Human tenacity is such that you can deal with any failure or problem in your life. For that you must have courage, confidence and belief in yourself. With determination and confidence in your skills, knowledge, and abilities, you can overcome any failure in your life and find solutions to every problem. A setback may temporarily upset your plans and halt your progress, but with determination, right effort and right state of mind, you can recover from even the worst failure. One effective way to deal with failure is to treat it like any other problem, and apply your knowledge and intelligence to find solutions.

Accept failure as normal: Society degrades failure, but you do not have to. If your car broke down while you were driving, it does not mean that it is worthless, but that it may need repairs and some maintenance work. The same is the case with failure. In any goal oriented action success and failure are just two possibilities. You must be prepared for both. We stumble before we learn to walk. We fail before we succeed. We cannot guarantee the result, but we can always guarantee a sincere effort. Our success and failure in any situation depend upon many factors which are not entirely within our control. Therefore, however hard we may try, we cannot be sure how our actions will turn out. A failure is success in the making; a phase within a process; a problem within a solution; and a disturbance within a dream. Each failure has a message to deliver and a lesson to teach. The good thing about failure is that it is temporary, manageable, and solvable with further effort.

Accept failure as a learning opportunity: You can either learn from your failures, or feel depressed or dejected and nurse your wounds. The choice is yours. Whether you are aware of it or not, you always have this choice. Your life is largely shaped by what you choose. We fail in our actions because we make mistakes. It may be caused by a wrong decision, a defective process, a bad judgment, or an incorrect tool we use. Since we are not perfect, we are bound to make mistakes. What happens when your computer develops an unusual glitch? You do some research and try various options before you find the right solution. If you cannot solve it, you consult someone or hire a professional. You just do not give up. Once the problem is solved, you use the knowledge you gained to deal with a similar problem next time. You can bring the same attitude into your other actions also. The cost of finding solutions and resolving problems in each case may vary, but the approach is the same. You should learn from your failures and mistakes, and move on. Failure grounds you in the reality of life, puts things in proper perspective, lets you know where you stand on the path to success, and what skills and effort you still need to move forward. In short, it prepares you for success. If you consider failure with this attitude it paves the way for your improvement and increased awareness, without lowering your morale and spirits.

Anticipate problems to prepare for them: Optimism is good, but it is always better to assess the risks involved in any situation and prepare for them. You should anticipate failure by identifying possible causes. You have to do it as preventive measure, just as you lock your house and start the security alarm before you leave. It is a proactive approach. Have you ever wondered why auto manufactures equip every vehicle with two headlights instead of one? Having one light is technically a good option because it prolongs the battery life. However, with two lights you can continue to drive in the night if one fails or is damaged. Systems are designed in such a way that for every failure there will be a fallback option. For example, even though most passenger planes are put on autopilot in the midair, for the safety of passengers they are always flown by two or more pilots. If one loses consciousness, the other can safely land the plane. Before you initiate any goal oriented action, anticipate what problems, bottlenecks, and possible breakdowns you may face in future and prepare for them with suitable alternatives and backup plans. It may not guarantee a hundred percent fail-safe system, but it will reduce your chances of failure.

Monitor your actions: In science fiction movies astronauts may travel to distant galaxies while they are asleep in frozen chambers, but in real life you have to be awake and pay attention to your actions, especially those that may affect your success. Negligence can prove very costly and time-consuming, besides distracting you from your main goals and tasks. When you drive a vehicle, you cannot fall asleep. The same degree of attentiveness is required when you perform any important action. Do you know what is common to many successful companies? They pay attention to quality and strive for excellence. They make sure that errors arising from human negligence or prevented or minimized. Even the most automated systems require human supervision to intervene and rectify errors and malfunctioning. If you have visited a factory or a manufacturing plant, you will notice how the machines are constantly monitored by qualified people so that the processes would run smoothly. Nothing works on its own, without human intervention. You cannot put your duties and responsibilities on autopilot. Successful small business owners know the importance of monitoring. They do not take anything for granted. They go to great lengths to keep their customers happy and settle their grievances. You can do the same to increase your chances of success and minimize the possibility of failures and setbacks.

Accept responsibility for your failure: You might have seen people routinely blaming others when things go wrong, even if they have nothing to do with it. It frequently happens in politics. It happens in personal, and family matters also if there are people with questionable integrity. When you lose your way in the middle of a desert, you will gain nothing by blaming the sun or the sand or fate. You have to accept responsibility for what happened, and try to survive. The first step in dealing with a setback or a failure is to own it. It is the right approach. There is no shame in forgiving yourself for your failures or faults. We all make mistakes and occasionally fail in our actions. In fact, our rate of failure depends upon the complexity of the tasks. If you are doing something which no one has done before, your chances of failure are even more. Hence, you must accept failure as the risk that comes with any action. If you are honest about your failures, you will increase the odds of finding better solutions, friends, and opportunities to resolve them. If you blame others, you may lose any support you may get from them. Even if they are at fault, you may have to forgive them because you may still need them to complete your tasks. Therefore, own your failures, keep an open mind, and move on with the task of fixing the problem rather than becoming stuck in fixing the blame.

Keep your emotions under control: Emotions are bound to flood your mind when you deal with problems, conflicts and failures. They do serve an important purpose in your life. They call your attention to the problems, flaws, and risks hidden in your plans, decisions, methods and approaches and alert you to situations that they might create. In every failure and setback there is a hidden message that wants to teach you something. You can decipher it using your emotions. There is an aspect of intelligence called emotional intelligence, which helps you to decipher situations and make sense of them. It is normal for people to feel depressed or dejected by failure. Fear of failure also prevents them from taking bold actions. Since each failure cuts into your self-esteem, with each failure you feel increased pressure and negativity to reignite your motivation. However, you can do it by increasing your enthusiasm for doing the task rather than for the results.

Do the task as excellently as you can and leave the results to God. You cannot control the outcome of your actions, but you can control your actions and approach. Have you seen how tight rope walkers manage to cross long distances on a thin rope without losing their balance? They focus on each step until they reach the other end. You can bring that kind of Zen attitude into your actions. If you focus on the processes, techniques and methods rather than the results, your actions will improve and you will be more balanced, peaceful, and less emotional. Therefore, keep your emotions under control and perform your tasks sincerely, without unduly worrying about the outcome of your actions.

Be persistent: Weak minds are disheartened by failure and give up after a few setbacks. When they face problems, they stop trying, or find excuses to blame others or circumstances for their failures. Several years ago my friend and I went to a remote place in India in the countryside to climb a hill. Since we could not drive the car all the way to the hill, we had to park it in a nearby village and walk a few miles to reach there. If you are familiar with Indian summers, you know how hot it can get. By the time we reached there, it was midday, and we were already exhausted as we walked in the glare of the summer sun on an uneven ground that kept rising gradually. From the ground up, the hill looked very steep at the top, foreboding the trouble we might have once we reached there. I enjoyed climbing hills both for the physical and mental challenges it posed. From each climbing experience I learned lessons about life, human behavior, and myself.

Halfway through the climb, we were exhausted by the heat from above and the heat from the rocks. My body refused to move as I felt no strength in my legs. My friend managed to reach the peak ahead of me when I was still struggling about twenty feet below. For a few minutes I wondered whether I should continue. My friend kept encouraging me to join him and see the beautiful panorama from up there. Although I was extremely tired, I managed to reach the top and saw the beautiful valley spread below. I was able to do it because by observing people, who were tenacious and perseverant, I learned not to give up easily. Some of my teachers in this regard were poor farmers whom you might not consider successful. But they had that tenacity, which taught them to survive the worst of calamities. You may even mistake them for being stubborn, but it is the same quality, which fuels their purpose and enthusiasm and keeps them focused upon their goals.

Sometimes you may not have friends or family members to encourage you when you think that you have reached the end of the road. It does not mean it is the end of all. You have to step back, weight your options, and move forward again in another direction. The end of a cliff is not the end of the world. In any discouraging situation, the strength and motivation to continue must come from within. In the face of failure, strong-willed people continue their effort, by keeping their hopes alive and their minds firmly set upon their goals. They respond to failure with actionable solutions. For them persistence means more than doing the same task again. They improve with each repetition, as they learn, adapt and try again, until they reach their goals.

Seek help from others: Successful people respond to failure positively. If they conclude that their failure was caused by a deficiency or defect in their methods, skills, or techniques, they either try to work on that area or seek other people's help. Prudence dictates that you should seek the help of those who are known for their integrity and reputation. Everyone is endowed with certain skills, strengths and weaknesses. Your strengths are your resources, which help you to reach your goals. Since your weaknesses may interfere with your strengths or success, you need to find people who can compensate for them, especially if they are going to interfere with your work. You can deal with your weaknesses by learning and training, which may require time and effort, or by seeking the help of those who are strong in those areas. When you seek help from them, you have to consider the risks and costs involved. For example, when you hire others you may have to share proprietary information, which may be used against you or shared with your competitors.

Be creative: We learn from history that under pressure people manage to find creative and inspiring ideas to overcome their problems. They survive under the most pressing situations by learning to use their minds creatively. It is true that some of the world's best ideas and solutions were discovered during difficult times when there were wars, natural calamities, or epidemics. Businesses routinely use adverse situations to improve their productivity or restructure their operations through innovation and creative solutions. You can follow the same approach and view your problems and setbacks as opportunities to think creatively and improve your methods and techniques. Psychologists recognize three phases in creativity, getting to know the problem, letting your mind rest and think of other things, and illumination when your mind suddenly becomes aware of the solution. You can follow the same approach to let your mind find creative solutions to your problems.

Think positively: Every significant failure brings out the worst in us before it brings out the best. In many situations when there are problems people experience negative emotions such as fear, anger, frustration, and low self-esteem. They may even begin to wonder whether their lives will ever be normal again. In the face of failure, you may become your own worst enemy and feel too critical of your abilities and actions. Out of frustration or anger, you may turn against your own friends and refuse to accept their help or advice. As we have seen before, people internalize success and externalize failures to protect themselves against their own fears and negativity. Even it does not guarantee peace because of the subconscious fears that people experience habitually about their own future. It is very difficult to live with failure when one has lost hope of resolving it. To overcome these habitual reactions, you have to train your mind to remain calm under pressure, focus on the possibilities and opportunities, and act rationally in the face of fear and dejection. You have to learn to dispute you negative self-talk, irrational beliefs and assumptions, and internalize positive affirmations. By staying focused on your goals and strengths, working around your weaknesses, increasing your knowledge and expertise, and improving your efficiency and effectiveness, you can keep your hopes alive and your chances of success.

Be systematic: If you organize your life and actions, you will greatly reduce the chances of failure. Being organized means keeping things in an orderly and verifiable fashion, having a place for everything and ensuring that everything is in its place. It means planning and performing your tasks with precision, imparting a method and structure to what you do and what you have, and keeping your work environment clean and manageable. It also means having rules, following discipline, enforcing order, prioritizing things, keeping task lists, following well laid out action plans, removing unnecessary clutter, and focusing only on essential tasks. If you are organized and systematic, you stay focused, conserve your resources and improve your performance. It helps you to remain in control of your environment, and maximize your effectiveness. With an organized and systematic approach, you will recover swiftly from your problems and failures, as you can identify the causes, locate and organize your resources and implement your solutions. It will also help you to plan and control your actions, conserve your resources, measure your progress, and stay on course.

Use the power of failure: Failure is not an option in a competitive world, where you are constantly challenged by people and circumstances to prove your ability and talents, and stay on top. When you are unable to reach your goals, you have to consider the options that are available to you and take right decisions, so that your failures will not hurt you or make you feel small and defeated. You have to use defensive pessimism to anticipate problems and stay prepared. To avoid repeating the same mistakes, you should improve your methods and processes constantly and minimize their occurrence. You can turn your fear of failure into a motivating factor to safeguard yourself from the risks that are inherent in your plans and actions. You must learn to face your failure with courage and accept the challenges they pose, without taking them personally. Each failure is like a storm in the long voyage of your life. In most cases you can anticipate its coming by noticing the changes in your environment and take precautions to sail through it safely. You may consider each failure a part of achieving success, which demands timely and skillful action, planned effort, positive mental attitude, confidence and conviction. It is part of the learning and perfecting process and a means to self-improvement. You have to face your failures with courage and right attitude to make them propel you towards success.

Planning Your Day

Life happens, but sometimes we are not mentally present to enjoy it. As we fall into routine, we ignore the hours and days that make up our lives. Time is one of the most valuable but misused resources on the planet. A lot of time goes into frivolous or repetitive tasks as many people live their lives routinely. For them time moves on without leaving any memories worth remembering.

This reminds me of a joke about the meaning of on the job experience, which I heard. Once, an organization promoted a junior employee who had just two years experience over a senior employee who worked in the same department for nearly twenty years. The senior employee was upset by this decision of the company as he was expecting a promotion which was repeatedly denied to him. Upon receiving the official confirmation, he went to his supervisor and asked him why he was not considered for promotion. He reminded him that he had been working in the department for nearly twenty years and none in the company qualified for a promotion more than him.

The supervisor listened to him sympathetically and agree that he did spend twenty years serving the company and appreciated him for his loyalty and dedication. However, he also asked him to analyze what he did in those twenty years. Did he ever come out with any solutions on his own? Did he ever make any suggestions to improve the systems, which the company accepted? He politely told him that although technically he worked for twenty years, in truth it was as if he was reliving one year experience twenty times. Experience mattered, but in his case he was not better off than his junior colleague who was not experienced but had more focus, involvement and initiative. This was not a real incident, but it does reflect an important truth about our lives and how we go about our tasks and duties.

Most of us live our lives rather routinely, performing the same routine tasks and letting life slip by. There is not much difference from one day to another because in routine tasks and familiar situations we find comfort and security. If anyone asks you to recollect the events that happened four days before or what you did on that night, you may not be able to answer clearly unless an unusual event happened or you found yourself in extraordinary circumstances. Indeed, in the long span of our lives we go through numerous experiences, but remember only a few. Technically, our personalities are largely shaped by such memories only. The rest may subconsciously influence our thinking and behavior, but what we consciously remember is what goes into our identities and behavior.

What does it signify? It means we must live with more awareness and sensitivity. If we live more consciously, we will have better awareness and understanding of ourselves and the world around us. Knowing yourself means being yourself. Being yourself means being authentic, genuine and truthful to your inmost thoughts and aspirations. It means giving expression to the best that is present in you and represents you. It is possible only when we spend our time wisely and mindfully, and increase our awareness and active participation in the events of life. It means that if you take care of your days, you will take care of the quality of your life. If you spend your days well, you will enjoy your life well, with purpose and awareness. In this regard the following points are worth considering.

1. Time is a limited resource, which is more valuable than money and other things. Yet, most of us do not think so, and spend our time in frivolous activities.
2. Much of our time is spent in either sleep and rest or routine activities that do not add much value to our lives, or knowledge and wisdom to our minds.
3. Each day must in some way contribute to your over all goals. Each day in some way must be connected to the rest of your life. Each day in some way must lead to your wellbeing, peace, and happiness. When these are present, your life will be structured and organized.
4. Those who work for others or organizations spend most of their lives contributing to their wealth and prosperity, with little time for themselves. They do not have much freedom over their time, since their lives are largely driven by other people's desires and expectations, rather than their own.
5. If you are self-employed and not answerable to anyone for your daily output, you need to be even more careful about how you spend your time, since people who work alone with no supervision and

accountability tend to take liberties with their daily schedules.

Here are a few questions for sincere introspection. Are you aware of how you spend your time? Do you follow any methods or system to plan your daily activities? Can you even remember which day today is? Does each day add any value to your life and contribute to your self-growth and progress? At the end of each day, do you review and analyze your daily activities? How many great moments of your life can you easily recall? Can you instantly recall, at least, one significant event per year in your life in right sequence?

If you answer these questions affirmatively, you may consider yourself organized and focused who know the value of time and live consciously and responsibly as part of a larger vision and purpose driven life. If not, you have to see how far you can take liberties with your life and afford to let go of the opportunities it gives you to learn your lessons and make progress.

Planning for incremental progress

The following suggestions are helpful to plan your days according to your chosen purpose and long term goals. With them, you can bring discipline and self-control into your actions and shake off any passivity that may settle into your thinking. If you feel that you are stuck in your career or circumstances, you can become unstuck; and if you are feeling lost and lacking direction, you can bring discipline and structure into your life.

- **Put the day in perspective**: Make sure that every day that you spend contributes to your long term goals and purpose. You can accomplish it best by planning your days according to your long term goals and organizing your actions around them.
- **Start the day cheerfully**: Start each day with as smile, even if you have to do it forcefully. As you wake up, remember inspiring thoughts, cheerful people, happy memories, positive affirmations, and moments of peace and joy.
- **Be thankful**: Express gratitude for the blessings you received and whatever that happened to you so far to be who you are today.

- **Keep yourself healthy**: You cannot ignore your health or leave it to chance. If your job is sedentary, you should find opportunities to participate in physical activities such as walking, helping others, using stairs instead of elevators, gardening and household work.
- **Fine-tune your mind**: Your mental health is equally important. You can relieve daily stress and accumulated negativity by relaxing your mind, listening to good music, praying to God, taking deep breaths, reading inspiring books and articles, or listening to inspirational talks.
- **Do something for your soul**: Listen to your feelings, emotions, intuition, and aspirations. Do something that uplifts you and makes you feel good, such as helping others, speaking good words, sending healing thoughts, listening to your heart, and feeling compassion for those who suffer.
- **Improve your knowledge and expertise**: Try to read every day something useful to nurture your mind and improve your knowledge and skills. Whatever you do, do it sincerely with full attention.

Celebrate all days

You should celebrate all days with enthusiasm and zest, not just birthdays and few anniversaries. Think of your life in terms of days rather than years. If the average life span of a person is 100 years old, he has 36,500 days only to live. Of them, at least for 5000 - 7000 days (say for about the last twenty years) he would be too old and infirm to undertake any vigorous activity. From the remaining days (about 29,500), deduct the number of days you have already spent, by converting your current age into days. Now, see how many days are still left. That is all that you got to enjoy your life or achieve whatever you want to achieve. Think how you would like to spend those days. Prepare a list of the most important things you want to do in that limited time and plan on doing them.

Dealing with emotions

Emotions add drama to your life. Without them, life would be dull and boring like an empty canvas. The Star Trek character Spock may be fit for an intergalactic voyage, but he will not make an ideal life partner in life because he cannot relate well to others emotionally. Emotions are at the heart of both good and bad relationships.

Emotional people are easy to get along, but they are also difficult to handle. Positive emotions bring people together, while negative ones tear them apart. People can communicate with others emotionally, but know little about emotions, and much less about how to deal with them, live with them, or keep them under control. Under their influence, people act strangely, as if they are different people from a different world. We have stories of divinities, saints and seers becoming emotional, losing their balance, and making mistakes.

Since emotions are viewed unfavorably in society, many people prefer not to speak about their emotional problems in public. The secrecy associated with emotions make it even more difficult to deal with the problems arising from them. Since emotions are an integral part of our lives and we all experience them, we need to know how to manage them and keep them under their threshold point. The following are a few suggestions in this regard.

1. Acknowledge and accept your emotions: Since emotions are not viewed favorably across all cultures, a lot of guilt is associated with them. People like to experience positive emotions, but do not like to deal with negative emotions or emotional people. However, you do not have to feel guilty about them because they make you human and impart meaning to your actions and situations. Your emotions are an integral and important part of your personality. They are essential to your survival, and serve a definite purpose in your life, which is to arouse you emotionally into a state of readiness and prepare you to deal with problems. They also help you to relate well to others and understand them. Positive emotions help you to feel good about yourself and pursue your goals and dreams, while negative emotions keep you within your limits and save you from harming yourself by taking undue risks. Therefore, you should develop a positive attitude towards your emotions, know them and use them where the situation demands. You should also allow yourself to frequently experience positive emotions by creating necessary conditions. If you frequently experience positive emotions, you will feel good about yourself and others and face your problems more confidently and spiritedly. Your emotional intelligence improves as you gain insight into your own emotional behavior.

2. Do not try to suppress your emotions: Because emotions create feelings of guilt and remorse, you may try to forcibly suppress them. Although it looks like an easy option it is not a good strategy, as it will lead to side effects and other problems. Although it may give you a temporary relief, the repressed emotions will resurface through other channels and trouble you in unrecognizable ways. When emotions arise, allow them to arise and subside on their own, using the opportunity to observe them and know their underlying causes. It helps you to know your vulnerabilities and prepare for them. Indeed, trying to control your emotions may not even work because during the initial rush of emotions the rational part of your mind remains inactive and does not regulate your emotional responses. Hence, even if you have trained well, when an emotional situation arises, you are bound to experience them both physically and mentally. Besides, emotions help you to make sense of problem situations. Therefore, it is not even a good strategy to control them. The best way to deal with them is to let them arise naturally and speak to you in their own way.

3. Experience your emotions fully: This is partly a continuation of the previous suggestion. Intense emotions like anger and rage are real killers. If ignored, they can cause great harm to you and others. If you direct them to others they will be hurt, and if you suppress them, you will be hurt. Therefore, you should learn to channel your emotions without hurting anyone and keep them under control. Just as you would respond to hunger, you should respond to your emotions when they arise and allow them to do their work. When you are upset, it is better to stay alone and let your emotions subside, or find a person with whom you can share your feelings. You can also observe them mindfully, or let them out through other channels such as exercise, going out for a walk, etc. By expressing your emotions in healthy ways you can lighten up. In doing so, you take out their excess energy and reduce their intensity or ability to hurt you or anyone else. Emotions generate intense levels of energy to prepare you to deal with threats. If you hold them inside you for long, they can upset in your inner balance. Therefore, it is better to bring them out and reduce their impact. By venting your emotions, you return to your normal, healthy mode and continue with your daily tasks. Emotions do not just go away if you interrupt their normal cycle. You have to let them pass through the three phases of eruption, expression and dissipation. When your emotions erupt, you should experience them here and now, and allow them to subside slowly without feeling guilty.

4. Maintain good health: Your mind and body are interconnected. Biologically, they represent one complex system. Your thoughts can influence your body functions and vice versa. Yoga proves that even your autonomous nervous system can be controlled partially by controlling your mind and body. Emotions have a physical and mental component. They arise physically as sensations and mentally as feelings. Some even suggest that emotions such as fear may have a certain smell, which may be even true because animals can smell your fear from distance. It is well known that emotions influence the body and the body influences emotions, while both are in turn influenced by the environment or the context in which they arise.

There is a direct correlation between health and emotional states. Certain physical activities such as exercise, yoga, healthy diet improves a person's emotional wellbeing and positive emotions. Healthy people counter negative emotions better than those who suffer from health problems. Health is a major source of worry and anxiety. Prolonged illness can induce depression, anger and resentment. Many psychosomatic disorders, such as high blood pressure, indigestion, and back-pain are caused by chronic negative emotions, as they cause the body to release harmful chemicals into the bloodstream, and weaken its immune system. A healthy body absorbs negative emotions more effectively. It is also conducive to produce positive emotions. Hence, you should take care of your health by making healthy lifestyle choices and living a disciplined life.

5. Stay in the present, here and now: Whether you are asleep or awake and you pay attention or not, life goes on. In your life's journey if you are lost in your thoughts, you will miss the journey and many precious opportunities to watch and learn. Your life is enriched to the extent you pay attention and live consciously. Most people do not live in the present. They keep thinking about their past or their future, troubled by worry, guilt, remorse, fear and anxiety. In the process, they lose touch with their current reality and their ability to respond to situations properly. Present moment awareness grounds you in the reality of the moment and enables you to control your emotions and find better solutions to your problems. It also helps you to observe your habitual thought patterns and repetitive emotional responses, and know about yourself and others with better insight. In our daily lives, we frequently lose present moment awareness, as we become engrossed in our thoughts and actions. On such occasions, a simple technique to return to the present is to pause and look around or take a few deep breaths. Listening to the sounds in your surroundings also creates the same effect. Another useful technique is to use all your senses when you talk to people, or listen to them. Yoga, relaxation, meditation and mindfulness practices also help. When you are in the present moment, you remain in control of your thoughts and actions, and act according to situations rather than your emotions.

6. Develop trust: People suffer from extreme emotions of fear and anxiety when they lose faith in themselves or in their cause. It happens because of repeated failures, circumstances or change in perceptions. Faith is your last resort, and your final sanctuary. When everything else fails, faith comes to your rescue and lifts you up from your self-inflicted doubts. Faith sustains your perseverance and resilience and helps you to keep going in great difficulties. It is important not to lose faith in yourself because without faith your life becomes a struggle. You will withdraw from fighting your battles and keeping your hopes alive. You must therefore keep the flame of your self-confidence alive in your heart and protect it well. You can develop faith in yourself, or regain it, by focusing upon your strengths and achievements, and by facing your fears and acting upon them. Having faith in God is equally morale boosting. The very belief that God is with you and helping you can increase your confidence and motivate you to keep going in difficult situations. History proves that people used this power in the past to overcome great suffering and even changed the course of history. Many great institutions that we have today came into existence because of it. Therefore, believe in yourself and in God, and keep your negative emotions out of your way.

7. Find mentors or better solutions: We do cope with many emotions every day on our own. It is part of our living. No one is ever truly free from negative emotions, or the suffering they inflict upon us. It is what makes us human in the first place. There is no shame or dishonor in having problems or suffering from emotional upheavals. Many people learn to cope with their emotional problems in their own individual ways. It is an ability, which you cannot buy with money or power, but which you can learn from your own experience by observing and learning. Emotions enrich your life and make you stronger and even wiser.

I learned most of my lessons from my suffering only. They opened my eyes to many hidden truths of life that I was unaware of. I learned from emotions to be myself, not to follow anyone blindly, be practical, and reserve my judgment until I ascertained all possibilities. Your experience teaches you valuable lessons. It is the best teacher. However, your own experience can blind you to certain truths. Therefore, it is better to know how others respond to their emotions and what they learn from their experience. You can do it by talking to them, observing them, reading books, or having mentors. Internet is another great source where you can do research about specific emotions and the problems that arise from them.

8. Acquire knowledge: Having more knowledge is not a guarantee that you will have better control over your emotions. You can tell it from the biographies of people who are well known for their knowledge and erudition. Many great authors, scholars and philosophers suffered from chronic depression. Some of them even committed suicide as they could not take it any longer. Even Freud and Jung, who are considered pioneers in modern psychology, were not entirely free from anxiety and neurosis. Their lives amply illustrate that knowledge alone cannot save you from emotional instability. In fact, it may even complicate matters further as you may develop a rigid mindset and refuse to acknowledge solutions that do not fit into your belief system. However, having right knowledge about your emotions, their causes and control has its own benefits. It may not guarantee you complete control, but gives you awareness about the possibilities and opportunities that you can use to deal with them. You can use the knowledge to find your own solutions and to know your emotions better.

9. Become a master of your emotions: Mastery does not mean forceful suppression. True mastery comes from self-knowledge or self-awareness. By knowing yourself and observing your thoughts and emotions, you can make peace with yourself. You should know which factors or situations may make you emotional, and how to cope with them. For example, if you know that in certain situations you are going to be vulnerable, you can either avoid them or learn to deal with them. When you are upset by an event or situation, you should identify the emotion and its causes, and let it dissipate until it no more troubles you. Mastery does not mean that you should know how to suppress your emotions, but how to deal with them effectively without negative consequences. It also means knowing how to deal with emotional people and situations, keeping your emotions well under control.

10. Examine the beliefs underlying your emotions: John was anxiously waiting in his office for Harry to arrive. Yesterday, he assigned him a task to finish a report and submit it by the next day morning. Harry had not yet reported for duty and did not leave any information about the status. Meanwhile, his boss called him twice from the headquarters and told him that he was going to LA that day by the afternoon flight and he needed the report before he left. More than an hour had passed since the office was opened and there was no sign of Harry. He was also not responding to his calls and text messages. As another hour passed by, John's anxiety began mounting up. He had a suspicion that Harry was unhappy with him because he was not promoted last year. He also never saw Harry praising his leadership. John felt that Harry delayed the report deliberately to cause him trouble and jeopardize his position in the company. As more time passed, John's concern turned into anger. He decided to call his boss and tell him that he was going to fire Harry for his negligence. At last, after another half an hour, Harry reached the office and handed over the report. He told John that he kept working until the morning hours to complete the report and fell asleep. When he woke up he realized that it was late. He also apologized for the delay and not responding to the phone calls promptly.

What happened here? John became angry and anxious as he believed that Harry was out to destroy his career and therefore did not arrive in time. The truth was that Harry spent the whole night trying to meet the deadline and help John. Your beliefs control your thinking and behavior. Positive beliefs produce positive emotions and vice versa. It does not matter whether the beliefs are true or false. They just trigger emotions according to the circumstances. You may believe that you are disturbed by others or external events, but it is not always true. Your beliefs influence how you think and act in different situations, how you receive and interpret information and how you bring out different emotions in response to them. They not only trigger various emotions but also help you to subdue them if you learn to dispute them and put them to reality check. If you change your beliefs, you may not experience the same emotions. For example, if you believe you are weak or you have no solutions, you will experience fear, but if you believe you are strong and you can deal with the situation, you will feel hopeful and encouraged to respond positively.

11. Change your thinking: Emotions arise because of the way you think, evaluate and judge to make sense of the world, people and events in your life. The events may be external, such as what someone said or did, or they may be internal such as an old memory about a past event. Since emotions arise in response to events, it follows that if you think wrongly you may also respond or react wrongly. In life many misunderstandings and conflicts arise because of this. It also follows that by changing your thinking, you can prevent certain negative emotions from arising in you. For example, imagine that you were driving on a double lane road at a normal speed when someone suddenly started tailgating you and gesturing you through the window saying something. When you see him through the rearview mirror, your spontaneous reaction would be to feel annoyed because of your feeling that the person was rude and aggressive. You would think that if he wanted to go faster he should have changed the lane and gone his way. Your anger in that situation is truly justified, provided your assumptions were true.

However, what if that person noticed that the trunk of your car was open and he was merely trying to draw your attention to it? If you know it, instead of feeling annoyed you will thank him for it. Thus, you can see that your responses and emotions depend upon your thinking and perceptions and how you interpret them, rather than what might have actually happened. If you gather information, analyze and ascertain facts, and change your thinking and interpretation based upon them, you can change your emotional response, and instead of feeling negative emotions, you can feel the positive ones.

Dealing with the Problem of Loneliness

A tree has better chances of surviving in a forest among other trees than when it stands alone in an open land, where most likely it will be cut down or stuck by a lightning. Most animals live in groups to ensure their safety and survival even if it means sharing food and habitat with others. Even insects, fish and several microorganisms live in colonies to ensure their safety and continuity. Somehow Nature induces this social intelligence in all living beings to improve their chances of survival. From this we may conclude that staying alone is not natural behavior, but mostly caused by external factors or personal choice. By nature, humans also prefer living in groups and assuming a group identity. Sometimes group identity becomes more important than personal identity. Group identity makes people feel secure and comfortable in their groups and compete for resources more organizedly. However, humans have a choice to live alone. Many monks and ascetics prefer living alone as part of the spiritual development. Solitary confinement is often enforced upon people when they breach the norms of society or government laws.

When loneliness becomes a problem

Loneliness is different from aloneness. Some people prefer staying alone to spend time in contemplation or know themselves. It helps them to gain insight into themselves and their problems, and experience peace and happiness. Occasionally, we need to be alone and find relief from the daily burdens of life. However, we cannot always do it, unless we choose to become monks. In fact, when we are in deep sleep, we are always alone. If you are able to sleep well, it means you are doing well. Choosing to be alone, therefore, is not a problem as long it is a conscious choice. However, feeling lonely and alienated is a problem. It is a morbid state of mind caused by negative thinking, whereby a person may feel lonely even in the midst of a crowd. People who experience it suffer from low self-esteem, do not adjust well to the world, or feel comfortable with themselves. Whether they are alone or with people, they experience the same feelings of alienation and loneliness, since they find the world too depressing or intimidating to relate to it. In solitude normal people may not feel lonely at all, even if they are alone, as they manage to communicate with what they love and experience positive emotions, whereas people suffering from loneliness prefer being alone because they are too afraid to open up and become vulnerable. Chronic feelings of loneliness may lead to psychosomatic disorders, suicidal tendencies, even antisocial and sociopathic behavior.

Causes

Loneliness may arise due to various external and internal factors. External factors include childhood experiences, traumatic events, chronic health problems, social causes, family problems, marital issues, physical abuse, loss of status or esteem, etc. Among the internal factors important ones are childhood traumas, depression, genetic factors, and low self-esteem. Fear is a major factor. Feelings of loneliness may also arise because of guilt, shame, rejection, dishonor, and distrust. In today's world, even children are not free from it. Single parenting, divorces, economic downturn, natural disasters, political upheavals, wars, terrorism, ethnic violence, religious and racial, discrimination, civil unrest, and several such factors force children to live in isolation and fear, feeling abandoned, lonely, ignored, and rejected. They carry forward such feelings into their adulthood and develop negative attitudes towards society and life. People like to be in groups and relate to others to fulfill their need for belongingness, recognition and approval. They would like to be loved, accepted, and appreciated. When it is not forthcoming, they develop resentment and apathy towards society and the world in general. Many celebrities and successful people go into self-imposed exile due to unjust criticism and constant negative publicity.

Coping with loneliness

You can deal with the problem of loneliness to some extent by taking control of your thoughts and actions and responsibility for your life and relationships. Undoubtedly, the world is not an easy place to live. We come across many people in our lives who can harm and hurt others with their words and actions. However, it not enough justification for us to shun the world or live in isolation. You may choose to be alone for professional or spiritual reasons. I personally prefer staying alone, when I have to write or think seriously. It is not because I dislike people, but because it helps me to focus upon my work and keep my mind receptive. The feeling of loneliness is different from staying alone. It is the feeling that you are missing something or someone in your life when you are alone, and not feeling comfortable when you are with the people you like. You experience it due to low self-esteem and negative self-talk. The following suggestions are useful to deal with it.

1. Have clear goals in your life: Having clearly defined, specific and long term goals keep you busy and focused. If you have goals and aims, you will not feel lonely or bored. Your goals fill you with passion and keep you active during your waking hours. A purpose driven and goal oriented life is the best antidote to loneliness. It does not matter what your goals you choose, as long as they are meaningful and relevant to you and your life and are aligned to your strengths and talents. If your goals are relevant to your life and personal beliefs, you are more likely to feel engaged, preoccupied and good about yourself. It is even better, if you include other people in your goals and make them partners in your success. Goals help you to explore your knowledge and potentials, express your thoughts and ideas, feel proud of your achievements, transcend your limitations, rise above mediocrity and provide meaning and direction to your life. Most importantly, they bring you into contact with others, as none has ever achieved success without the help and cooperation of others.

2. Stay out of abusive relationships: Prolonged abusive relationships and interaction with negative people can break your zest for life and trust in relationships. Relationships are important, but no one should stay with habitually abusive people and repeat offenders. An abusive relationship will undermine a victim's self-esteem and individuality and cause loss of hope and faith in the humanity. Many people continue to stay in bad relationships to avoid feeling lonely or rejected. They patiently bear with the anger and resentment shown by their victimizers, in the hope that things would change and the relationship would improve. In a prolonged abusive relationship, the abused person develops a submissive and dependent relationship with the abuser, and may even develop a liking for the person.

One should stay away from such one-sided and painful relationships. With their uncontrolled anger, violence, and aggression victimizers can harm themselves and others, or commit crimes involving their victims, causing even more trouble. Hence, it is better to be alone and find your own voice rather than seek their company, even if they happen to be your close relations. As a precaution, stay away from people who are too critical, self-centered, selfish, immoral, unethical, mean, and prone to frequent mood changes. Avoid those who make others unhappy for no particular reason, with their envy, resentment, anger, aggression and frustration. Seek legal protection if necessary, and do not let them trample upon your life and liberty. They are not the right solution to the problem of loneliness.

3. Learn to like yourself: You may avoid the company of others, but you cannot escape from yourself. If you feel good about yourself, chances are you will like others and prefer their company. If not, you will feel inadequate when you are with them and miserable when you are alone. Everyone has an inner critic, who keeps passing harsh judgments and creating negativity. If you let your inner critic speak to you constantly, telling you how clumsy and imperfect you are or how guilty you should feel about your thoughts and your actions, you will undermine yourself and your self-worth whether you are alone or with others.

Your inner critic is a relic of your past. He represents an outdated value system, inherited from your peers and parents. He reinforces your negativity using both your positive and negative thoughts about yourself. It means you cannot escape from the negative consequences arising both from positive and negative situations. You will feel guilty, depressed when you make mistakes or fail in your expectations. You will also feel inadequate, unsure, and unappreciated when you achieve success. Thus, whether you succeed or fail, your "pathological inner critic" keeps you constantly under a cloud of negativity.

You can counter his criticism by disputing your negative thoughts, removing "musts" and "shoulds" from your vocabulary and by doing a realistic assessment of your strengths and weaknesses to know yourself and developing compassion for yourself. You can also use positive self-affirmations to reinforce your feelings of self-worth.

Your life is mostly a reflection of you. What you find in your heart and mind, you will find in the world. If you open your heart to yourself and accept yourself unconditionally, you will extend the same generous attitude towards others. You will realize that others are not much different from you and have the same problems and concern as you have. If you want to avoid loneliness, you must accept yourself unconditionally and project the same attitude towards others. The person whom you need to appreciate and accept most in your life is you only. Love yourself unconditionally, suspending all the judgment, which your inner critic uses against you. Know that you do not need to be perfect and do not have to have an extraordinary resume. You can be ordinary, as long as you are happy. You can be who you are and still learn to accept yourself and lover yourself. Strive to improve yourself and excel in some field, not because you think that you are imperfect, but because you want to realize your true potential and express yourself.

The relationship that requires the best attention and respect in your life is your relationship with yourself. Spend time, appreciating your own achievements and rewarding yourself suitably. Be compassionate towards yourself, forgiving your own faults and expressing gratitude for all the blessings you have. Focus on your strengths to overcome your low self-esteem and self-criticism. Self appreciation does not mean complacency. There is always scope for improvement in your life, and you can always choose to grow and improve not to impress anyone but to progress in the direction of your goals.

4. Be observant: Pay attention to your thoughts, feelings, emotions, and various sensations that arise in your mind and body during your waking hours. If you are observant, life offers you many lessons to learn and progress, and many opportunities to know about yourself and your deeper thoughts. Use every disturbance you experience as an opportunity to learn about yourself and your behavior. Life will unfold itself to an observant eye. To a sensitive person, each day is a unique experience which brings its own rewards and insights. Some people have an eye for unusual things. They know how to appreciate the beauty and diversity of life, even in ordinary circumstances. They enjoy their lives fully, feeling vibrant and alive, because they make the best use of their minds and senses, and increase their knowledge and sensitivity. If you are observant and attentive, you will not feel loneliness as you are drawn into the present moment and feel connected to the world. From observation arises the power of discernment, whereby you know who your true friends are, whom you can trust, what to keep, and what to avoid. You can cultivate the habit of mindful observation by learning to sit back, watch and enjoy, opening your mind and senses to the world around you and in you. From time to time pause in between and look around.

5. Live in the present: When you are in the present moment your right brain becomes active, and you feel connected to the current reality impersonally, without the need to judge anyone or define and defend yourself. However, you cannot practice it effectively if you are disturbed or preoccupied with your past or future. You enter present moment awareness by waking up to the moment, respecting the reality in front of you, and valuing your time. Not paying attention to others is a form of selfishness. When you are full of yourself, you do not listen to others or pay them attention. If you have this tendency, you need to step out of your shell and pay attention to others rather than becoming lost in your own concerns. It also grounds you in the reality of the people and situations you deal with. By staying in the present, you can be in touch with the happenings, observe your reactions and body sensations, and control your thoughts and responses according to the situation. It gives you an opportunity to step out of your habitual frame of mind and deal with the situation realistically and thoughtfully.

Here are a few simple techniques, which you can use to practice mindfulness. Next time when you sit down for a meal, eat your food as if it were the last meal of your life and as if every morsel of the food counts. Another simple technique is to spend a minute or two as if your life depends upon it and every moment counts. You can also occasionally focus upon your breathing when you have time to enter present moment awareness. You do not have to be always in the present moment, but you should be when the occasion demands. The third technique is listening to your heart, which means paying attention to your emotions and feelings when they arise.

6. Develop healthy relationships: These days, it is difficult to find good people and even more difficult to know them and form a relationship with them. Every young woman of present generation knows the perils of dating and the difficulties in finding a suitable partner. It is always riskier to become intimate with people you do not know much since you may become vulnerable and get hurt. If you are not watchful, you may even become involved with abusive people or dangerous characters. Relationships that arise from birth cannot be avoided altogether. You have to live with your brothers, sisters, parents, and other relations until you become independent and learn to create and sustain your own relationships.

Human beings are unpredictable, independent minded and prone to their own beliefs and prejudices. Hence, human relationships rarely run smoothly. You cannot keep them going unless your learn to adjust, compromise, bring out your best behavior and manage your true feelings. At the same time, intimate relationships thrive only on trust, love, openness, freedom, understanding and acceptance. Discretion, therefore, is the basis of lasting relationships. Whatever may be the methods you follow, make sure that you do not seek relationships out of desperation or sense of dependency. Try to know the people who matter to you. Be generous to them in giving, caring and helping and show them compassion for their weaknesses and vulnerabilities, without letting them exploit you emotionally or use you as a punching bag to take out their anger. It is a delicate balance, which you have to practice.

7. Help others: Helping others is the best cure for loneliness. It ennobles your character, makes you feel good about yourself and increases your opportunities to interact with people of various backgrounds. Those who help others are seldom lonely. They are respected, loved and sought by people. Studies prove that happiness comes from helping and serving others. You can reach out to people and help them in the following ways.

- Volunteer to help needy people.
- Donate the things that you do not need.
- Give charity.

- Become a mentor to children who come from broken families. There are organizations which can help you to mentor such children.
- Write a blog or a book sharing your experiences, insight and wisdom.
- Help your family members if it is possible.
- Find a good cause and work for it.
- Frequently send blessings and healing thoughts into the world.
- Help yourself and others by practicing compassion.
- Take up a cause in which you believe and keep posting about it on the social networks.

8. Be creative: In simple terms, creativity means the ability to see patterns and connections where others do not. It is perceiving and interpreting your reality and resolving your problems uniquely and differently by transcending your ordinary and habitual mindset. With creativity you can transcend your routine thinking, and mental filters to see the world from unique perspectives. If you are creative, you will find innovative solutions to the problem of loneliness and deal with it effectively. Within your means and limitations, you will find opportunities to establish positive relationships on a long term basis and increase your social interaction and sphere of influence. You can improve your creativity with the following.

- Read books and articles on creativity.
- Think about a problem from different perspectives.
- Keep an open mind.
- Avoid being judgmental.
- Do not jump to conclusions.
- Do not go by surface impressions. Think deeper.
- Understand your mental filters, selective thinking, stereotyping and other prejudices.
- Believe in yourself and be yourself.
- Do not seek others' approval.
- Make a firm commitment to be creative.
- Gather as much information as you can about the problem you want to resolve.
- Give your mind occasional rest.
- Keep a journal and note down your thoughts.
- Avoid authoritarian, critical and judgmental people.

Your creativity stems from fluid thinking when you suspend judgment and negative self-talk. Your mind must also be positive and cheerful. When you are unhappy or feel disturbed, you should learn to see things from a comic perspective, as if you are watching a cartoon movie.

9. Loneliness is a state of mind: Loneliness is a state of mind, or a feeling that persists because of your thinking and attitude rather than what the world does to you. You choose to be lonely because either you find comfort and security in it or you choose to avoid hurting yourself. Since the causes are mostly internal, caused by your beliefs and attitudes, you can deal with them by changing them. For that you have to identify the distortions in your thinking, and how they aggravate your persistent beliefs and fears about yourself and others. You have to dispute your own thoughts, assumptions and conclusions, so that you can see things differently and clearly. Secondly, you should focus upon your strengths and use them to your best advantage to feel good about yourself, accepting at the same time your weaknesses as opportunities to improve yourself. Finally, whatever may be your past, you should wholly accept yourself, forgive yourself and tolerate your own faults and failures.

When you become your own good friend and establish a healthy relationship with yourself, you will gradually open your mind and heart to others and learn to deal with them as your equals. Whatever may be your personal beliefs and lifestyle, you cannot remain alone forever. Even if you escape into a cave, the world will follow you in your thoughts and imagination. You may despise and distrust the world, but a part of you will still yearn to be with it. By prolonging your loneliness with self-deprecating thoughts, you will only aggravate your depression, isolation, and negativity. Therefore, it is better to take a few courageous steps to move forward, and learn to be a little vulnerable so that you can feel connected to the people around you and find social acceptance and belongingness in the company of others.

Health and Fitness

Exercise is an important aspect of physical and mental health. Regular exercise keeps the body in shape and leads to increased immunity, muscle strength, weight control, fitness, metabolism, and positive self-esteem. Irrespective of your age or occupation, with its help you can overcome many problems associated with stress, blood pressure, obesity, and heart diseases. While the benefits are many, you should not ignore the problems arising from doing wrong exercises or those that do not suit your body or age.

Although, Nature protects you from many threats, your health and fitness depend a lot upon your own effort. In this regard, your mind plays an important role. As it happens in case of many, unless you are mentally ready and willing to make necessary effort you will not continue with your fitness program. In other words, your commitment and involvement with your fitness must be total and your participation must be wholehearted. The motivation to do it and sustain it must also come from within yourself.

Many people live sedentary lives due to lack of knowledge and motivation. This, coupled with unhealthy food habits, has led to the problem of obesity in many parts of the world. According to a survey conducted by the National Health and Nutrition Examination (2003-2004), about 66% of adults in the USA between the age groups of 20 and 74 years were either overweight or obese. Studies indicate that the number of obese people has been growing steadily since 1976. Obesity is caused both by internal and external factors and cannot be fully resolved with exercise alone. However, where it is caused by lifestyle choices, it can be effective. Obesity is not the only problem which can be addressed with exercise. The following are the direct benefits of regular exercise.

- Improved blood circulation.
- Stress reduction.
- Lower risk of heart disease.
- Improved mood.
- Weight loss and weight control.
- Increased bone density and reduced bone loss.
- Restful sleep.

- Increased muscle weight and strength.
- Higher energy levels and stamina.
- Reduction in blood cholesterol.
- Healthier skin and body vigor.
- Reduced blood pressure.
- Relief from depression and anxiety.
- Positive self-image.
- Enhanced feelings of optimism and happiness.
- Know which exercises are good for you.

Types of exercise

We can divide the fitness exercises into aerobic and anaerobic, which are also called dynamic and static. The names are misleading because in both cases you have to breathe in a lot of fresh air. The names are given based upon how they induce and activate the metabolism of the body.

Anaerobic exercises build muscle mass so that the body will become strong, healthy and fit. Muscles consume a lot of energy. Hence, when you increase the muscle content in your body, your body's metabolic rate automatically goes up. Thus, Anaerobic exercises may not reduce your body weight immediately, but help you to sustain and maintain your body fitness on a long term basis by increasing your body's overall metabolism. Besides making the body strong, they also help you to control and manage fat and cholesterol ratios in your blood.

Aerobic exercises increase the metabolic rate instantly for the duration of your exercise and contribute to immediate fat burn, provided your calorie intake is under control. They induce your body to inhale more oxygen and release more glucose into your bloodstream to sustain your increased physical activity and prevent physical exhaustion. If there is not enough glucose in the blood stream it will break down fat reserves to continue the supply, which automatically leads to fat reduction.

Both types of exercises are good for the body in the long run as they improve immunity and health. In the initial stages, you may feel stressed by the effort since you have to force your body to adapt to increased physical activity. However, in the long run both exercises contribute immensely to your health and self-esteem. In today's world, fitness is the best healthcare insurance. It does not cost you much other than the time and energy you spare for the exercise.

If you are in good health, you do not have to make frequent visits to hospitals. In old age you will have better control over your life and freedom. The condition of old people in many parts of the world is deplorable, as they are neglected by their own children and forced to live in age old homes or in isolation. Many are forced to go there by their own children because they cannot take care of them or they feel that their parents cannot look after themselves and cannot be left alone. If you are healthy, you can keep your independence even in old age and it is possible through healthy lifestyle choices and regular physical activity. Therefore, unless you have strong reasons such as health problems, you should use exercise as the easiest and cheapest option to improve your health and fitness. Even if you have health problems, you can devise suitable strategies to work your body muscles and keep them strong. There are indications that even visualizing exercise routines can temporarily increase your body metabolism.

In anaerobic exercises you have to stress, stretch or contract your muscles to increase your muscle mass and body strength. You do it by pulling, pushing and stretching your muscles using various weights which make your muscles stronger and sturdier. Pushing exercises strengthen the front muscles of your body, especially those in your hands, shoulders, neck, chest, arms and legs, whereas pulling exercises strengthen the ones in the back. Stretching exercises make your muscles supple by toning and relaxing them, and prepare your body for increased physical activity.

Apart from strengthening the muscles, they improve your breathing and blood circulation, which lead to increased vigor, peace, relaxation, and mental stability. Those who practice yoga regularly, may use the postures (asanas) as stretching exercises. Aerobic exercises increase your pulse and heart rate as your body consumes more calories to cope up with increased physical activity and body metabolism, which reduces the chances of excess fat from accumulating. It also purifies your blood by reducing sugars and toxins present in it. Common aerobic exercises include cycling, jogging, pedaling, rowing, dancing, swimming, climbing stairs, jumping and playing games like tennis, racquet and basketball. Common anaerobic exercises include all weight exercises, pushups, etc.

Create the right fitness program

For better results, any fitness program should incorporate both aerobic and anaerobic exercises. With aerobic exercises you will burn fat, but loose muscle weight also, which is not good for your overall strength and stamina. Anaerobic exercises, on the other hand, increase your muscle weight and thereby make it harder for you to lose weight. Besides, prolonged and daily practice of weight exercises is also not good since it can lead to muscle fatigue and even injury. Therefore, to derive benefit from both and protect your body from possible harm and injury health experts suggest that they should not be practiced every day, but only on alternate days. This is known as cross training. As you practice them alternatively, your body will gain strength and loose fat, without side effects, fatigue, and muscle loss.

The purpose of doing exercise is to improve your health and fitness. Many people forget this goal after they start exercising and get hurt as they exercise improperly or use wrong weights to impress someone or gain attention. Therefore, balance, discipline, regularity, and self-control are very important in any fitness program. Before you begin any exercise, your body should be tuned and prepared to withstand the rigors of exercise. It means you should eat adequately, drink enough water and do some stretches before you get into heavy routine. To avoid injuries, muscle tears, and even fractures, you should choose your exercises according to your age. Unless you exercise regularly for a long period, you cannot develop a perfect body. Hence, instead of pu(ni)shing yourself, choose your exercises carefully and allow your body to regain its strength and stamina in due time.

Understand your body

Your body is a natural machine. No matter what you do, it will try to protect you from possible threat and even from your own actions. It has an intelligence of its own, which it uses effectively to protect you from all possible dangers. It is not entirely under your control either, while you can control some of its functions only partially. It has an amazing self-repairing mechanism. There is even an argument that the cells in your body may have their own intelligence and can repair themselves without your knowledge.

Your body senses the changes in your physical activity and energy consumption instantly and adjusts its metabolic rate accordingly. If you increase your physical activity, it slows down to compensate for the fat loss and maintain the energy reserves. If you reduce your physical activity, it senses an opportunity to store even more reserves. This is why many people experience frustration when they begin doing dieting or exercise. They notice that although they are exercising vigorously their weight is not coming down. It also happens that in the beginning you lose weight rapidly, but as you continue doing your exercises, you do not lose weight at the same rate. It happens because while you are trying to lose weight your body keeps protecting you from excess fat burn and energy depletion.

The best way to deal with this problem is knowing your body's metabolism and making it your ally in your fitness program. Instead of fighting your body's natural tendencies, you should keep the metabolic rate at a certain level, while allowing it to gradually adjust to the new lifestyle you have chosen. An ideal solution is you should vary your exercises or their sequence, and avoid doing the same exercises regularly. This strategy makes it harder for the body to anticipate its energy requirements and adjust its metabolic rate. It is also important not to stress your body with over exertion and under nutrition.

Choose your nutrition program

We have already mentioned the importance of food and nutrition in improving your physical wellbeing. The body needs a good mixture of proteins, vitamins, minerals, carbohydrates and other nutrients for its immunity and proper functioning, more so when you are doing regular exercise. Any dietary plan, therefore, should include healthy foods according to your body requirements and exclude those that harmful and unhealthy. For example, dietitians and nutritionists recommend drinking plenty of water, eating fruits and vegetables, avoiding foods that are rich in fats and sugars. They also warn against the consumption of alcohol, beer, and other intoxicants, which can cause irreparable damage to various organs in the body. A good nutrition program should take care of the requirements of both the body and the mind. Of all the parts in your body, your brain needs maximum supply of glucose and other nutrients, besides a constant supply of purified blood. Preventing bone loss is another important goal that cannot be ignored especially in old age. Thus, nutrition is as important to your fitness as any exercise.

Sustained physical activity improves the functioning of the heart, lungs, joints, digestive system, lungs, kidneys, and other parts of your body, which means you may have to make lifestyle changes to meet the demands of your body instead of focusing upon a few narrow aims such as improving your looks or reducing weight. Your efforts to lose weight and improve your health should be part of a holistic lifestyle. It cannot be and should not be done in isolation. You can always lose weight rapidly by taking some diet pills or eating less, but in the long run it will not work as your body regains weight as rapidly as it lost. Dieting and exercise should part of your overall health goals. According to the U.S. Department of Health and Human Services a good dietary program should aim to "maintain a healthy weight, promote health, and prevent disease." Apart from these, it should "reduce the risk of major chronic diseases such as heart disease, diabetes, osteoporosis, and some cancers." Their guidelines aim to "balance calories to manage weight" to prevent obesity and body weight to increase physical activity and maintain proper calorie balance during each stage of life.

Your calorie intake depends upon your body conditions. You have to find out what suits you. Studies show that it is good to occasionally starve yourself, so that you can get rid of the toxins that accumulate in your body. However, one cannot solely rely upon such a limited approach. In a holistic weight reduction program, you have to focus upon overall health to ensure that each component of your program contributes to your overall fitness. Hence, choosing and eating right food in suitable quantities at regular intervals and in right combinations is important. You have to know which foods are good for you, and how you can put together a dietary program that can maximize the benefits of exercise and minimize side effects. It is true that with so many proprietary programs in circulation, choosing the right one that fits your needs is a challenge. Some programs recommend purely vegetarian food, some suggest a combination of proteins and carbohydrates, while others recommend fruit and milk diet, or a combination of all these. We do not have enough evidence to determine which of these food combinations are good for you. Cultural and social factors also matter in choosing your diet. When you practice weight exercises you will need more protein, whereas you may have to drink a lot of water and protect yourself from hot and humid climates when you practice aerobics. In short, you should choose your diet according to your exercise goals and nutrition requirements.

Seek help

The human body is a complicated system, with many interdependent parts and processes that need constant care and attention. It is subject to limitations and vulnerable to many threats and weaknesses. Whether you like it or not, your body is your abode and your ally, which serves dutifully as your vehicle of movement, action and communication. It is where you experience everything about life, love, and suffering. Certainly, it is much more important than the house in which you live or the cars you use. It defines your existence and connects you to the world. Without its support, you cannot exist at all in this world. Therefore, you cannot ignore its value to your life, or its needs that are central to your happiness and well-being. Whatever may be your priorities, and preoccupation you have to protect it and preserve it for your own good.

Your body has certain limitations, which you must respect. For example, it cannot withstand the extremes of anything. Whether it is food, activity, alcohol, or weather, you have to practice moderation to avoid falling sick and staying healthy. One of the immediate effects of exercise upon your body is increased stress and physical discomfort, which means when you start exercising regularly you should take adequate rest and eat well to allow your body to repair itself. It also means that you have to avoid hurting yourself by taking necessary precautions.

Human beings vary in their ability to cope with the pressures of physical activity. Some health problems will not be known until you begin doing exercises. If you have excess cholesterol in your body, you may be prone to heart problems and rigorous exercises such as jogging and weightlifting may be unsuitable for you. You should always consult your family physician before doing any exercise and ask for any precautions that may be specific to your health conditions. You should also decide whether to join a gym or be on your own. Joining a gym has its own advantages. The gym atmosphere keeps you motivated, besides offering you several options to practice your exercises. Nowadays modern gyms offer a number of facilities to keep you focused and entertained while you exercise. They also offer qualified trainers whom you can hire to know the basics of weight exercises. With a trainer by your side, you can keep yourself motivated and get on with your fitness goals.

Change Your Mindset

In this age where families are breaking apart, living is becoming increasingly tough for old people, and where health costs are skyrocketing, we cannot ignore the importance of staying healthy and fit. The best way to achieve it is to devise a proper fitness program and a dietary plan according to your age and health. If you have mostly lived a sedentary life, you will find it hard to change your mindset and get into a fitness program. Old habits are difficult to break, especially when they become an integral part of your daily routine. You may begin by making a few changes to your current lifestyle such as climbing the stairs instead of using the lift, or walking in your spare time. From there you can add more activities to make it a wholesome practice. The best way to keep yourself motivated and bring a fundamental change in your thinking and attitude is to become health conscious. You can do it in any of the following ways.

- Have clearly defined and measurable fitness goals and frequently remember them.
- Check your weight regularly at least once a day.
- Read health information or watch fitness related videos.
- Use positive self-affirmations.

- Try to remain physically active during the day by finding opportunities.
- Play some sport.
- Have friends who are fitness conscious.
- Check for calorie values and fat and sugar content when you buy foods.
- Practice yoga and meditation.
- Focus on the benefits of exercise.
- Reward yourself when you reach milestones.

Because of low motivation, disinterest in looking attractive and low self-esteem, many people do not pay attention to their physical fitness. Your health and hygiene are an important part of how you present yourself to world. It shows up in your thinking, attitude, lifestyle, relationships and habits. Ignoring your health is a form of physical self-abuse. It means you do not love yourself enough and do not consider that you deserve a good life. To change it you have to examine your beliefs and attitudes and your motivation in following such a self-destructive path. Take that one step forward and commit yourself to a robust and healthy lifestyle centered on healthy diet and physical activity.

The Power of Your Thoughts

Abundance is a state of mind. You conceive it with your thoughts, intentions, desires and beliefs. You realize it with your actions, dedication, resolve and commitment. Just by sitting somewhere and day dreaming, none can become successful or rich. Saying so would be naive. Our thoughts precede our actions, almost always. We think before we act, even when it appears we are not. Everything begins as an idea in a fertile mind and materializes through actions. Thus, there is a thought process behind every action we indulge in. When our thoughts and actions are in harmony with our deepest aspirations and intentions and when we are attuned positively to believe in ourselves, we make possible our hopes and dreams.

Our thoughts have a power of their own. If we know how they work and how to make use of them effectively, we can accomplish a lot more in our lives. Our thoughts reach out to others, through our words and expressions. They influence people both positively and negatively. They help us to make sense of the world and interpret our experiences according to our emotional states and perceptions. We value people, who are good thinkers and who have an exceptional ability to express their thoughts and resolve problems.

People are successful or unsuccessful, rich or poor, mainly because of the differences in their thinking. Our mental states influence our circumstances and together they create the experience we call life. Positive thoughts lead to positive states of mind, bringing us their rich rewards. Negative thoughts influence us in negative ways, bringing us pain and suffering, subjecting our minds to destructive thoughts and distracting emotions and reducing our ability to think normally or function effectively.

An idle life is a product of morbid thoughts. A mind fired by the power of imagination and the desire to achieve finds little value in harboring idle thoughts. When matched with corresponding effort and enthusiasm, it will lead to greatness, transcendence and abundance. By changing your thinking and beliefs, you can overcome the limitations of your mind and your circumstances and achieve an expansive state of mind. Your mind is the key to your success and progress. It is the powerhouse of your thoughts and beliefs. It is where your dreams and ideas take shape. Hidden in it are your immense potentials and unknown possibilities. It makes possible who you are and what you can do. Because of that we have awareness, knowledge, sensitivity and intelligence. Because of that we experience and control the very process of existence and intelligent awareness.

If you know how to manage your thoughts to achieve desired results, you will transcend your ordinariness and bring order and discipline into your uncertain life. When there are problems and difficulties, you will not feel paralyzed by your fears and self-deprecating thoughts. You will have an edge over those who surrender to their weaknesses rather than to their strengths and you will reach your goals with conviction and confidence. When you energize your actions with your thoughts, determination, clarity and clear purpose, you unleash your mind's immense power to manifest and make possible your intentions. You increase your ability to reach your goals with purpose filled and pointed actions. With each success, you will become effective, task oriented, and hopeful.

Our perceptions, thoughts, attitudes, feelings, emotions and perspectives, manifest our reality. It is where our convictions gather strength and our progress gains momentum. Others may interfere with our lives, but only in a limited way. They may become part of our lives or partners in our success, but only with our consent and willingness. The healing thoughts that come to us from outside do not heal us, unless we deserve help and are receptive enough. It is with our thoughts that we set the tone and direction of our lives, attracting or repulsing the abundance of the universe and opportunities. Knowingly or unknowingly, we harbor thoughts that shape our destinies. We allow them to build our hopes and aspirations as well as our fears and doubts. Our thoughts may not have the miraculous powers to manifest reality instantly. But they do so, slowly and gradually, according to our faith and effort. If you know how to use your thoughts effectively, you will multiply your energy and your chances of your success.

Here are few questions that are worth examining to know whether you are prepared for success and happiness in your life. What type of mindset do you have? What type of thoughts do you entertain most of the time? Are you able to control your mind and its activities? How easily are you distracted? How focused are you in your life? Are you resolute enough to carry through your actions? How do you react to the problems that arise in your life? How frequently do you suffer from negative thoughts and actions?

We do not frequently ask ourselves such questions, but they are worth examining and remembering to remain positive and hopeful. If you want to find lasting solutions to success and happiness, you need to do introspection on these lines and find your own truths according to your experience and circumstances. Your findings may not help you to deal with every situation in your life, but they will prepare you mentally to take control of your life and manifest your dreams and desires according to your beliefs. A room which is decorated with an abundance of roses is bound to emit the fragrance of the roses. Your mind acts similarly, it reflects what it has. If it has knowledge, it radiates knowledge, and if it has ignorance it radiates the same. If you keep it clean and organized with the fragrance of positive, constructive and empowering thoughts, you will smell the sweet fragrance of success coming out of it. Similarly, if you have peace, harmony and happiness inside you they will manifest in your life too. Therefore, if you want to achieve success in any venture, you have to prepare and train your mind to contain the seeds of it.

Success and achievement are transformative processes. We achieve success when we translate our thoughts into actions and our actions into desired results. Every action begins in our minds first as an idea or a plan and becomes an action only when we apply our energies to it. Otherwise, our actions will remain as mere thoughts or wishes. In doing things and achieving things, we transform our energies by using our resources. We exchange them with the universe in return for gains, approval, and recognition. The universe is always willing to help you as long as you are willing to work with it positively. In life it may seem that you deal with innumerable things and people, but in reality you deal with but one, which is the universe. He appears to you in innumerable forms and guises and creates in you the illusion of dealing with many. In your dealings with the world, you should always remember that fundamentally only two realities exist, the universe and you. The rest is all a play of names and forms. You may think you are dealing with others, but you are dealing with yourself or the universal Self.

Hence when you exchange things unfairly, you become responsible for your actions as the law of compensation is set in motion. Therefore, when you deal with others try to be fair and generous, knowing that the universe keeps a watch on all and settles the dues. You are never separate from the universe. You look at the screen and forget that you are in the theatre. The universe is your witness, and your partner in everything you do. He dutifully balances your account as your resources and energies are but His. You may mistake the aspects of universe as different, but such distinctions do not exist in the domain of the universe. If you are unfair or unjust to others, know that you are unjust and unfair to the universe. When you hurl abuses at others, know that you are hurling abuses at the universes. The universe is the otherness. What you do to others will bounce back to you. Everything outside you is one; everything inside you is one; until you know that everything is one.

Our thoughts create our actions, and our actions precipitate reality. This is the underlying mechanism behind every self-willed and self-directed manifestation. What we call planning is actually an exercise in manifestation. We use it to give a definite shape to our thoughts and desires as the blueprint of our future. It is an organized effort to remain committed to our goals and aspirations. Our thoughts are thus our prime resources, the raw material, with which we manifest our dreams and desires. We are what we think and believe to be. We make things possible or impossible through our beliefs. If you want to achieve something in life, you must first believe in it and work for it with conviction. When you set out on a course of action, you must resolve your doubts and fears. Otherwise, they may become your actions.

Our failures and successes, and so also our experiences and circumstances are mostly products of our consciousness. Superficially it may appear that events happen randomly, but in reality through our thoughts, desires, beliefs and decisions we create them. The world is beyond our control, but not entirely beyond our influence. Knowing your limitations and opportunities, and what you can and cannot do is important. Even in the most helpless change others or your circumstances but you can change your thinking and decisions. You may not have full control over Nature, but you can adapt to it. You may not change others according to your wishes, but you can always decide which relations to keep and which to ignore. The world may not listen to us, but we can pay attention to it and learn from it. Thus, whatever may be the circumstances and difficulties, you can always act to feel empowered and optimistic.

Truly speaking, we are all great survivors. We survive against great odds. We can adapt to circumstances and survive in difficult environments. People have been doing it for ages. We may not be able to change the course of the planets, but we can change the course of our lives. With positive thoughts and aspirations, we can bring light into our hearts and minds and change our destinies. Your thoughts manifest your desires. Since they are not always under your control, you should know how to attune them to your goals and aspirations. You have to learn how to think positively and keep your mind focused on your goals. In this regard, the following suggestions are helpful

- Pay attention to what you think mostly. Avoid frivolous thoughts.
- Believe in your ability to manifest your thoughts.
- Clearly know what you want and focus on it.
- Dispute your negative thoughts using positive ones.
- Think deeply until you have weighed all the options.
- Be realistic, but know you can create magic with your thoughts and actions.
- Do not let others control your life. Empower yourself.
- Cultivate relationships with people who are successful and positive.
- Stay focused on your strengths and positive outcomes.
- Avoid people who are by nature negative and critical.
- Organize and prioritize your resources and tasks.
- Frequently visualize your goals to remember them.

- Use positive affirmations to reinforce your thoughts and beliefs.
- Keep an open mind to see new possibilities and alternatives.
- Improve your vocabulary and communication.
- Practice meditation and mindfulness techniques to remove negative energy from your mind and body.

If you truly want to succeed in your life, you should mentally prepare for it and develop the necessary strength to withstand the problems and challenges that arise from it. You should use your intelligence to find your purpose, define your goals and develop suitable means to reach them. No one is perfect. You must be willing to forgive your faults and imperfections, without taking them personally and being stuck in them. You must keep your mind in a certain positive frame of mind and fuel your actions with positive thoughts. This is the proven way to reach your goals. There is no magic wand other than this. You may not have the wings of angels, but you can wing your thoughts and dreams with your beliefs and let them fly. What you think you are, and what you stand for in your life determine what you will ultimately become. If you are in harmony with yourself, you will be in harmony with others. If you are confident of reaching your goals, you will improve your chances of success. If you remain in a positive state of mind, you will harness your energies with minimum friction.

You are the source of all that happens to you. You decide what will happen to you. You are the sum total of all your thoughts, feelings, emotions, beliefs, expectations, intentions, goals, memories, knowledge, ability, skills and energies. Your ability to control and regulate your life, your capacity to face adversity, your willingness to learn from failures, your interest in forging healthy relationships, your integrity, personality, balance, character, and attitude are shaped by them. They make possible what you desire in your life, how you relate to your world and experience the joys and sufferings of life. Some people work less, accomplish more. There are some who toil day and night, but remain unhappy and unfulfilled. Some, despite their great riches, do not experience prosperity. Driven by insecurity, they live like poor people. For some, life is a rewarding experience. The mere sight of a flower or a sky fills them with joy and wonder. When you interact with some, you feel energized, peaceful and spiritually uplifted, but when you meet some, you feel disturbed and depressed, as if something has been taken away from you or drained out. These differences exist because of the differences in thinking and perceptions. It is for us to decide what we want to do with our lives and in which direction we intend to go. It is up to us to decide whether to take control of our minds and thoughts or let them control us.

The Power of Attraction

Planets use gravitational force to keep things together and stay in equilibrium. Although they compete with one another, plants of each species prefer living in the same habitat. In the attraction of things is the seed of life. In life we use our thoughts and emotions to attract things and hold on to them. If you smile, the world smiles back. If you frown, the world frowns back. If you are likable, your circle of friends expands; if you are disliked you will be left alone. This is the principle of attraction in play. You can build such power and your influence by radiating positive thoughts and bring light and happiness into your life.

You can be the magnet for a good life

You can attract good things into your life by energizing your mind with positive thoughts. This is not a magical shortcut to success. It is possible if you can train your mind to think positively and believe in the possibilities even in the worst difficulties. For it to happen you have to overcome your inner resistance and believe positive outcomes. You can test it right now with this simple exercise. For the next few minutes, look at yourself in a mirror and keep smiling. See how you begin to experience pleasant feelings. You can also test it by calling a person who helped you in the past and whom you did not talk for a long time, and tell him how happy you were to talk to him and how grateful you felt for his help. When you make other people happy, their happiness makes you even happier. It is again the power of attraction happening in the reverse.

A cheerful, friendly and benign attitude invokes positive reactions from others and strengthens your relationships with them, while critical and negative attitude isolates you from them and leaves you alone and unhappy. Love and compassion open many doors, while hatred and resentment shut them down. There is no dearth of good friends for the positive and amiable people, while those with anger and hatred may attract a similar kind. We all possess the power to attract what we desire strongly. You can use it to achieve your goals and dreams, and find happiness and fulfillment. With compassion, generosity, understanding, empathy, charity, courage, and sacrifice, you can set in motion the higher powers of your mind and find peace and happiness.

You can manifest your reality

The human mind has many abilities. Of them one is the power of manifestation. Due to lack of conviction many do not use it. When you energize your thoughts and desires with your imagination and intention, they manifest according to your convictions. In this world, you are the sum total of your thoughts, beliefs, desires, emotions, hopes and fears. You attract and manifest what you think and desire according to your beliefs, emotions, passions and intentions. You also attract and manifest what you fear and resist. If your fear arises from your subconscious mind or from your repressed thoughts, you may not even know why your life is not happening the way you wanted to.

You subconscious mind is the graveyard of your forgotten and repressed memories, thoughts and perceptions. It is like an ocean of consciousness in which your wakeful mind floats like a land mass. You cannot reach it as easily as you can reach your conscious mind. It is not directly under you control, but listens to you and manifests your predominant and thoughts and desires. You can make it your friend or enemy, depending upon what you think, and how envision your future. If you think positively and see positive images in your mind, it will manifest them unconditionally. If you have doubts and fears, it will manifest the same confusion in your life.

Your subconscious mind is your obedient and silent partner in your life. It does not question you, judge you, or use its discretion while executing your intentions. Other than whatever you feel, think and expect, it does not create any negativity, filter your perceptions, or alter your thinking. It accepts you unconditionally and manifests your desires according to your hopes and expectations. Since fear is a dominant emotion, many people fail to harness the true potential of their subconscious minds. They sabotage their own success as they fail to resolve their fears and doubts.

You can control your life and destiny

What you think and believe is therefore important. If you want to achieve success and positive results from your actions, you have to train your mind to think positively so that it can send clear signals to your subconscious mind and direct it without conflict. To think constructively and creatively and keep your mind free from negativity, you have to overcome your prejudices, negative attitudes and unverified assumptions, irrational beliefs and preconceived notions. With open and receptive mind prepared thus, you can manifest the life you want to lead. The following suggestions are helpful in this regard.

- Use positive affirmations to stay positive and direct your subconscious.
- Believe in your ability to manifest reality.
- Each road leads to many destinations. Hence, you need to know where you want to go.
- Begin your day with positive thoughts, an inspiring message or a sincere prayer.
- Express gratitude for the blessings you have, the lessons you have learned, and the progress you have made.
- Bring clarity into your thinking, purpose, aims and vision, so that your subconscious mind knows what to manifest.
- Visualize your goals vividly using your imagination, and envision how you intend your life to be when you achieve them
- Focus on your strengths and potentials.
- Practice possibility thinking.
- Look for opportunities in every situation.
- Keep motivating yourself with books, articles and inspirational audios.
- Remember your goals as frequently as possible.
- Avoid negativity towards wealth and wealthy people.
- Appreciate your happiness. Understand your suffering.
- Keep your mind focused on solutions and opportunities.
- Know what you want and let your subconscious mind decide how to achieve it.
- Thank for everything even when you have problems and difficulties.

- Open your mind and heart to the beauty and wonders of life.
- Remember good things about people, and when you are with them appreciate their positive qualities.

Your subconscious mind gets things done for you. It knows what you want and manifests it. It is more active when you are restful, positive, confident and cheerful. Therefore, stay positive and use possibility thinking to see opportunities, find solutions and reach your goals.

The Power of Determination

You quest for success and happiness begins with right intentions. It culminates when you reach your chosen goals. What sustains your effort in between is your determination. What carries you towards your goals is your determination. If mankind has reached the moon or is planning to land on Mars or another planet someday, it is because some people, somewhere, are determined to make it happen, with firm conviction. Determination means the firmness of purpose or intention. It is the strength of your will and focus to remain steadfast in your effort. It means having the ability to stay on course, remain focused on your goals, stand up to the problems and obstacles with conviction, stay fixed and firm about your decisions, solutions and intentions and apply the power of your will to your dreams and desires with resolve, grit, fortitude, faith and courage.

If there is one gift that you can give to yourself in your life to be what you want to be, it is the power of determination. Without it you are a mere passive spectator in the drama of your life. If there is one quality that makes a difference between a winner and a loser or a leader and a follower, it is the power of determination. Without it, you may dream wild dreams, but you will not accomplish much in life. If you have determination, nothing can stop you and deter you from following your course of action to achieve your goals or realize your dreams.

Obstacles may arise and obstruct your progress. They may delay your success, disturb you temporarily, and may even mislead you, but they cannot withstand the power of determination. It is the power that you generate within yourself to remain committed to your path and conviction, and march towards your cherished goals. Determination is a strength and valuable resource in itself. If you have it, you can aim for the stars. You are successful or unsuccessful to the extent you are determined and committed to your goals. With determination we can accomplish many goals in our lives. With faith in God and confidence in yourself, and with strong determination, you can achieve the impossible, realize the most difficult dreams and achieve excellence and incredible success in your life. Remember the following formula. Write it down and frequently refer to it until the idea is firmly implanted in your mind. The first one leads you to success, and the second one to nowhere but into a fantasy land.

Idea + Determination + Effort = Success.

Idea - Determination - Effort = Wishful thinking, fantasy.

Before you take up any project or goal, you should know whether you have the determination to stick to your plans and reach your goals. Your determination has to arise from within and derive its reinforcement from your thinking and beliefs rather than circumstances. Only then you will be able to sustain your effort, even when the going gets tough. Determination is your inner strength. Like the hardwood inside a tree, it gives you the power to stand tall and face the winds of turmoil. The following factors strengthen your resolve.

- Clear goals.
- Knowledge and skills.
- Self-esteem.
- Positive mental attitude.
- Courage.
- Faith in yourself and God.
- Self-motivation.
- Visualizing the end.
- Positive self-affirmations.
- Supporting people.
- Empowering thoughts and beliefs.

With determination you can crush the mountains of fear and doubts in you. You can find your way through the most difficult situations. Determination does not mean you will be insensitive to the reality of the situation. A determined person is also an adaptable and flexible person. He is not interested in being tough for toughness sake, but to overcome obstacles and reach his goals. Hence, he remains open-minded about possibilities and opportunities, but firm in his commitment and convictions. Discipline and determination go together. If you have them, you become unstoppable.

The Power of Positive Affirmations

An affirmation is a positive thought, or statement that you repeat to yourself frequently and embed in your inner consciousness for inspiration and motivation to overcome negativity and sustain your interest and enthusiasm to perform actions. When you affirm a statement repeatedly, it becomes a part of your consciousness and guides your behavior. You can use affirmations to overcome undesirable behavior and negative and habitual thought patterns, which prevent you from effectively using your full potentials.

They are especially useful to overcome fear, self-doubt, low self-esteem, lack of confidence, initiative, and anxiety. You can also use them to reinforce positive thoughts such as compassion, love, courage, confidence, amiability, and positive mental attitude. Affirmations are found useful in helping patients to recover from psychosomatic disorders and certain illnesses. They are also called auto-suggestions because they work like subtle commands with which you can retune your mind.

Why affirmations?

Your mind is a vast storehouse of accumulated knowledge and learned responses. It is programmed to act in certain mechanical and predictable ways. It relies upon certain learned responses and perceptual filters to make sense of the world. Since it has to cope with large volume of information from the outside world and much of it is either routine or irrelevant, it learns to filter the information according to its importance in your survival. In this your desires, beliefs, thinking, and attitude play an important role. For example, if you are a painter you may see the world in terms of colors, shades, and perspectives. If you are a writer, or a reporter you may look for a story angle.

Your mind is thus shaped by your interests, desires, past actions and experiences. If you have visited the same place several times, you may pay much attention to it as you assume that not much has changed. However, a new visitor to the same place may find there many attractions. Since your mind is conditioned by several experiences and cultural influences, it is not easy to control its movements or break its conventional habits. Using affirmations you can instruct your mind and body to act in desirable ways and overcome the barriers that stand between you and your ideal personality. By sending subtle auto-commands into your mind you can empower yourself in the following ways.

- Powerfully change your thinking, beliefs and behavior.
- Heal your mind and recover from pain and suffering.
- Dispute your negative self-talk to improve your self-esteem and morale.
- Empower yourself to deal with the problems and challenges with increased confidence, enthusiasm and determination.
- Control your thoughts, emotions and irrational beliefs.
- Channel your energies in the desired direction.

Following are a few important positive changes you can bring using positive affirmations.

- Lose weight in a natural and healthy way through gradual lifestyle changes.
- Excel in sports or academic achievement.
- Start and complete a project such as writing a book, which you thought was difficult.
- Overcome certain fears and anxieties, and feelings of inferiority and low self-esteem.
- Cure certain types of sickness and weakness.
- Improve performance and efficiency.
- Strengthen your will power and determination.
- Learn a new skill or subject.
- Improve your memory, listening, and perception
- Change your attitude, behavior, emotional responses.
- Change your habits and daily routine.
- Improve your social intelligence and interaction.
- Heal your past relationships and traumas.

Positive affirmations may not get you everything you wanted in your life, but they can help you to build on your thoughts and achieve self-mastery. They can change your thinking and beliefs, and align you to your goals and aspirations. With their help, you can overcome your negativity, fears and frustration and feel responsible for your actions and thoughts. You can face the challenges of your life more confidently, with the conviction that your destiny is in your hands. Using affirmations, you can practically do anything that's humanly possible and within your capacity. You can change the way you think, act, and relate to yourself and others. You can become the person you want to be. However, to make it happen, you should know how to make the affirmations work for you. The following suggestions are helpful in this regard.

- **Know what you want**: If you clearly know what you want or expect, you can frame your affirmations correctly to address the problems and goals that are specific to you.
- **Use positive words and phrases only**: Positive affirmations keep your expectations positive. You should avoid negative expressions since your subconscious mind may become confused. For example instead of saying, "I don't want to be nervous" you may say, "I am feeling confident about this."
- **Keep your affirmations simple and clear**: Vague and ambiguous words may create confusion by sending wrong signals to your mind. Therefore, use concrete and specific actionable words that directly appeal to your mind and senses.
- **Write down your affirmations**: Write down your list of affirmations on a piece of paper or in a notebook and refer to them frequently so that you can use the same wording each time you go through them.
- **Remember your affirmations regularly**: You should frequently remember them until they are firmly remembered. Revisit them every day whenever you find time to make them a part of your active memory.
- **Update your affirmations**: As you make progress, your affirmations may require revision to reflect the changes that happen during the transformation. Therefore, update your list of affirmations according to your progress.
- **Counter your negative self-talk**: Self-talk is the best part of your mind. Affirmations are meant to

artificially improve the quality of your self-talk so that it will be supportive and relevant to your goals. However, negative self-talk can ruin your efforts. Hence, use positive affirmations to counter your inner critic.

- **Use affirmations to remember your goals**: Create them in such a manner that they remind you of your goals or the actions you need to perform to reach them.
- **Change your habits**: Use your affirmations to change your negative, emotional and habitual responses as well as you negative and self-destructive habits.
- **Use emotions**: Use powerful, and positive emotions along with your affirmations. Studies show that when affirmations are combined with emotions they yield better results.
- **Own your affirmations**: Make your affirmations personal by crafting them in first person so that you can relate to them directly and take responsibility for the changes they bring. For example, "I am happy I am making progress."
- **Use the present tense**: Use the present tense as if your affirmations are already working for you and yielding positive results. Express gratitude for the transformation that is happening.
- **Invoke the power of God**: If you believe in God, bring Him into your affirmations and energize them. Combine the power of prayer with your affirmations. Affirm your faith in God and ask Him to manifest your goals, expressing gratitude for the help you are already receiving.
- **Use visualization**: Add imagination to your affirmations and pour life into them to make them effective. Visualize how they are manifesting the change you want to see in your life or in you.

Build your life with positive affirmations

A pointed well-crafted affirmation is more powerful than a missile because it creates rather than destroys. You have many options to achieve success and happiness in your life. You can take charge of your life and realize your goals in various ways. You may choose any method or path that suits you according to your knowledge, abilities and circumstances, but if you combine your methods with positive affirmations, you will vastly improve your chances of success. When positive affirmations are reinforced by strong emotions, faith, and corresponding effort, they will bring you rich rewards. They enhance your self-esteem, reduce your negativity, and pave the way for success and happiness. As you change your thinking and behavior, you become a new person and develop a new perspective about yourself and the world. You become the source of your success and happiness and empower yourself with positive and transformative self-talk. As you pour energy into your thoughts through affirmations, they manifest your desires and goals and lead you towards success and happiness.

Positive Thinking in Daily Life

Positive thinking is a powerful thought force which helps you to go the extra mile by expecting more and achieving more in your life than normally possible. With positive thinking you can rise from the ordinary to the extraordinary and deal with your setbacks and negative emotions. You can set higher standards of performance to manifest your goals and accomplish difficult tasks. Positive thinking arises from the following.

- **Your attitude**: It shapes your worldview and determines how you process and interpret your perceptions and experiences, and regard the world and yourself in empowering ways.
- **Your self-image**: It determines how you feel about yourself and how you think others might see you. It influences your decisions, actions, and your relationship with the world and the people in your life.
- **Your beliefs**: They shape every aspect of your life. It is not even an exaggeration to say that your attitude depends directly upon your beliefs. Since beliefs do not depend upon reality, attitudinal problems arising from deep-seated beliefs are difficult to resolve.

Positive thinking means

Positive thinking means living in the hope and expectations of the good things to come, without losing faith in your ability to deal with problems and make use of opportunities. It is seeing solutions in problems and opportunities in threats. It is making peace with the world and finding your way through resistance. A positive thinker look at his perceptions, experiences and actions as empowering and learning opportunities to sustain his morale and motivation. He looks at the events and situations in his life with a hopeful, cheerful and positive frame of mind, despite any negativity and uncertainty that may be present them.

Positive thinking helps you to position yourself positively towards others and the world in general. It empowers you to deal with your problems and challenges with hope and courage, and believe in yourself and your abilities. When you are positively inclined, you see opportunities instead of problems and use the possibilities life offers to you as challenges and obstacles. Positive thinking also means jumping the sinking ship at the right time hoping to find a raft or a boat. A positive thinker is not delusional or unrealistic. He uses defensive pessimism to prepare for contingencies. He knows how to adjust his plans and actions according to the circumstances.

40 ways to remain positive

Positive and negative thinking are learned responses. Certain factors such as chronic illness or depression can lead to prolonged and deep-seated negativity. Certain events and situations in life may develop in some people a deep distrust towards others and the world in general. Repeated failures and setbacks in life can break one's confidence. The world takes its own time to acknowledge you and accommodate you. You have to keep faith in your methods and keep trying.

It is difficult to generalize solutions for problems such as these. However, it should be comforting to know that positive thinking can be cultivated. Here are a few suggestions to develop and maintain positive mental attitude. Not all of them may be suitable for you. You may also need to customize them according to your needs. However, practice the methods you choose sincerely until they become part of your conscious thinking and behavior.

1. Believe in your ability to achieve goals and dreams and manifesting your destiny.
2. Believe in your ability to control your thoughts and emotions.
3. Believe in your ability to resolve your problems and difficulties.
4. Believe in yourself. Keep remembering, "Yes, I can."
5. Know that you deserve the best.
6. Know that you are unique, and none but you can live the life that is given to you.
7. Focus on your achievements, strengths, talents, skills and past successes
8. Remember the problems you solved and the difficulties you overcame.
9. Focus on the possibilities and opportunities while planning and preparing for problems and threats.

10. Learn to appreciate instead of criticizing.
11. Smile frequently and keep your cheerful mode.
12. Occasionally pause and say thank you for the blessings you received.
13. Stop mind reading and attributing negative motives to others without evidence.
14. Give benefit of doubt to others when you do not have all the information.
15. Focus on your merits, strengths and achievements.
16. Give yourself credit where it is due.
17. Forgive yourself for your past mistakes and weaknesses.
18. Focus on what you can do, and what you can control in a given set of circumstances.
19. Balance your life and make provision for relaxation.
20. Do whatever is possible, instead of worrying and giving up. However, challenging a situation may be, try to find a solution and do something about it. If you cannot control a situation, control your responses.
21. Do not give up hope when results are not forthcoming. Keep trying alternatives.
22. Treat others fairly and generously, keeping an open mind and focusing on their merits and the good they have done.
23. Help others when they need your help or when they are in difficulties. Show willingness to resolve conflicts and grievances.
24. Avoid critically harsh people who do not appreciate others, and those who indulge in backbiting and rumor mongering.
25. Acknowledge and appreciate what you have and make use of them.
26. Think as if you have already achieved what you are aiming for.
27. Believe in the power of your subconscious mind and its ability to manifest your desires.
28. Make peace with your past and resolve the negativity associated with it.
29. Stay in the present and remember that your past is behind you.
30. Counter negative self-talk with positive affirmations. Boost your self-esteem by believing in yourself and remembering your strengths.

31. Read books and articles on positive thinking and fill your mind with positive thoughts.
32. Cultivate friendship with good people who are positive and appreciative.
33. Always try to frame your words positively.
34. Change the way you talk to yourself and others. Practice positive communication, using positive words and statements and avoiding harsh and negative words.
35. Stop being judgmental and critical unless it is necessary for a higher purpose.
36. Learn to laugh at yourself. See the world and events from a comic perspective.
37. Seek forgiveness when you make mistakes without taking it personally.
38. Learn to ask fearlessly and confidently to overcome your fear of rejection.
39. Take failure as a learning opportunity.
40. Face your fears and learn from them.

Defensive pessimism

It may be impractical to practice positive thinking without considering the pros and cons a situation. Positive thinking should not be a delusional effort to escape from reality. It should not be used to indulge in magical thinking. There may be situations in life, like a debilitating illness or a psychological problem, where positive thinking may be ineffective, if not tiring and distracting. There may be times when we have to admit failure and defeat, and surrender to the facts of life, in order to avoid further complications, failures and losses. In tough situations, pessimism may even be required to balance our thinking and arrive at right solutions. When we practice positive thinking, we have to keep such realities in mind and aim for right balance. We should manage our expectations and emotions in different situations, without losing faith in the value of positive thinking and without feeling frustrated or angry about our circumstances. Sometimes we need defensive pessimism to anticipate problems and difficulties and develop suitable preventive measures or contingency plans. No plan is complete without them.

Positive thinking is an internal response to external situation. It is what we can do about ourselves rather than the world in response to an event or a problem. Positive thinking cannot remove the harsh realities of life. It cannot change people instantly or make miracles happen. People may even misunderstand it as your weakness. At times, you may need patience and perseverance to make things happen. However, what it can do is that it can change your attitude towards external situations and make you adaptable, flexible and hopeful. It can help you to absorb the shocks and tragedies of life, with forbearance and dignity. It can help you to nurse your wounds and march on with increased determination and hope. With its help, you can view the problems in your life with a positive frame of mind and deal with them with courage and conviction.

Priority Areas of Life

Life is complex. There are many aspects of your life which require your time and attention. With limited time and resources available to you, it is impossible to pay attention to everything that goes on in your life. Therefore, it makes sense to focus on certain areas and work on them to improve the quality of your life and your chances of success. Have you ever wondered to which aspects of your life you should pay maximum attention and consider them your priorities? From my study of successful people, I have identified the following eight priority areas, where I believe one should focus to achieve balance, harmony, success and happiness.

1. Health
2. Career
3. Family
4. The Wider World
5. Your Finances
6. Relationships
7. Your Thoughts
8. Spiritual Life

Health

Your health is important in your life. It contributes to success, happiness, and fulfillment. One should be healthy not only physically but also mentally and spiritually. It means one cannot ignore the importance of discipline, values and clean habits. Good health depends upon a combination of genetic, personal and environmental factors. It is sustained by lifestyle choices, positive thinking, healthy habits and self-control. If you are in good health, you will have the added advantage to work for your goals with focus, perseverance, energy and enthusiasm. It saves you money, energy and peace of mind. In this regard your own habits, attitude and personal hygiene play an important role.

Many people neglect their health in the pursuit of success or just take it for granted. It is not a good choice. You should give priority to your health and health matters. It becomes even more important as you age and grow and as your body loses the ability to rebuild and regenerate. Good health is more important than material wealth because without health you cannot enjoy life. Hence, pay attention to your health and keep track of the changes that happen in your body.

Career

Career is what you do out of interest or for your livelihood and survival. It may be a job, some business or professional activity or an artistic effort, which you may pursue. For most people it is their main occupation, which keeps them busy and consumes their time, energy and resources. The career you choose is important because it defines and adds to your identity. Your status, self-esteem, wealth, level of satisfaction, relationships and recognition in society depend upon it. Depending upon which career you choose and how seriously you pursue it, you become rich or poor, a winner or a loser, successful or unsuccessful, and happy or unhappy. Most of us spend our lives in pursuit of success and happiness through our careers. Some people over do it and pay dearly for it. You cannot make your career a substitute for your life. It may bring you wealth and success, but it does not contribute to your relationships or inner happiness unless are not balanced and careful. The workplace is not an ideal place to look for relationships. It is a place where you compete with others and where your success may not be appreciated genuinely by all. Yet, your career is an important part of your life. You have to pay attention to your career goals and build your career to achieve excellence, without ignoring your relationships and self-actualization need.

Family

Studies show that the early development of children is influenced by the attention they receive from not only their parents but also others who frequently interact with them. Having more people around and interacting with them make the babies feel more assured and comfortable. Those who are deprived of touch and feel sensations and who do not get enough attention in the first few months of their lives develop emotional problems at a later stage. In this the family plays an important role. Thus, from childhood, family plays a crucial role in our lives providing us with numerous opportunities to experience the feelings of being loved, cared for, nurtured and assured. It is where we learn our social skills and the dynamics of human behavior and relationships. It also serves as our sanctuary. When we are hurt, defeated or depressed, we turn to our families for advice, solace, and comfort. Since your family is crucial for your happiness, it is important that you make your family part of your success. Some people ignore their families as they become successful and busy. It may lead to problems. Make your family a part of your success journey. Let them share the fruits of your achievements. Spend quality time with them and make them feel part of your life. It will keep you and your family happy and strengthen your relationship with them.

Your finances

Money may not make everyone happy, but it is essential for our wellbeing. For many, success means having a lot of money. The world is ambivalent towards wealth. Money is scorned in spiritual circles, but venerated by the public. Many believe that poverty is a virtue and wealth is a trap. Yet, we all know in our hearts how important wealth is and what misery poverty can bring. Our attitude towards wealth becomes reflected in our lives. If you feel negative about money or wealthy people you may not manifest much wealth in your life. The same is the case with self-limiting thoughts about money, which lower your expectations and your earning potential. You must believe that you deserve wealth and you are ready for it. You must use strengths, since they are your natural wealth, as your resources to create wealth. Wealth is created not only by earning but also by saving. A high income does not necessarily lead to creation of wealth. You must manage your expenses wisely and save. If you want to borrow, it should be for productive purposes. Whatever you do, keep your future in mind. If you save more in the first half of your life, you will be more comfortable with your finances in your retirement. Increase your income and accumulate wealth, investing on a long term basis and overcoming your self-limiting thoughts. Make sure that you fulfill your family obligations and do not leave those in dark who depend upon you.

Relationships

Success is not achieved by your efforts alone. It needs the active cooperation and contribution of others. You may achieve excellence in your education, but would it be possible without the help of your teachers, parents, and those who encouraged you and motivated you? The so called self-made success in anyone's case is not possible without the involvement and contribution of countless people, who include your family, friends, colleagues, business partners, employees, government, and even unknown people you might have never met. Think of those who maintain law and order, who keep the roads clean, who ensure your water supply, and who pick your garbage. They perform their duties to let you focus on your work. Also think of those who make available to you the finished products that you purchase in a store. You might have never met them, but they help you to enjoy the comforts of life and keep yourself nourished.

Different people thus play a significant role in your life. They help you to concentrate on your work and live in peace and happiness. They also help you negatively by criticizing you, opposing you and challenging you, teaching in the process valuable lessons about friendship and enmity. Your relationship with yourself is also important because it determines your overall happiness, attitude and emotional wellbeing. You will not establish positive relationships with others, if you do not feel good about yourself. You will not accept others if you do not accept yourself unconditionally. Therefore, examine your feelings about yourself and resolve them to improve your social skills and establish healthy and positive relationships in your life.

Your thoughts

Your reality is shaped by you. Your thoughts and actions produce consequences and precipitate reality. There is no exaggeration in saying that we reap what we sow and realize what we think and deeply desire. You create your future through your thoughts, beliefs and actions. The one thing that may throw a spanner in this process is a random event or an act of God. You manifest your hopes and aspirations as well as your fears and doubts according to your attitudes and beliefs. If you are undecided and feeling helpless, it may be because you are stuck. If we are motivated and inspired, we persevere and make progress. Your life is thus mostly your creation. Your mind constantly churns out thoughts, which manifest reality. If you want to know where you are heading in your life, spend some time observing your thoughts to know where your attention is and what consumes you most of the time. If you do not have goals and if you do not feel passionate about anything, very likely you will be leading an aimless life.

To mold your life, you have to control your thoughts first. If you want to be a different person, you have to change your thoughts right now. You can change the course of your life, by changing the way you think about people and things. You achieve success when you direct your thoughts in the direction of your persistent desires. Your dominant thoughts manifest always. Therefore, reinforce your mind with positive thoughts about your goals. Think positively about your abilities and self-worth, so that you can remain focused and confident about reaching your cherished dreams. Surround yourself with things and people, who keep your mind in a positive state of mind and encourage you to work for our goals. Read books about inspiration to remain motivated. Practice meditation to improve your thinking, understanding and mental clarity, so that you can envision your future clearly. Become a creator of your life by empowering your thoughts with vision and purpose.

The wider world

The world very much lives inside us. It grows in strength as we grow older. The world inside us draws us out into the world outside. We begin to chase our dreams in the world we see. Until you become a perfect adept, the world never leaves you. Although, we all seem to be independent beings, we are interdependent and cannot live without the world. Our seemingly independent and isolated actions affect others in countless ways. A cyclone or a hurricane may hit a faraway place, but the ripples it creates touch all of us in due course. Slowly and steadily individual actions contribute to life upon earth both positively and negatively. If a majority of us indulge in destructive thinking, chaos will spread in the world. If we make the world a difficult place to live through our collective actions, we will have to share the consequences of such actions. It is imperative that you will not willfully cause harm or hurt to others or take away what does not truly belong to you. You may not be immediately haunted by negative actions of your past, but the world keeps its count and settles the balance. If there is only one pond in a village and it is the only source of water, everyone has to keep that water pure. The world is the only lake we have. We have to keep it pure. When we share the resources of the earth, we have a responsibility to keep it clean and balanced. Since the world gives us so much, we have to keep it free from evil and maintain peace and harmony. Through acts of kindness, generosity, understanding and compassion we should reach out to others and strengthen the interconnectedness of the world. By knowing how the world contributes to our welfare and happiness, we can transcend our selfishness make the world a better place to live.

Spiritual life

Material wealth is important. At the same time spiritual wealth is also equally important. One is for the mind and body and the other for the soul. We have a right to enjoy the riches of the universe, but we should not do it at the expense of our spiritual wellbeing or others. Material wealth satisfies our need for comfort and happiness, but true fulfillment comes only when we realize our spiritual nature and final purpose. Spiritual life contributes to increased self-awareness and self-knowledge, which make people feel more responsible towards themselves and others and accept life in its totality. People who pursue spiritual aims look at life in a wider framework by transcending their individuality and seeing the whole creation as one. As their vision widens, they transcend their egoism and selfishness and accept life as an opportunity to learn and grow.

Materialism and spiritualism together make life complete. A person who practices both finds no contradictions in their ultimate aims. Both are meant to help us to grow and increase our knowledge and wisdom, without soiling our hands. It is difficult to purse self-actualization needs when the basic needs are not met, or practice meditation when one is hungry and miserable. We grow towards light and wisdom in stages, learning our lessons and resolving our problems and setbacks. In all this you should not ignore your spiritual responsibilities or your higher nature. Do not degrade yourself or others thinking that humans are just animals. It is your frame of reference which guides your destiny. Aim for balance in your life and know that your deepest aspirations are your soul's aspirations.

Simple Relaxation Techniques For Your Eyes

Your eyes are your windows to the world. About 85% of your sensory input comes from them and the rest from other senses. Having normal vision is, therefore, a great blessing. Your health, habits and lifestyle choices influence your vision and the condition of your eyes. Since your sight is vital to your survival and wellbeing, you have to take every possible precaution to protect your eyes from harm and injury, and keep them in good health. Your eyesight is effected by many health conditions. Of them stress is a major factor. Prolonged stress causes vision impairment and leads to their wear and tear.

Studies show that you can improve your eyesight by relaxing your body and mind. Regular exercise, adequate sleep, moderation in your habits, relaxation techniques, healthy diet and lifestyle choices, regular physical examination of your eyes, contribute greatly to your overall health and minimize harm to your eyes. Your eyes have a direct connection with both your mind and body. Hence, you should focus upon both to improve their functioning.

The following suggestions are meant for healthy people with normal vision to practice relaxation and keep their eyes healthy and stress free through normal and harmless ways. If you suffer from any eye problems, you should consult your physician and seek his advice. The techniques suggested here are not substitutes for medical advice or treatment. For any problems related to your eyes, before taking any action, you must invariably consult a doctor or an eye specialist and seek advice.

1. Sleep well: Since your eyes remain open and active when you are awake, you should give them adequate rest. Lack of proper sleep can lead to tiredness, irritation in the eyes, stress, headaches, drowsiness and even migraine attacks, which in turn may result in sight problems. If you have sleep problems, you must address them first. Many factors interfere with your sleep. If you have worries and anxieties, you will not be able to sleep well even in the most peaceful environment. Therefore, if you are suffering from lack of sleep, you should ascertain the causes and find a suitable remedy. For example, eating before going to bed or watching television late in the night may result in disturbed sleep. It is also not a good practice to take medicines, drugs, and alcohol to sleep well, since it can lead to long term adverse effects. On the other hand, meditation, healthy diet, and regular exercise can greatly help you to improve your health and experience peace and happiness.

2. Learn to relax: Stress builds in your body gradually during the day as you spend the day dealing with problems, making decisions, and performing tasks. If your day job is stressful, you are likely to suffer even more. Unfortunately, you cannot just run away from your job or avoid doing it. You have to find other ways to cope with job related stress by using your ingenuity to find opportunities to relax even amidst work. For example, a friend of mine who worked in an accounting firm had to check everyday hundreds of receipts and certify them before entering them into ledgers. As the business increased, his workload also increased. He devised his own method to avoid stress. In between his work, he would stop doing everything, close his eyes and briefly relax. It helped him to keep his stress under control. Another friend of mine worked in a warehouse as the delivery man. He had to drive almost eight hours each day to transfer packages from the warehouse to customer's place. Driving in busy lanes and frequent traffic jams caused him a lot of stress and affected his sight. He too found a way to reduce his stress. Whenever he had time, he stopped his vehicle somewhere on the way at a quiet place and relaxed there until he felt fine. His supervisor allowed him to do it since he knew how stressful the job was. If you are a busy person, you can find your own ways to relax while performing your job. For example, you can use your breaks to relax and relieve stress. You can also occasionally pause in your work, take a few deep breaths and stretch your body. By relaxing intermittently you can decrease the stress that builds in your body.

3. Use cold water: Cold water can have a very soothing effect on your eyes. You might have noticed how relaxed and refreshed you feel when you use cold water to wash your face. Your eyes are the most delicate part of your face. The touch of water can increase the blood flow to them and provide the much needed relief. Hence, to feel refreshed, wash your face with cold water, or take water in your palms and gently press your eyes against them. Water is both a healer and a purifier. It will take away not only the impurities from your face but also the negativity and stress that builds up in you, apart from making your feel energized and relaxed. There are no fixed rules regarding how many times in a day you can practice this. Practice it three or four times every day, depending upon how stressed you are. However, make sure that the water is clean and you do not have any make up on your face or eyelids.

4. Get your eyes checked: Your eyes need care and attention. You have to get them examined regularly, or whenever you feel your eyesight has deteriorated. After a certain age, you must invariably get them checked every year. In some people, eye sight stabilizes after sometime and in some it continues to deteriorate. Many eye problems develop slowly and almost silently. The checkups help you to detect any hidden problems in time and avoid complications. The U.S. National Library of Medicine and the National Institutes of Health categorizes eye care specialists in the following manner. Choose them according to your need.

- Opticians who dispense glasses, but do not diagnose eye problems.
- Optometrists who perform eye exams and may diagnose eye problems. They prescribe glasses and contact lenses, and in cases may even treat eye diseases.
- Ophthalmologists, who actually diagnose and treat, eye diseases. They may also provide routine vision care services such as prescribing glasses and contact lenses.
- Primary care physician, who may provide additional assistance when the eye problem is part of a general health problem.

5. Blink consciously: Your eyes are one of the most active organs in the body. Nature has provided them with certain mechanisms to relieve strain. Of them blinking is one. Your eyes keep blinking regularly, whether you are aware of it or not. It keeps them moist and reduces the tension that builds in the muscles that are connected to it. The blinking is more regular in people who have normal vision, whereas those with sight problems develop the habit of staring at things to see them more clearly. It increases strain to the eyes. See how frequently you blink. If you are not in the habit of blinking regularly, you should try to blink consciously to provide the relief that they need.

6. Practice eye exercises: Certain eye exercises are prescribed in the holistic medical systems and alternative therapies, which can relax the eyes and relieve the strain. They have been used for long in traditional medical systems and alternative therapies. There is no empirical evidence to suggest that they all work uniformly for everyone. However, several people found them effective in improving their vision. Some even claimed to have regained their vision fully after practicing them and done away with their glasses. The following exercises are recommended by many to improve vision. When you practice them, make sure that you will not unnecessarily strain your eyes as it may prove counterproductive.

- **Palming**: In this exercise, you use your palms to cover your eyes fully and stare into the darkness that appears in front of you until you are completely relaxed. Try to see as much darkness as you can since it puts you in more restful state. When you do it, make sure that your palms do not press your eyes or cause any strain. If you practice it regularly and correctly it will relax your eyes and improves your vision. After practicing it for a few months, some people said to have reported that they were able to see normally without wearing any glasses.
- **Moving your eyes**: This exercise is meant to strengthen your eye muscles. You have to practice it either by standing or sitting. Keep your head straight and move your eyeballs, up and down a few times. Then repeat the same moving them sideways, and finally in circular fashion. When you move them in circular fashion, you may do it visualizing zero or eight. Again, it is important that you will not strain your eyes when you do it. You should also keep your head straight and not move it when you move the eyeballs.
- **Focusing far and near**: This exercise also meant to increase the flexibility of your eyes tone the connected muscles, and improves blood circulation in them. You can practice it either in open or in

indoors. For this exercise, you may either stand or sit comfortably, and choose two objects for focus, one that is far away and another that is very nearby. Briefly, look first at the faraway object and next quickly look at the nearby object. Repeat it for a few times in quick success. Some people hold their hand or a finger in front of their eyes and use it as the close object and choose a tree or a hill or some landmark as the faraway object. You can any choose any objects you like for this exercise, as long you alternate the focus and do not strain your eyes.

- **Massaging the eyes**: This is a delicate exercise in which you gently massage your eyes and the surrounding areas with your fingers or palms, accompanied by deep breathing and relaxation. You may even do it as part of your facial massage or extend it to other areas in your face such as your forehead, cheeks, and eye sockets. Additionally, for increased relaxation, you can use your fingers to gently press various pressure points in your cheeks, forehead, near the eyes and ears, and back of the head, without pressing them hard.
- **Effortless focusing**: This exercise is meant to improve your peripheral vision. In this exercise, you can sit or stand in a relaxed manner, but you should keep your head straight and your eyes wide open. Now, without turning your head or making any effort to look at any object directly, you should become aware of all the things that are present in your field of vision. You should see as far right and as far left you can without moving your eyes. This is called effortless and aimless focusing, which improves the fluidity of your eyes, whereby you can see without any desire, intention, or interest, and become aware of your surroundings without being particularly interested in any specific object.
- **Deep breathing**: This is similar to the breathing exercises, which you might have practiced in yoga. Sit in a comfortable position, holding your head straight. Close your eyes and relax your mind and body, as you take few deep breaths in and out. Alternate your breathing pattern, with long and short breaths, until you are fully relaxed and enter a restful mode. The more your relax, the better it is

for your eyes, mind and body. When you do this exercise, do not fight any thoughts. Just focus on your breath and breathing pattern. If you do it sincerely, your thoughts will take care of themselves.

- **Meditation**: This is also similar to the meditation exercises taught in yoga. In this exercise also you sit comfortably in a chair or on a mat. Close your eyes, take a few deep breaths and relax your entire body from toe to head, focusing on each part. After a few minutes as you enter a fully relaxed and restful mode, you may begin to observe your thoughts and emotions as they rise and fall, without offering any resistance, making any judgments, or becoming involved with them. If you are lost in your thoughts, try to bring your mind to the present moment and start again. The idea is you must become a mute witness to your own thoughts and allow yourself to become fully relaxed and refreshed.

8. Use the warmth of the sun: In this exercise, you use the warmth of the sunlight without directly looking at the sun. Go out into the open, close your eyes, and turn your face towards the sky in the direction of the sun. Let the warmth of the sun touch your face, eyelids and gently relax them. Feel the heat in your face, eyes and other parts of the body. This exercise is meant to increase the blood flow to your eyes and create soothing effect as your bask in the light of the sun. It is however important that you will not look at the directly at all, as it can permanently damage your eyes.

9. Protect your eyes from the sun: You may use the warmth of the sun to improve your vision, but never directly look at the sun. You should also avoid going out frequently into the open when the sun is bright, without wearing dark glasses. Sunlight contains harmful ultraviolet radiation, which can damage your retina. Some people claim to have developed mystic powers by directly gazing at the sun. However, it is a dangerous practice, which should be avoided by all means. Prolonged exposure to bright sunlight, even when you do not look at the sun directly, increases the incidence of cataracts and macular degeneration, while exposure to ultraviolet light may lead to benign growths on the surface of the eyes. Therefore, protect your eyes from the sun and the ultraviolet radiation, by wearing sunglasses whenever the sun is bright.

10. Eat healthy food: Certain fruits, vegetables, nuts, eggs, fish, oysters and milk are found to be good for your eyes because they are rich in vitamin A, C and E, anti-oxidants, and minerals such as zinc and selenium, which are required by the eyes. They not only improve your vision but also reduce the incidence of cataract, night blindness, macular degeneration and corneal ulcers. However, you should avoid foods that are found harmful to your eyes such as sugars, carbohydrates, alcohol, coffee, fried food, hydrogenated oils and margarine. Prescription drugs that are used in the treatment of chronic diseases like arthritis, depression and high blood pressure, may produce side-effects that increase the incidence of cataract, glaucoma and blood clotting. When you have to use them, consult your doctor and seek advice.

11. Avoid injuries: Since your eyes are delicate and vulnerable to injuries, you should take proper precautions to protect them. Every year, millions of people suffer from eye injuries, which often lead to partial blindness. Children who play games with darts, toy guns, and sharp objects are especially vulnerable. Those who use welding machines, cutting machines, flammable materials, and harmful chemicals, or those who play dangerous sports, or games where physical contact is unavoidable, should invariably wear protective gear to protect their eyes.

15 Effective Ways to Deal with Adversity

Adversity strikes us in many unpredictable ways. Much of our fear and anxiety arise because life is uncertain and we do not know clearly about the forces that govern it. In the face of adversity, we turn to God or become philosophical, wishful, or depressed. Since we do not have control over many things in life, we cannot always effectively succeed against the devastating forces of Nature. Our knowledge, skills and achievements may increase our chances of survival, but do not guarantee protection against adversity. When adversity knocks on our doors, many are unprepared and find their lives turned upside down. Adversity comes into our lives because we are weak and imperfect and make mistakes.

Each adversity tests our ability and strength against the forces of Nature and the world itself. With each adversity we can become better and wiser, by dealing with our imperfections and weaknesses that are primarily responsible for our suffering and adversity. It continues, in most cases until we develop the needed perfection. While we seek happiness instinctively, our progress takes place mainly because of adversity, as it molds us into perfection in the crucible of life. The following principles are useful to deal with adversity. They stand the test of time and can be used in many situations to deal with problems, difficulties and obstacles.

1. Learn from your past: You can consider adversity an opportunity to know something about yourself, especially your failings and shortcomings that stand in the way of your success, so that you can work on them to improve your life, thinking and attitude. The suffering that arises from adversity teaches people a lot about themselves, which they are not otherwise willing to learn. It increases to the degree they are unwilling to respond to it or change themselves, and remains so long as they are stuck in their lives and refuse to move on. Most of our suffering arises from the choices we make and the things we choose. What we ignore or neglect or what we love or hate or what we desire or detest, usually becomes the cause of our suffering. In an adverse situation, we should always remember this.

We have to introspect and find out which qualities, weaknesses, choices, preferences and actions of ours have precipitated the situation, why we caused it and what important lessons we should learn from it.

When you have a serious problem or crisis in your life, ask yourself, "Why have I created it and what lessons I can learn from it?" If you accept responsibility for it and think about it, you will certainly find an answer. By this method, you will go to the root of the problem that lies within you and understand it comprehensively. Once you find an answer, you can work on the solution so that it will not recur or become more serious. Most problems in our lives can be traced to our thoughts and desires because they are responsible for our actions and circumstances and the destiny we manifest through them. Critical self-evaluation will help you to find out the root causes that originally led to adversity. If you are not convinced, think of any serious situation that happened to you before, or happening right now, and analyze why it happened and what actions and decisions of yours might have contributed to it.

In critical situations it is normal for people to lose their balance and think emotionally or irrationally, without focusing on the facts or understanding their implications. Letting out your emotions may give you temporary relief from the feelings of guilt and inadequacy. However, in the long run it makes matters worse, because the problem itself is not addressed and resolved. In difficulties it is important to remain calm and composed and search for solutions through introspection and analysis. It is equally important to be resilient and responsive and act rationally, despite emotional pressures arising from the situation.

2. Accept responsibility: People tend to internalize success and externalize failure. It is normal for people to assume that they are responsible for their successes and others or external events are responsible for the problems and failures. This is how we naturally protect our self-esteem and avoid getting hurt or feeling guilty. While such self-defensive strategies may shield you temporarily from negative feelings, they also prevent you from facing the reality and taking responsibility for your life and actions. A student may blame her teachers, the school or the education system for her poor grades, ignoring that in the same class other students might have done better than her.

By shifting the attention from her to others, she may find temporary relief, but eventually she has to realize that the problem will not go away until she accepts responsibility for it and takes steps to improve her grades. Many parents tend to blame the education system or society for their children's failures. They overlook that many people who study in ordinary schools and grow up in deplorable social and economic conditions achieve success and excel in their lives despite the conditions. Their lives are a proof that you are not entirely at the mercy of your environment.

When people accept responsibility for their problems, they also feel responsible for their solutions. They rise to the occasion and accomplish their goals, finding solutions and inspiration on their own, but seeking help from others where necessary, without losing their independence. Self-reliant people think for themselves and show initiative on their own. They are not afraid to speak their minds or take responsibility for their actions and inactions. Accepting responsibility does not mean that you should blame yourself for your problems and failures. It means you take responsibility for your life and accept the consequences arising from your actions, without negative judgment and self-deprecating behavior. In other words, in both failure and success you look to yourself for solutions and initiative, and do not blame anyone for your actions and inactions. When people blame others for their problems and adversity, it is a sign that they are in a denial and have not yet found freedom from the sense of dependence they cultivated in their childhood. It is a sign that they have not grown up mentally and accepted the burdens and responsibilities of adulthood. When you look to others for direction and help and hold them responsible for your circumstances, you give them control over your life. You let them victimize you and feel obliged, helpless, and dependent. While it may help you to justify your failures, it does not help you much to resolve your problems.

In a competitive world, you will always find people who are deceptive, harmful, and even destructive. You should not attribute your successes and failures to them, even happen to play any role in your life. Many lives are destroyed because of troubling relationships and marital problems between spouses. We cannot stop living because of them. We cannot let mean people win, by playing into their hands, and become cynical or apathetic. Success is the best answer you can give to those who want to see you fail. In life, people come and go. Situations that arise in our lives, would not last forever. Our lives are mostly in our hands. Unless we hand over the reins of our lives willfully to others in abdication of our responsibilities, we have to carry our torch and saddle in the darkness of life.

3. Seek help: Although you are responsible for your life and actions, you cannot do everything on your own. You need to seek help from others where you do not have the means or the knowledge to act on your own. When we are in difficulties, we tend to avoid people and withdraw into a mental shell to nurse our injuries and feelings of hurt. As situation gets worse, many people lose their zest for life, become depressed and defensive. They withdraw into themselves, avoid personal or social contact, and become indifferent and reclusive. It is a sign that by letting depression settle in, they have surrendered to their negativity, and internalized their failure.

In adversity people feel small and hesitate to ask for help, whereas they should actually do the opposite. They should wisely and promptly approach others without hesitation or embarrassment, especially those who may have the resources and knowledge to resolve their problem, either for free or a fee, and ask for their assistance. They should build an effective network of relationships for help and guidance when needed. In adversity people usually avoid asking for help, due to low self-esteem and fear of rejection, whereas prudence suggests that they should do the opposite and actively seek help from others, especially those whom they can trust, who are known for their knowledge, principles and integrity.

4. Stay on the right side: Equally important is avoiding shortcuts and questionable methods to overcome your current problems. Many people resort to illegal and fraudulent activities to avoid personal failures and financial difficulties. They may also manipulate others or exploit them for personal benefit. They are not going to be happy in the end because they miss an important truth regarding adversity, which is that it is a consequence of wrong actions and faulty thinking. It arises to teach people important lessons about their weaknesses and shortcomings and change them for better. Instead of learning the lessons to improve themselves, if people persist in their imperfections, in the end they would face more troubles and trap themselves into even more difficult situations. Adversity is meant to open our eyes to the truths concerning us and strengthen our character and behavior. It aims to elevate us, not degrade. Therefore, in adversity people should try to improve their conditions and work against destabilizing forces, without undermining their values or their aims.

5. Do not miss opportunities: In adversity, you will not have many opportunities to improve your situations. When they arise, you should not miss them. Wherever possible, you should try to create opportunities. It is equally important to remain level headed since you cannot afford to make too many mistakes or create more enemies. In adversity, many become rigid and negative, whereby they cannot see possibilities and opportunities, think rationally, work for long term goals, or see the bigger picture. Repeated failures and setbacks break their morale, and make them feel less confident, insecure, and depressed. The harsh realities of life shake their confidence and beliefs about people, making them cynical and critical towards themselves and others. Many succumb to the feelings of rage, frustration and helplessness as they develop negative attitudes towards the world and people, whom they once trusted, whereas in such situations they have to remain in control, focus upon their goals, and keep moving forward instead of becoming stuck. In a survival mode you should constantly look for opportunities, prioritize your tasks and responsibilities according to their importance, and do everything possible to increase your chances of survival. You should not just wait for opportunities, but create them wherever possible.

6. Conserve your resources: Adversity and scarcity go together. When problems arise, you will have an abundance of difficulties, but limited opportunities and resources to turn the tide. As your influence wanes, the people who want to support you and work with you also disappear gradually. When you are walking through a desert, you have to conserve your energies and use your drinking water sparingly until the journey lasts. In adversity, you have to follow a similar policy. You have to cut your costs, prune your budget and keep a tight control over where your money is going. Whether in business or in personal life, when your survival is at stake, you cannot afford to be extravagant or careless. You have to make wise investments, cut your losses, and maximize your returns.

7. Manage your relationships: Another important area you should focus in difficulties is how you manage people and relationships. In adversity your influence weakens, and your word does not carry the same weight as before. Many friends become enemies, and your enemies may gain strength to trouble you more. In adverse conditions, you have to fight many battles on several fronts at the same time, which you cannot do all by yourself. Hence, in difficult situations you have to deal with people with more humility and build bridges of understanding and cooperation. You have to create friends and secure support and cooperation from everyone who matters to you and whose help you need. No matter what happens, you should build your network of relationships and secure their support, protecting yourself from your enemies, and staying within your limits to avoid rancor and misunderstandings. At the same time, when the going gets tough, you should not lose your heart or hope, and try to keep working for your goals, with your head down, focusing upon your tasks, and choosing your actions and options wisely according to your needs and priorities.

8. Prepare for a long battle: Desperate situations call for desperate measures. No one knows how long an adverse situation will last. Situations may sometimes get worse or go beyond your control, despite your efforts and good intentions. None can predict future, or how things will eventually resolve themselves. Therefore, when there is a crisis, you should not take it lightly or underestimate its power and ability to destabilize your life and activities. Instead, you should be mentally ready to deal with it on a long term basis. As you tackle the problems, do not be distracted by small victories and lower your guard, unless you know surely that you have achieved the final victory. In life, actions have consequences. The problems that you solve may create newer problems. You can never be sure what future may bring. Therefore, do not be under the illusion that if you address current issues your difficulties will disappear. Prepare for a long term battle with precautionary and proactive measure. Gather necessary resources, build necessary defenses, and keep a close watch on the happenings, even when conditions have improved.

9. Be objective: Emotions complicate life and make matters worse. Instead of resolving problems, they create confusion and prolong their continuity. Many people take adversity to their hearts and hold themselves personally responsible for it. As a result, they suffer from low self-esteem, fear, shame and anxiety, and begin to live in denial or frustration. It distorts their thinking and decision making, and their ability to deal with their problems rationally. In difficulties when your survival is as stake, it is difficult to be rational and objective. Yet, you have to be level headed, practical and objective, and avoid being careless or delusional. Your thinking and actions must be grounded in reality, and you must face your challenges squarely, without any illusions. Objectivity is your best shield in the battlefield of life. You can have faith, believe in God and pray for miracles, but you must not lose sight of ground realities. It helps you to weigh situations realistically and solve your problems, without feeling guilty, remorseful, or victimized. When you objectively analyze and study any problem, your solutions will be better and your approach will be practical. You will see possibilities and opportunities, without losing sight of your limitations, circumstances, and consequences. Objectivity means seeing things as they are, not as you want them to see or believe them to be true. You see them with clarity, discernment, detachment, maturity and balance. When people are objective, they learn from their problems and mistakes, overcome their weaknesses and improve their techniques. Their thinking and judgment also improves as their perceptions and understanding improve.

10. Be optimistic: When circumstances are unfavorable, you should not lose hope and courage, but believe in your ability to resolve them and reach your goals. Without optimism, it is difficult to face adversity and endure the suffering it brings. In difficult situations, you should keep fighting until the end, even if the odds are stacked against you, which you cannot do unless you believe in positive outcomes. Life on earth is both precious and precarious. You can take nothing for granted, since the world is subject to change and impermanence. Its impermanence is a cause for hope and a reason to feel anxious. It is a cause for hope because like everything else even adversity cannot continue forever. Someday it has to fade away and yield place to better conditions. It is also a reason for worry and anxiety because you do not know whether things will change for the better or worse. In these circumstances, the best thing you can do is to live with optimism and make peace with impermanence, doing what you can within your means. While you cannot be sure of the outcome of your actions, you can view the world with optimism and perform your actions with hope and enthusiasm. Even if situations are not fully under your control, With optimism you can still explore alternatives and find a way out. Therefore, when things are not going well for you, make sure that you do not lose hope, and take things in your stride with courage and confidence.

11. Keep an open mind: Adversity leaves behind its own trail of destruction and feelings of devastation. It creates such bitterness in people that they become defensive, distrustful and suspicious of everything that they perceive as potentially harmful, building walls of isolation and distrust around themselves, and closing their minds to new ideas, possibilities and relationship with new people. It is difficult for those who close their minds to venture out of their comfort zones, and deal with unfamiliar situations about which they have no experience. They also find it difficult to build bridges of understanding with strangers if they have certain reservations against them and cannot think with an open mind.

Being open minded does not mean being reckless. It means you explore possibilities and opportunities, suspending your judgment and without losing sight of your objectivity and pragmatism, so that when they present themselves, you do not miss them or ignore them. It also means that you would keep an eye on both opportunities and threats and make use of them to your advantage. People who suffered adversity before, or who are going through it presently feel uncomfortable to deal with new people or readily accept new ideas or untested solutions unless they are pushed into a corner. While such defensive attitude keeps them safe, it also limits their options to deal with the problems and challenges they face.

In difficulties, people should explore every opportunity to overcome them. They have to find as many ideas, friends, well-wishers, opportunities, solutions, resources and alternatives to increase their effectiveness and chances of success. They cannot do it, if they remain confined to their small world, nursing their grievances and feeling victimized by people and circumstances. Instead, they should take control of their minds to overcome their fears, prejudices and assumptions. Keeping an open mind, they should think of possibilities rather than threats.

12. Keep your faith: In any adversity, you are your own sanctuary. If you do not believe in yourself, trust yourself or depend upon yourself for initiative and action, no one else can help you much. The loneliest person is not the one who has no friends but the one who has lost faith in himself. If you want to resolve any problem, you should believe in positive outcomes and in your ability to make them possible. Without it, you cannot also persevere. Adversity breeds its own monsters of doubt and despair. Depending your attitude towards yourself, it can throw you into depths of confusion and self-doubt, or raise you to the heights of glory and courage. What makes the difference in both cases is whether you still believe in yourself, and how sure you are about your core values, beliefs and abilities. You may lose everything, but if you have faith you can still hope to make progress and find solutions. Without it you will give up even trying.

Having faith also means having faith in your methods, decisions, and solutions. In life, there is no one particular way of doing anything. There are as many solutions as there are people. What is right for you may be a problem for another. What worked well in one situation may not work in another. What helps you to move forward in this zigzag course of uncertainties is your faith in your abilities, thinking, solutions and choices, and the conviction that somehow you will find the right solutions and reach our goals. In difficulties, faith is even more important. It is in the sanctuary of faith that you will find the soothing and comforting assurance that your destiny is in your hands and you can manifest your dreams.

13. Be Steadfast: When you are in difficulties and circumstances are unfavorable, you should remain firm in your effort to overcome them. You should not admit defeat easily even if there are initial setbacks, because rolling back your plans may prove costly and more problematic. Action is the best antidote to fear and failure. Before taking any actions, take all the possible precautions. Weigh all the options, cots, risks and threats. However, once you make a decision and set your mind upon a particular course of action, you should persevere and break through all barriers. Sometimes, people give up just before they were about to overcome a major hurdle or achieve success. When it happens, they do not even know what they missed. If you are steadfast in your aims, you will have fewer regrets in your life. You will not worry about missed opportunities and failed schemes. Therefore, spend as much time as you can analyzing problems and finding solutions, but once you make a decision, do not easily give up. If you face resistance, you may make some changes to your plan and methods, but you should not abandon the whole plan or your goals.

14. Know your goals: Life is very much like a journey. You need to know to where you are heading and how you intend to do it. More than 90% of people plan their journeys but do not spend even half of that time to plan for their lives. They drift aimlessly from one day to another, not knowing where they are heading, and become stuck in the same routine they hate to repeat every day. Adversity is prolonged by confused thinking and lack of specific goals and purpose. An aimless life is at the mercy of chance and fate. Aims or goals prepare us well to meet our challenges and remain in a state of readiness. They also minimize our chances of failure. Absence of goals indicates disorganized effort and lack of specific interest.

Life is precious. In a way, it is a battle, because here you are in conflict with many forces of Nature and with others. It is also an opportunity to learn from your experiences and become a better human being. No one can sleep through life because each has to fulfill his destiny and perform certain obligatory duties for himself, his family and society. We do not live in isolation, as our lives are interconnected. What we think, do, or do not do, have an impact on others in substantial ways. You should therefore live responsibly and dutifully with consideration for yourself and others and knowing in advance what you want to accomplish in life.

Whatever may be your situation and personal difficulties, you should have specific goals, according to your philosophy and aspirations. Goals are the hands that shape your dreams in the world of reality. Without them, you remain small and mediocre. If you have never cared to establish goals in your life, analyze and find out whether having them would have made any difference. If you have clearly defined goals and if you are determined to realize them, you will be surprised to see how energized and organized your life and thoughts will become. With goals you will lead a purposeful life, driven by specific needs and a clear vision. When you have goals, you will see opportunities, which you ignored before. Therefore, stay focused on what you want to achieve and spare no effort to reach it. Have clearly established goals and bring them to life through your actions. Focus on them and make them an integral part of your life, so that you remain committed to them.

15. Control your fears: If you observe your thoughts and actions intensely for a day or two, with detachment and objectivity, you will realize that most of your actions and reactions are driven by fear or its various forms. In this respect, you are not alone. Most people are motivated more by fear than anything else. Fear limits and shapes your actions in various ways. Because of fear people work, enter relationships, accumulate wealth, or succumb to self-destructive habits. Because of that, they wear masks and rarely show their genuine sides. The way we dress, communicate, establish relationships, take decisions, express opinions, are influenced substantially, if not completely, by our fear of society or criticism from others.

Fear is also responsible for many health and emotional problems. Restlessness, anxiety, stress and depression are caused by fear. Our religions do not provide enough comfort in this regard, as they always reminded you of how evil the world has become and how near the final destruction is. The media takes advantage of our insecurities and keeps churning out negative and disturbing news to keep it exasperated. In adversity people experience fear and anxiety more frequently as they lose their confidence, faith and self-esteem. Because of that they also become distrustful of others and their intentions, ignoring in the process many opportunities and solutions that might have benefited them. Therefore, in adversity it is necessary to keep your fear under control and take calculated risks. When you take decisions or perform actions, dispute your irrational fears and doubts, while taking precautions and preventive measures to minimize risks and threats.

Conclusion

Adversity happens to almost everyone. Impermanence is the nature of our existence and therefore everyone is vulnerable to loss, aging, sickness and death. In an uncertain world, the best way to deal with adversity is to keep your courage, faith and confidence as you establish definite goals, work out a suitable plan of action and make a sincere effort to reach them with hope and perseverance, overcome obstacles and resistance. Suffering is inherent in life. It is caused by the forces of Nature, which uses adversity to test and weed out weaker creations from its inventory. All religions acknowledge suffering as the essential nature of our existence and recommend various methods to overcome it and become free from the control of Nature. The best way to deal with suffering at the human level is to follow Nature's own methods to weed out your deficiencies and improve yourself constantly using adversity as a test. There is a method in the wilderness of Nature. It has goals, which are not immediately perceptible. It preserves the best, conserves its resources and utilizes every opportunity to minimize its losses and maximize its efficiency, by constantly removing all the clutter and waste from its assets.

How to Manage Your Self-talk

The great war, mentioned in the epic, Mahabharata, was fought between two groups of cousins, five brothers called Pandavas on one side and a hundred brothers called Kauravas on the other. Almost every king and warrior who lived in that era in India participated in the war, which was fought for 18 days. The name of one of the brothers in the Pandavas was Arjuna. He was a great archer. He was a great archer. He was assisted by Lord Krishna, an incarnation of God, who agreed to act as his charioteer in the war. Arjuna had an opponent, who was also a great warrior, born with the brilliance of the sun. His name was Karna. He was assisted by another well-known person of that time called Salya. Salya was no friend of Kauravas or Karna. He was a sympathizer of the Pandavas, who he believed were wronged. However, due to obligations of relationship and duty, he agreed to act as his charioteer.

In those days, charioteers played an important role in the battlefield and contributed greatly to victory of their masters. They drove with dexterity in the enemy lines, encouraged their masters to fight well, cautioned them about the dangers, and tried to rescue them from grievous attack when their defeat was imminent. The charioteers also occasionally fought to protect themselves from direct attack. Thus, a charioteer was not just a driver, but a friend, ally, and benefactor in the wars. After entering the battlefield, when Arjuna became confused and despondent about the prospects of fighting his own kin, Lord Krishna reminded him about his duty as a warrior and urged him to fight injustice with detachment and dispassion and without worrying about the consequences. Throughout the war, He stood by Arjuna and helped him with good counsel. In the end, the Pandavas won because of his moral and spiritual support.

His opponent Karna was not so lucky. When he was ferociously fighting his opponents, his charioteer kept willfully discouraging him and criticizing him, expressing his doubts and disapproval, with an intent to damage his morale. Listening to the negative talk, in the end, Karna lost his focus, his skills, his chariot and his life. Salya broke his morale, confidence and his will to fight, and contributed in no small measure to his downfall and the defeat of his side.

Here is an important lesson which we can learn from this episode of the Mahabharata, which is relevant even today. In each of us, there is a personal charioteer, who talks to us every day and every minute. He tells you what to do or what not to do, or whether you did something right or wrong and whether you should feel good about it or ashamed of it. He is intolerant of your failures and not very appreciative of your achievements. His job is to ensure that you live in a certain way and according to certain standards as prescribed by your parents, peers, society, or your own idealism so that you will not embarrass yourself with thoughtless actions. If you do not listen to him or follow him, he will oppress you with negative and self-deprecating thoughts. He is your inner voice or the self-talk. Some even call him the pathological, inner critic, whose aim is to keep you on a leash and control your life. Your life and destiny depend upon how you deal with him and respond to him. You are either happy or unhappy and confident or despondent according to the messages and judgments he delivers.

Your self-talk runs in the background all the time. Whether you are alone or in the company of others and whether you are idle or doing something, it continues to assert itself through a barrage of judgmental thoughts and opinions. It may not always communicate with you verbally, since it can reach out to you variously as your thoughts, fears, doubts, opinions, feelings and emotions. It tells you what is right or wrong, what you can or cannot do, whether you did something perfectly or imperfectly or how you should feel about yourself or your actions in a given situation. It is your inseparable twin with which you have to live for the rest of your life. Through a constant barrage of opinions and judgments, it subjects you to a wide range of conflicting moods and emotions. Whether you are married or unmarried, alone or in the company of others, it is your invisible but troubling partner. In extreme cases it develops a life of its own and creates a split personality.

Your self-talk is an integral and essential part of your consciousness, and you have to live with it throughout your life. It is a part of your survival mechanism, which runs mostly on autopilot. Your self-talk in itself is not a problem, except when it becomes negative and unleashes the inner critic, which tries to help you when you do not want or when you need to focus upon more important tasks. You may escape from others, but you cannot escape from it. Being the most irreverent and unrelenting critic of your internal world, it has the power to take you to the heights of excellence or drag you down deep into the depths of fear and guilt. Your self-talk is part of your self-preservation instinct. A great deal of your success depends upon the way you talk to yourself. Your motivation, enthusiasm, interest and perseverance are largely influenced by it.

You largely rely upon your self-talk to make sense of the world and relate to it. You use it to intuitively know how people act and react and how they are responding to you. You use it to guide yourself and manage your thoughts and actions. With some training, you can also control it. For example, when you are down and defeated, you can change your thoughts and moods by changing the way you think about yourself, others, or your actions. You can talk yourself into performing difficult tasks which you may not willingly perform without self-motivation.

It is good to have an inner power that acts as your internal guide and compass and keeps you trying against odds and pushing forward. Great people and leaders reach their heights by managing it. They know how to talk to themselves into dealing with difficult tasks and problems, how to remain safe and detach themselves from controversy, doubt and despair. It should be reassuring to know that you can control your self-talk and change your responses to what happens in your life. You may not have control over the world or the events that take place in the world, but you can change your thinking and regulate your thoughts, emotions and responses. Here are some of the ways in which you can do it.

1. Examine your beliefs: You can change your self-talk, and your self-image by knowing the early influences that shaped your personality and by examining your unverified beliefs and assumptions against your current reality and personal experience. Most of your opinions about you and your self-image were formed in your childhood when you internalized your parental instructions and opinions and forgot the source. Your parents and your peers created your values and guiding principles when you were too small to think independently about anything. Now, they become the constitution for your self-talk and inner critic to judge you and your actions.

If you are told repeatedly that you are good or not good in anything, that thought takes a life of its own and stays in your memory as a judgment or standard for the rest of your life. If you are constantly told that certain types of people are untrustworthy or unethical, you will distrust them even after you become an adult unless you examine that deep-seated belief against your own experience. Childhood beliefs and habitual thought patterns stay with many people for the rest of their lives, unverified and unexamined, like some baggage that they keep carrying but never open. As a result, they remain immature and childish in their thinking and attitude even after they grow up. Some of it shows up in their attitude towards their own children like a family legacy. Most likely, their children also continue the same tradition.

Thus, irrational and unexamined beliefs remain in circulation for generations and become part of the culture of a nation, group, or a community at the collective level. To break this chain of legacy, you have to examine the beliefs and attitudes, which your parents imprinted in you, and cleanse them through a rational and objective self-analysis. You have to verify the belief system which you inherited from them, and subject it to reality check against facts, reason and your own experience, so that you can free your mind from the contamination caused by it. You have to process the irrational thoughts and beliefs that are currently interfering with your thinking and replace them with the information that is based upon your own experience and observation.

2. Dispute your negative thoughts: You have an inner critic who makes you feel miserable with constant self-criticism. He is destructive because he fills your mind with negativity, self-hatred, doubt, guilt, and low self-esteem. As explained already, it thrives on the strengths of your unexamined beliefs and parental commands. Therefore, to stop victimizing yourself and free yourself from its tyranny, you should counter your inner critic effectively, questioning its assumptions, seeking proof, and finding counter evidence. By doing the reality check you will weed out the irrational thoughts that you inherited from your parents. You will take control of your mind and thoughts as you change your thinking and attitude according to your current circumstances and experience. Here are a few examples to suggest how you can dispute your negative thinking by asking questions and finding answers based upon your personal experience.

The negative thought	Disputing questions
I cannot do this. I am not fit for this task.	Why cannot I do this? Where is the proof? Have I done anything similar to this before? Have I ever failed to do it in the past? If it is so, what were the reasons? Was there anything I could have done differently? Can I do it differently now? Is it possible humanly? Has it been done by others in the past? Then why am I not fit for the task?
I am not good at it. I am clumsy. I am stupid. I am foolish.	Why am I not good at it? Why do I think so? What is the proof? What if I do it? Have I done it in the past?

I do not deserve this. I cannot own this.	Why not? Why should I believe it? Where is the justification? Who is responsible for this belief in me? Did anyone make a similar comment about me in the past?
I do not have the strength or the ability. I do not have the means. I do not have the skills. I do not have the resources. I do not have the qualifications.	Is it true? Can I acquire the required skill? Can I overcome the weakness?

3. Learn from your criticism of others: Your self-criticism manifests itself as your opinions and judgments about others, which is called projection. Whether you are aware or not, your world is more or less a reflection of your personality. You pay attention to that which is familiar to you or which predominates your mind. You see in others what you see in you. You dislike in others what you subconsciously dislike in yourself. Your parental beliefs, which we discussed before, also show up in you as your assumptions about others. This is a common behavior, since it is how we perceive the world and use our experience as a measure to make sense of it.

Therefore, if you want to know about your negative side, see what you criticize or whom you frequently criticize, and vice versa. Know that very often you may find yourself in your reflection of others and you can know your weaknesses by examining your critical nature and what upsets you and torments you. Next time, when you start judging and criticizing others, remember that you may be voicing your inner critic's opinion of you and projecting your own feelings of guilt and sadness into others. See what is common between the person you criticize and you, and what conclusions you can draw from it for your own self-growth. You can also neutralize your negative thoughts about others, by focusing on their positive traits and remembering that by criticizing others you are just reinforcing your inner critic and justifying his criticism.

4. Know your strengths and weaknesses: If you know who you are, you will not accept any criticism against you without scrutiny or believe in your self-talk blindly. You may even replace your negative thoughts about you with positive appreciation and improve your self-esteem. When you are self-aware, you will act according to the situation rather than your negative thoughts, irrational beliefs, and habitual responses. You will show tolerance and compassion towards yourself and others, and objectively weigh the criticism leveled against you. If it is genuine, you will learn from it and move on, but if it is false you will ignore it or reject it, rather than suffering from guilt and self-deprecating thoughts.

Thus, cultivating self-awareness is the best solution to the problem of negative self-talk. Many people know little about themselves. Other than what they see physically in the mirror and having a few preconceived notions, they do not know much about themselves. If you want to cultivate self-awareness, you should become your own observer, know your strengths as well as weaknesses, and clear any assumptions and erroneous beliefs you may have about them. You have to know how you regard yourself in your own esteem and how you value your own thoughts and opinions. If you hold them in good esteem, you will not look to others for approval or validation. You will follow your own judgment and act according to your values and standards.

Although knowing yourself seems easy, it requires a lot of courage, honesty, and objectivity on your part, for which you have to overcome several physical, mental and emotional barriers. They world may regard you in great esteem, but unless you believe in it wholeheartedly, none of the appreciation and you receive from others will make you happy. Here are some ways by which you can cultivate self-awareness.

- Start with an honest assessment of your qualities, strengths and weaknesses. Know what makes you

happy or unhappy and how you react in different circumstances.
- Examine your past to understand what factors influenced you and shaped your personality and behavior.
- Examine whether you look to others for inspiration, appreciation and approval and whether you are unduly influenced by the expectations of others
- Prepare a list of your beliefs, assumptions and parental commands that have become part of your consciousness and influence your thoughts, and actions. Examine them against your own experience.
- Constantly question the assumptions that go into your decision making.
- Pay attention to the feelings caused by your self-talk. Become familiar with them.
- Practice meditation to dig deeper into your mind and know the basis of your self-talk.
- When you are in doubt, ask others for opinion and verify it against yours.
- Try to understand why others evoke in you various emotional states and whether it has any connection with your self-talk and self-image.

Since our personalities are very complex with a lot of unknowns and hidden aspects, it may not be possible for anyone, even with professional help, to know oneself fully. In fact, a lot of information about us remains buried in our consciousness beyond our reach. The task of knowing yourself becomes even more complicated with each passing day as you gain experience and accumulate more knowledge and memory. Self-discovery, therefore, is a continuous and never-ending journey. To expand your self-awareness and become a better human being, you have to keep looking into yourself constantly, with your mind firmly rooted in reality.

5. Learn to accept yourself: Everyone in this world, including you, deserves love, compassion and appreciation because living and surviving in this complex world is in itself a great achievement and a reason to rejoice. You can compare your actions and achievements with those of others whom you may consider as ideal, but it should never be the cause for feeling negative about yourself.

If you felt that you were unloved in your childhood, very likely you will bring that attitude into your life and relationships, especially those that you form with your closest people, and try to protect yourself from them by remaining aloof or defensive. Your self-esteem is a direct result of your self-talk. It is negative to the extent you accept its judgments and deprecate yourself. If you want to feel good about yourself, you have to accept yourself unconditionally, forgiving yourself for your weaknesses, imperfections, mistakes and wrongdoings, and appreciating your talents abilities, and any good that comes out of you every day and touches others. You can practice self-appreciation in many ways. Here are some.

- Make peace with yourself even if you had a terrible past.
- Acknowledge and accept the negative aspects of your personality, as part of your learning, growing, and improving.
- Let go of any bitterness you may hold in your heart against others for being wronged or ill-treated. Forgive them for your own good.
- Unconditionally forgive yourself for all your faults, negativity and bad behavior.
- Keep your promises and honor your commitments. It will make you feel good about yourself.
- Respect your opinions, values and judgment, without the need to impose them upon others or earn their approval.
- Celebrate your successes and victories by rewarding yourself suitably.
- Stop being apologetic for your faults and failures or desperate for the approval of those whom you hold in higher esteem.
- Use positive self-affirmations to change your thoughts and feelings about yourself.
- Appreciate your uniqueness and achievements.
- Always speak positively about the people you love and respect, and avoid criticizing others habitually.

As you accept yourself unconditionally, you accept your imperfections and shortcomings and reflect the same attitude towards others. You will also stop reacting to your negative self-talk and do not let it influence your thoughts and actions.

6. Stay in the present: When you are in the present, you will more likely act according to the circumstances and the current reality, rather than what happened in the past. You will be guided by your best judgment, rather than your prejudices, beliefs and preconceived notions. As you focus upon reality, your inner critic will gradually lose his voice and receded into background. Here are a few suggestions which will help you to develop present moment awareness.

- Pay attention to the happenings around you and the sensations you feel in response to them.
- When you are with people, observe them closely, and try to fathom their hidden intentions.
- Become your own observer to learn how you act and behave in different situations.
- Whenever you are lost in your thoughts, focus on your breath. It will bring you back immediately into the present.
- Whenever you find an opportunity, use all your senses to observe the world around you.
- Increase your attention span by paying attention to specific details in your field of vision.
- Cultivate genuine interest in knowing people and things.
- Take adequate rest to heighten your sensory experience during waking hours.

7. Use affirmations: Using powerful affirmations, you can counter your negative self-talk and correct the negative impressions it leaves in your mind. Identify the areas where you are uncomfortable about yours self-image and use suitable affirmations that suggest their opposite to overcome negativity or change your thinking and behavior. Repeat them until they are firmly implanted in your mind. To know how to create powerful affirmations and to use them effectively, please refer to the articles about positive affirmations presented in this book.

Successful people know how to condition their minds. They repeatedly send powerful messages and subliminal instructions into their subconscious minds through auto-suggestions and carefully framed positive self-talk. With their beliefs and positive attitude, they overcome their mental blocks and negative behavior. They know how to live consciously and responsibly, making wise choices and using positive expectations. They know how to dispute their negative self-talk, using powerful suggestions and visualization. They know how to transform their thinking and behavior according to their goals, dreams and vision. Most importantly, they know how to silence their inner critic, by staying in the present and knowing who they are and what they can do. They know that our self-talk can be our strength or our weakness depending upon how we use it wisely and judiciously. They learn to use their self-talk selectively to their best advantage.

Mental Maturity and Adult Behavior

Sally is a mother of two grown up children. She is well mannered and presents herself nicely in parties and social gatherings. However, her husband Vivian believes that she is immature and does not really act like an adult when they talk about important matters. He feels that she has frozen a part of her childhood memories and stuck in that, which makes her easily emotional, insecure, and irrational. He says that whenever she sees her parents or close relations, she becomes a different person, as if something came over her, and acts like a child in their presence. He believes that when they are around she becomes a child and relives her past. Sally is a perfect example of how some people do not grow up mentally with age. They remain immature in some aspects of their thinking and behavior, which can often lead to problems to themselves and others.

Immaturity is not confined to individuals alone. Often groups and even nations act immaturely, which results in misery and suffering to millions of people. It happened several times in the past, and it is still happening today in some parts of the world, causing a lot of agony and bloodshed to millions of people. Frankly, many leaders and celebrity figures, who are the icons and role models of our civilization, are immature. They hide it behind a façade of pomp and power, but betray their immature behavior through their actions and emotions.

We see or hear about incidents where public figures display immature behavior in front of others rather inadvertently while playing games, giving interviews to the press, debating with political opponents, participating in competitions, or attending meetings and public forums organized by government bodies and even the UN Security Council and general assembly. Immaturity shows itself in the way people react to things and situations, the movies they watch, the words they use, the lifestyle choices they make, the emotions they express, the causes they support, and the way they manage their health, relationships and finances. Truly speaking on a cosmic scale ours is still an immature civilization. We are not yet fully in control of our thinking and behavior. We may need at least a few more centuries to think and act with objectivity and maturity and cope with our emotions and conflicts in healthier ways.

Physical and mental growth

From physical appearance and the telltale signs of the body, we can discern whether a person has physically matured and reached adulthood. By just looking at a person, we can estimate his or her approximate age. Almost everyone attains physical maturity after a certain age, with minor variations. However, mental growth does not happen in the same manner. Some people attain mental maturity at an early age, while some take time. Due to various internal and external factors, a few may not mentally grow up even after they reach middle age. Potentially we can keep growing mentally until the end, depending upon our interests, and personal habits. Our brain cells do stop multiplying after a certain age, but it does not arrest our mental growth. In the short span of life that we live here, it is not possible to know everything. However, even in that limited short span, practically there is no limit to what you can learn and choose to learn. You can keep learning as long as you care, and as long as you keep learning you can keep growing mentally.

Mental growth and mental maturity are not the same. Hence, mental growth by itself does not guarantee mental maturity. A person may have a lot of knowledge and solve many complex problems and riddles, but in his personal life may show lack of maturity and childish behavior. Mental growth refers to an all round development of various mental faculties, whereas maturity refers to the use of reason, objectivity and commonsense in thinking and behavior. It also refers to self-control, rationality, and emotional maturity. Maturity comes from using the higher faculties of the mind and having control over the baser instincts of human behavior.

Some people attain mental maturity at an early age, while some remain predominantly immature even after they become adults. It is difficult to find people who are always mature and fully mature. Occasionally, everyone regresses into childish or childlike behavior. Depending upon their upbringing and other factors, people display different levels of maturity at different times. For example, the same person who displays a lot of maturity in his thinking and behavior before his coworkers at workplace may act like an adolescent in the presence of his friends and family as he opens up in their presence and feels comfortable with his hidden nature. Because of social pressures, a number of people mask their true nature in public and act differently. Thus, it is difficult to quantify a person's level of maturity and know when and whether he has reached the threshold of mental maturity.

What is maturity?

Maturity does not necessarily increase with age. It arises from thinking, knowing, perception, understanding, analysis, discretion and being practical and realistic. A matured person depends upon his own perceptions and experience in evaluating truth and situations. He keeps his mind free from illusions, unrealistic assumptions and irrational beliefs. Maturity develops to the extent we organize our consciousness, according to our experiences and perceptions, and to the extent we keep our minds free from irrational thoughts, beliefs, prejudices, notions and emotions, which we accumulate due to the mental filters we create. There is also no consistent correlation between physical growth and mental maturity. Sometimes a young adult may show more maturity than a grown-up person. Two people in the same age group may also have different levels of maturity. It is because, mental maturity arises from many factors such as age, awareness, intelligence, education and upbringing. Since they vary from individual to individual, people differ in their levels of maturity.

The Oxford Dictionary defines 'maturity' in the following words, "deliberateness of action, mature consideration, due deliberation, fullness or perfection of natural development, ripeness, due promptness, the state of being complete, perfect, ready," and so on. This is the literary definition. In a general sense, maturity means complete, physical and mental growth, or the state of adulthood. It is the ability to act rationally and realistically, rather than emotionally and irrationally. From a behavioral perspective, to be mature means the following.

- To be realistic, to be in touch with reality and guided by facts.
- To accept responsibility for one's own actions and behavior.
- To be willing to analyze and verify one's beliefs, prejudices and assumptions against facts and one's own experiences, and change one's thinking, aware-

ness, judgment, behavior and understanding accordingly,
- Being guided by reason rather than emotions, with the ability to distinguish the difference between the two and at the same time accommodate one's feelings and emotions appropriately and intelligently in one's life.
- To be assertive, without being aggressive; to be friendly without being self-centered; to disagree, without being insensitive; to ask, without the fear of rejection; and to act, without fear or anxiety.
- To be flexible and open-minded, instead of being rigid and judgmental; to be receptive to new experiences and new people; and to be willing to learn new skills and acquire new knowledge.
- To be curios, inquisitive and exploratory, seeking answers, gathering information, and weighing the options, before arriving at conclusions.
- To be open minded, free from mental conditioning, and act spontaneously according to the reality of the situation, without prejudice and preconceived notions, without the compulsion to be perfect or correct and without indulging in habitual actions and responses.
- To be in touch with the current reality or the present moment and learn from it.
- To know what is possible and achievable according to the circumstances, and accept the limitations.

Who is a mature person?

Here is a brief description of a mature person, and how he thinks and acts.

- Is concerned with facts.
- Goes by personal experience rather than beliefs.
- Relies upon reason rather than emotions.
- Thinks before acting.
- Uses resources wisely, according to the realistic needs and demands of the situation
- Weighs each situation carefully, before drawing conclusions
- Lives in the present.

- Is open-minded, willing to learn and explore other possibilities, view points and alternatives.
- knows the limitations
- Is flexible.
- Is spontaneous.
- Has a healthy self image and sense of self.
- Takes practical decisions, according to the situation.
- Knows how to deal with anxiety, fear and worries.
- Believes in human dignity. Respects self and others.
- Listens, pays attention and learns from experience.

Suggestions to practice adult thinking

Maturity is accepting what is, willing to change what can be and letting go of what cannot be. It is to make peace with yourself, by agreeing to follow reason, acknowledge emotions and rely upon your own experience. Mature people free themselves from the compulsions of their past and the anxieties of future, staying in the present and acting spontaneously. They cultivate a balanced view of life by detaching their minds from things and expectations and enjoying life as it happens. Here are some useful ways by which you can make mental maturity as the guiding force of your life.

1. Be Realistic: A matured person's mind is exploratory, unassuming, and rooted in reality. To develop your mind in that mold, you have to be sensitive and responsive to the reality around you. You may daydream, have plans and goals that are difficult to attain, may be driven by idealism in some aspects of your life rather than the pragmatism, and may even accept few assumptions about you or your life as the basis for your beliefs and actions. All of it is acceptable as long as you rationally know what you can and cannot, and know the difference between reality and illusions. In other words, you should rely primarily upon reason, and facts, rather than assumptions and beliefs. When you have to go by your assumptions because do not have facts or correct information, you may do so, but with the understanding that your conclusions may not be final. Most importantly, you have to focus upon facts and think rationally. By staying in touch with reality and controlling your thoughts and emotions, you will keep the adult in you active, responsive and in charge, and control your immature responses and reactions in critical situations.

2. Control your emotions and irrational thinking: You might have noticed from experience that knowledge and education in themselves do not guarantee mental or emotional maturity. Whether you are educated or not, occasionally you are bound to experience emotional and mental instability. When you are emotionally disturbed, you are bound to lose control over your thinking, actions, and reactions. One of the practical ways to overcome your emotional and irrational behavior is to examine your past beliefs and assumptions, in the context of your current knowledge and experiences and discard those that do not stand the test. You can do it by preparing a list of your beliefs, biases and assumptions and validate them against facts. You can dig deep into your unexamined past and challenge the cultural beliefs and assumptions you might have inherited from your parents and peers to free yourself from the conditioning to which you were subject as a child.

Other important ways to develop rationality are, not to accept any opinion blindly, finding logical fallacies in your thinking, looking for evidence and validation, asking questions, challenging opinions, not falling for surface opinions, using experience, being yourself, seeking information, and challenging your beliefs and assumptions underlying your decisions and conclusions.

3. Be curious and open minded: Apart from the child, we also have a parent component embedded in our consciousness. It is a remnant of the past, inherited by us from our parents and authority figures. When you were a child it might have helped you to make sense of the world, and guide your actions and behavior in socially acceptable ways and find approval and appreciation. However, since most people in their childhood accept their parental commands without questioning them, it becomes the unexamined part of your consciousness and your inner parent. Since it is created from your childhood memories, your inner parent prefers controlling and dictating rather than listening. As it regulates your thinking and behavior from inside, you become judgmental and opinionated in your thinking and act according to your deep rooted beliefs and prejudices rather than your current reality. In some cases, the inner parent pushes the adult into the background and assumes control whereby they become rigid and inflexible and develop the-know-all attitude.

People, in whom the parental part is strong, live rigidly, and place a high value on obedience, loyalty, attention and respect from others. They prefer safety to risk and convention to freedom. They move in familiar circles, visit known places, deal with their own kind, and show great reluctance to forge new relationships or experiment with new ideas. They also tend to advice, rather than listen, and criticize, rather than appreciate. They resent criticism and avoid those who disagree with them. They are also offended by the ideas and people who may seem to threaten their very lifestyle and the values they stand for.

If you let your inner parent dominate your thinking, you will bring all its associated qualities into play and act like them. You will become judgmental, close minded, and opinionated in your thinking and attitude. Since your parent also makes your self-talk negative and unbearable, you suffer from guilt and low self-esteem. Hence, you cannot let the parent in you to control and regulate your life, unless you prefer reliving their lives and values and ignore your current reality. You may use some aspects of it, but you cannot give it full control. Instead, you should allow the adult to stay in charge and rule your life since the adult is open minded, inquisitive, and rational.

4. Understand your emotions: Our emotions have a life of their own, or so it seems. Although we are rational, in difficult and critical situations we become emotional and even irrational. Emotions take time to subside, because of various, biological, and physiological factors and the changes they induce in our bodies. Suppressing them forcefully may also lead to many mental and emotional problems. Hence, when emotions arise, there is not much we can initially do other than trying to observe them and understand them. Emotions add color and drama to our lives, apart from helping us in our survival. They help us to perceive changes in our environment and make sense of the situations. Therefore, suppressing them is not a good strategy.

The best way to deal with your emotions is to pay them attention and become familiar with them, by knowing what causes them and how they rise and subside. Once you are familiar with their mechanism, you can let them express themselves without upsetting your inner balance. This is the matured way to manage your emotions and dissipate their destructive energy. Accept your emotions without feeling guilty and observe them to know their causes and underlying purpose so that you can manage them and control them.

5. Be in the present: Our lives are precious, and every moment counts. What appears to be a single continuum between birth and death is actually a series of moments, one following the other. The apparent continuity of time is an illusion. Each moment is separate and complete in itself, although we do not see it because of our beliefs and conditioning. If we remember it and stay in the moment we can control our emotions and think rationally. When we are lost in the thoughts of past and future, we become emotional and suffer from worries and anxieties. The present moment offers us a great opportunity to return to the reality and break free from such thoughts.

When we are caught in the momentum of life, we need to slow down, pause, take a deep breath and look around. In such moments, we can experience relief and regain our composure and inner balance. In such moments we realize the importance of being and the feeling of being alive. As we become busier and stressed, we lose control over our emotions. Small things can weigh heavily in our minds and upset us. The best way to recover from it is to return to the moment and let the reality soak in.

We do not have be always immersed in the present moment because we have to catch up with the world and live our lives normally. However, you can return to it whenever you feel that you are lost in the drama of life and need to recharge yourself mentally and emotionally. When you are in the present, you experience peace and think rationally according to the situation. You see the world and people with clarity, respond to situations correctly, avoid making mistakes, and become efficient and effective. With your emotions under control, you also learn to evaluate problems and situations realistically, finding solutions to your problems based upon your observations, rather than your fears and hopes. Therefore, when you are performing critical tasks, stay with the moment and flow with the events. Watch your own emotions, thoughts and feelings as you perform your daily chores, opening your eyes to the reality of the present moment.

6. Practice detachment: Detachment means staying mentally free from people and things, without responding or reacting to their presence or absence. Much of our suffering in life arises from our attachments, which in turn cause attraction and aversion to things and people. You are happy when you are united with the things you love, and unhappy when you are separated from them. Thus, your attachments subject you to the duality of pleasure and pain. You cannot escape from them until you cultivate detachment.

By practicing detachment you regain your inner freedom, overcome your sense of dependence upon things, and experience peace and inner stability, which in turn help you to deal with the world objectively and rationally. As you liberate your mind from the attractions and distractions of life, you accept things as they are, without judgment, emotion, and desire. Your awareness and understanding of the world and people improve, and so also your insight and intuition.

We are not only attached to worldly things, but also to the notion of success and failure. When we live with expectations and perform actions with an eye upon results, we are bound to experience disappointments and frustrations, since we do not have control over every aspect of our lives and we can keep nothing forever. If there is one strong justification to practice detachment, it is the impermanence of the world. Hence, it is wiser to focus upon what you can control and do within your abilities, rather than what you may gain or lose out of them. In short, do not be troubled by the presence or absence of things, or gains and losses. Adapt yourself to circumstances and make the best out of whatever life offers to you. Aim for success, but be prepared to accept failure as a learning opportunity.

How to Cultivate Mental Peace

Whatever may be your circumstances, invite peace into your life. Embrace it. Make it the very state of your mind and an integral part of your daily life. Put peace in every word you speak and every expression you make, so that the peace that you send out into the world through your thoughts and intentions create similar vibrations elsewhere and make a difference to someone somewhere.

In the present day world, to remain peaceful and stable, while performing our daily tasks is a great challenge. It is difficult not to be swayed by emotions when we are deeply involved with life. If you are in conflict with yourself, striving and struggling to reach somewhere in your life, seeking attention, promoting your interests and chasing your goals, dominated by your egoistic thoughts of separation and isolation, you are bound to experience inner turmoil and live as if you are under a siege.

Fear, anger, guilt, envy, remorse, pride and greed are a few emotions that keep your mind churning and boiling and do not let peace in. Peace comes with awareness, acceptance, surrender, compassion, understanding, discipline, control, detachment, moderation, balance, virtue, healing, forgiveness, trust and faith. They are the prerequisites that bring peace into your life permanently and allow you to experience it under all circumstances. If you are not ready for them, it will be very difficult to silence your egoistic mind and bring peace into all aspects of your life. Peace means freedom from emotional imbalance and mood swings, experiencing inner calm, enjoying the present moment and remaining equal to the ups and downs in your life.

We may occasionally experience peace when things are going well or when we are in a relaxed state of mind. However, without preparation it is difficult to always remain peaceful. A truly peaceful person experiences peace as his natural condition, not temporarily when the world is at rest or situations are favorable. Real peace means being neither happy nor unhappy, but always calm and stable, independent of circumstances. You can have it only when you can control your desires, choose peace over turmoil and accept life unconditionally. You may not experience the profound peace of a great yogi or stay peaceful forever.

However, with effort and right attitude, you can develop emotional resilience and experience peace and happiness.

Cultivating peace

The following suggestions are meant to invite peace into your life and keep your emotions under control.

1. Let go of things: It is difficult to let go of things and people when you feel that you are wronged or victimized or subjected to unnecessary suffering. You will find no value in seeking peace when your mind is filled with resentment and vindictiveness, against those who have wronged you, and it is very difficult to sleep well, when such destructive thoughts keep repeating in your mind and torment you with their heaviness. We all can make choices when life deals us with difficult cards. We can seethe with anger and frustration or learn to let go of those emotions to protect ourselves from their harmful effects and further consequences. But how can we let go when we are conditioned to react and resent? What logic can soothe our anger and bring comfort to our minds? Where is the justification to show your other cheek when you are slapped? How can we let go injustice, falsehood, deceit and meanness we find in others when it leaves such unpleasantness in us?

We cannot have peace, unless we accept responsibility for our lives and actions. Our actions and reactions are equally in our hands. How you respond to others depends upon the choices you make. You always have the choice to respond or not respond, forgive others, or act vindictively. You can let go of them or continue to seethe with anger to the point where it impairs your health and inner balance. Like many people, you can also choose to carry the emotional baggage of your past or drop it to walk freely on the path of your life. You are endowed with the freedom and intelligence to make such choices at each step in the journey of your life. These choices are entirely in your hands, and whether you want to make them or not is also in your control.

Our happiness and inner peace depend upon how we represent and interpret our experiences and perceptions. Some people can frame even the darkest of the incidents of their lives in a positive way that would let them absorb the suffering they create. For them a misfortune is a blessing because they use it to overcome their weaknesses and strengthen their virtues. They regard a person who causes them suffering as a gift from God who has been sent to teach them the virtues of patience, forgiveness and compassion. To experience peace we need to cultivate such an attitude. We have to learn to forgive ourselves and others, overcoming our prejudices and preferences and accepting everything as a learning opportunity that can elevate and expand our consciousness.

2. Have faith in yourself and in God: If you are an atheist, you can ignore this suggestion and go to the next suggestion. However, if you believe in God, it is worthwhile to spend some time here. Faith in God can work miracles. With faith and confidence in yourself and God, you can deal with many problems and challenges successfully. From faith arises courage and confidence, with which you can remain steadfast in difficulties and follow your goals with perseverance, courage and determination. In difficulties faith helps you to hold on to your hopes and dreams and your self-worth. Faith takes you closer to your heart, shows you the possibilities and opportunities hidden in a situation, and lets you channel your energies in the desired direction. When you believe in God and identify yourself with Him, you will live with the assurance that you are not alone in your journey and you have Him watching you, helping you and guarding you. The best way to experience peace is to surrender to God and offer Him all your actions with an attitude of sacrifice. Accept Him as the real Doer of all your actions, relinquishing your egoistic attitude. Perform your actions sincerely, letting Him decide their outcome. Offer your negative thoughts and emotions about others to Him and seek His help to transform them. Express your gratitude for everything that happens in your life.

3. Cultivate positive mental attitude: Positive thinking means focusing on the positive aspects of life, ignoring the negative, representing and interpreting your perceptions and experiences positively, with compassion and tolerance towards others, and faith and conviction in your ability to resolve problems and achieve your goals. Positive thinking does not mean that you have to gloss over facts and indulge in self-deception, but to accept the harsh realities of life without feeling oppressed by them, and deal with them appropriately, with faith and confidence in yourself.

You will not suppress negative emotions, but rather learn from them and tolerate them as a part of your self-transformation. Positive thinking is possibility thinking. There is a definite correlation between positive thinking and achievement. It also contributes to good health and thereby to inner peace and happiness. Positive thinking gives you courage and strength to take risks, cope with failures, control your self-limiting thoughts, establish enduring relationships, and feel good about yourself and achievements. In a positive state of mind, you are aware of your problems and at the same time hopeful of their solutions. You can control your thoughts and manage your reactions, expressing gratitude for the opportunities and blessings that you had to realize your dreams and enjoy your life. In a difficult situation, what keeps you from breaking up from inside is your positive mental attitude. What helps you to endure an ordeal is your positive thinking. What distinguishes a winner from a failure is positive thinking.

People fail or succeed in reaching their goals to the extent they keep their hopes and aspirations alive, by countering their negative thoughts with their positive thinking. If you develop a worldview which cannot be shaken easily by negative thoughts and emotions, you can remain peaceful and stable in any situation, independent of circumstances and pressures of life. If you have faith in God, in yourself, in the good you find in others and in the values of human life, you will deal with your negative thoughts and emotions positively and create conditions that bring peace and harmony into heart and mind. The following suggestions help you to control your negativity and inner critic and remain in a positive state of mind.

- Overcome your negative and oppressive emotions with positive mental attitude, not by ignoring them, but by paying attention to them and listening to their underlying messages to take appropriate action.
- Make a resolution to remain positive despite challenges and obstacles.
- Dispute your negative thoughts and doubts with facts and reason.
- Feel good focusing on the positive aspects of your life and what you like.

- Use words that are positive when you talk to people, appreciate them or interpret your own experiences.
- Look at benefits, opportunities and possibilities in various situations, problems and challenges you face in your life.
- Suppress the impulse to criticize or speak negatively about others.
- Dispute the inner chatter that is harsh and self-deprecating.
- Use visualization to counter your negativity. Replace negative thoughts with positive ones.
- Avoid people who are negative. Go against your negative thoughts, by doing their opposite.
- Find time to relax and energize yourself, by expressing gratitude and appreciation for everything that happens in your life.
- Invite peace into your life, sending out good thoughts and wishing the welfare of one and all.

4. Have realistic expectations and plans: Sometimes out of greed, desperation, ignorance or ambition, we take up more than what we can chew. Because of fear or hesitation we may promise others more than what we can deliver, knowing well that we cannot keep our promise. We exceed our limits of spending or affordability to impress others or satisfy our vain thoughts. When we indulge in such unrealistic and exaggerated attitudes, we suffer both physically and mentally from their consequences and experience pain, suffering and humiliation. When we fail to reach our goals or deliver our promises it will cost us not only credibility and relationships but also peace of mind. If you want to minimize problems, negativity, stress and strain you have to set realistic goals and expectations and plan your actions accordingly. You should know your strengths and weaknesses based upon your experience and draw your plans around them to use your strengths and manage your weaknesses. You should identify the right kind of people who can help you to further your goals, and know when to reply upon them and when to be on your own. By toning down your expectations according to the situation and setting up realistic goals according to your strengths, you can focus upon your tasks and perfect your methods instead of suffering from fear, uncertainty and anxiety. When you are grounded in reality, you will have peace, balance and harmony, and your relationships and attitude towards others will improve as you make better decisions, and understand objectively their motivation and behavior. You will also respond to problems and situations with the right mindset. Therefore, set your mind in reality and keep your eyes wide open as you negotiate through life.

5. Give unconditional love to one and all: Bring love into your life and experience the lasting impact it creates upon you and others. Let love flow from the depths of your heart into your life and world like an ethereal fragrance that knows no boundaries and preferences. Start with your family, friends and close relations and show them your love and kindness, accepting them and giving them benefit of doubt. Learn to forgive them for their mistakes and ignorance. Find time and opportunities to help them. Helping others is the best way to release stress and experience peace. You can do it variously. Become a volunteer in a philanthropic organization. Adopt a pet and give it your love. Through prayers and good wishes send the healing energy of love and blessings to those who need your help. Pray for those who are in adversity. Help them without expectations and without seeking publicity. Widen your heart to appreciate people and feel for their suffering. Instead of seeking love and attention from others, give them your love, compassion and understanding. As you let go of your selfishness and forgive them for their human frailties, you will experience peace and harmony in yourself.

6. Express gratitude: You are not independent in the real sense of the world. You are part of a larger life. All beings and things are interconnected. There is an underlying unity in the diversity of life. Your success and happiness are not yours alone. They are made possible by a million factors and forces. Whatever you experience, suffer, achieve or enjoy, is caused by your effort and the effort of a million others whom you may not even know. Your parents give birth to you. Your elders nurture you. Your teachers educated you. Numerous friends and family relations enrich your life and perceptions as you grow, through their words, actions, examples and even their negative behavior. You learn many lessons from the world and life in general. You have opportunities to learn from others and also teach them. You are helped by countless people and in turn you help many of them. Thus, you are indebted to the world and owe them gratitude.

From the time you were born until now, realize in how many millions of ways you have received help and encouragement from others. You may not even know personally most of them. Think of the books you read, the knowledge that you accumulated, the lessons you learned, the money and other resources you received and the inspiration you got. If it was not for them and circumstances, you would not have been where you are today and you would not have been who you are. We always compare ourselves with others and feel unhappy because we are lacking in some resource, comfort or advantage. We do not realize how fortunate we are to be even here, alive and enjoying the precious moments of life.

To be born as a human being and remain alive to the dangers to which we are constantly exposed is in itself a great gift. You will understand how precious life is when you realize that in all the known galaxies and planets, so far, life is found only on earth. People do not usually realize how fortunate and blessed they are until they are struck down by a health problem or a calamity. It is natural to feel disappointed, disturbed and even envious when you focus on what you do not have rather than on what you have. Count your blessings, appreciating all that has been given to you. Even a misfortune is a gift from God. Negative people and situations come into your life because God wants to remind you through them that you need to improve in some aspects of your life.

There is a purpose behind every important event in your life. You are here for a reason. You are reading this book for a reason, and why it has reached your hands. It wants either to teach you something or to teach something to me through you. Discover the purpose of your life and try to fulfill it. When you live with a sense of gratitude, you channel positive spiritual energy into the universe so that others may receive it to become centers of gratitude. When you bless others without any expectations, you reconnect yourself with the world and the Creator and invite peace and harmony into your life. Through your loving nature, compassion and understanding, you provide relief to the suffering souls and become a source of peace and inspiration to them.

7. Transcend your ego: Your ego is your personal identity. It is responsible for your seeking and striving. It thinks in terms of "me-and-them" and acts according to its limited vision, beliefs, fears, and doubts. It thrives on the illusion of separateness, which is responsible for your suffering and feelings of loneliness, fear and alienation. It seeks to find freedom and happiness, by having more and seeking more of the things it loves and avoiding those that tend to cause pain and suffering. This preferential approach evokes many positive and negative responses and emotions in you, causing instability and turmoil. The human ego likes to expand its sphere of influence, by asserting its dominance and establishing its mastery over others or the environment. In the process, it makes use of every opportunity and available resource to further its cause. It is the archetype which may religions perceive as the enemy of God. Our egos are responsible for our suffering. Because of them we go through many disturbing emotions and upsetting thoughts. Unfortunately, while the ego is a problem none can live without it because it is not possible to live in this world without any identity.

Your ego is responsible for your thoughts, desires, actions, and relationships. It controls your life, shapes your destiny, defines the boundaries of your perception, acknowledges your limitations, duties and responsibilities. It reveals to others who you are, what you are, and how they can relate to you. Therefore, you cannot do away with your ego by any chance. It is even impractical to try it unless you want to become a monk and withdraw from the world. However, you can transform the unpleasant and undesirable aspects of your ego by changing your behavior. With sincere effort you can transcend your lower nature and undesirable qualities.

By knowing who you are and why you are here and what you can do, you can transform your inner life. You can overcome your fear and doubt by dwelling deep into yourself and finding your connection with God or the universe. You can surrender yourself to the flow of life. Therefore, let your soul be the center of your life. Become a witness to yourself to understand your behavior and motives and avoid your negative emotions, critical nature and self-defeating behavior. Practice meditation in quiet moments to stabilize your mind and experience peace. Rest your mind in silence and mindfulness. Learn to give without expectations. Make others happy, without being intrusive. Help the poor and the needy, like an angel, without their knowing. Surprise someone with your generosity. As you center yourself in your higher consciousness with such liberating actions, you will experience peace and happiness and an expansive vision of your soul.

Morals from Aesop's Fables

Aesop's fables are as relevant today as they were centuries ago. Like the Panchatantra or the Jataka Tales of ancient India, they have fired the imagination of generations of young minds since ancient times, reminding them of the moral values and the importance of virtue, spirituality and character in a world filled with illusions, temptations and distractions. The fables are remarkably simple in their narration and presentation, but convey deeply appealing truths about human nature and behavior, leaving a lasting impression upon the readers and listeners alike. Although the stories were set in ancient times, they are as relevant today as they were then. Many people do not know that several popular sayings and expressions such as "self help is the best help" or "much ado about nothing" or "look before you leap," are drawn from Aesop's Fables only.

Who was Aesop?

Not much is known about Aesop or his personal life. As in case of Homer, personal details of his life are shrouded in myth and legend. According to some versions, he lived in ancient Greece about 6th century BC, first as a slave, serving two masters. After he was freed from slavery, he became popular for his fables, wit and wisdom. We have controversial and conflicting accounts of his last days and death. According one version he was killed by an angry mob at Delphi due to a misunderstanding. After his death, his fame spread and his fables found their way into many ancient cultures.

Authorship

Of the several fables that presently attributed to him, we do not know how many were original and how many were ascribed to him later by his admirers. Storytelling was a common pastime in ancient times. During their long sojourns, merchants and nomadic tribes who frequently traveled from place to place gathered around story tellers under starry skies to listen to them. They might have heard the fables of Aesop and took them with them to narrate elsewhere. It is also possible that Aesop himself might have compiled his stories from various sources and improvised them, adding his own creativity. We have reasons to believe that some of the fables were drawn from the literary and folklore traditions of ancient India.

Since earliest times, even before the invasion of Alexander, relations existed between India and Greece through Persia. The geographical connection facilitated exchange of ideas and free flow of information between the two. Aesop might have heard Indian tales from visiting merchants, bards and monks directly or through other sources, and incorporated them into his narrative. . The Gandhara region, which is now located in Pakistan and Afghanistan, was once a famous learning center, where scholars from all wakes of life gathered to teach, learn, or participate in debates. Its proximity to the famous ancient Silk Route, and the striking similarities between some stories from the Panchatantra and Jataka tales, and those of Aesop lend credibility to this theory. India was subject to many foreign invasions in the past, especially by Bactrian Greeks, Scythians, Huns, and Kushanas, who also employed Indian soldiers. It is possible that the exchange of stories might have happened through them during such interactions.

Morals

Aesop's fables are filled with profound wisdom, with such directness and simplicity that they can be understood by people of all ages, even by children and those who lack proper education. Their narration, context and character, still invoke awe and inspiration in the minds of children and adults alike. Their message and morals are still relevant even today. The world would be a better place to live, if a majority of people choose to reflect upon them and follow them sincerely in their day today lives. Our thinking, attitude, values, morals, decisions and relationships will improve for the better, if we frequently remember them.

The following list of morals from Aesop's fables is an attempt in this direction. They are worth reading and remembering. We have included them here to remind ourselves of the simple morality that guided the ancient people and helped them to live a life of virtue and practical wisdom without the burden of erudition and scholarship. You can use them for reflection and contemplation. See whether you can recall any incidents from your life to which you can apply them. If you can reflect upon them in the context of your own life and experiences, you will develop further insight into them and remember them better.

The tyrant will always find a pretext for his tyranny.

Like will draw like.

In serving the wicked, expect no reward, and be thankful if you escape injury for your pains.

If you were foolish enough to sing all the summer, you must dance to bed without supper in the winter.

Slow but steady wins the race.

Self help is the best help.

Birds of a feather flock together.

The greatest kindness will not bind the ungrateful.

No arguments will give courage to the coward.

Fair weather friends are not worth much.

Do not make much ado about nothing.

If men had all they wished, they would be often ruined.

Pleasure bought with pain, hurts.

One story is good, till another is told.

If words suffice not, blows must follow.

Look before you leap.

Misfortune tests the sincerity of friends.

Those who suffer most cry out the least.

Zeal should not outrun discretion.

Change of habit cannot alter Nature.

Do not attempt to hide things which cannot be hid.

He is wise who is warned by the misfortunes of others.

The value is in the worth, not in the number.

Do not attempt too much at once.

No one truly forgets injuries in the presence of him who caused the injury.

Seek Harm. Find Harm.

Evil companions bring more hurt than profit.

Do not be in a hurry to change one evil for another.

Little liberties are great offenses.

Old friends cannot with impunity be sacrificed for new ones.

Notoriety is often mistaken for fame.

Whatever you do, do with all your might.

Those who seek to please everybody, please nobody.

Pride goes before destruction.

There is no believing a liar, even when he speaks the truth.

Time and place often give the advantage to the weak over the strong.

Example is more powerful than precept.

Better poverty without care, than riches with.

Harm hatch, harm catch.

Benefits bestowed upon the evil-disposed increase their means of injuring you.

Equals make the best friends.

Hypocritical speeches are easily seen through.

What is bred in the bone will stick to the flesh.

Abstain and enjoy.

The memory of a good deed lives.

Children are not to be blamed for the faults of their parents.

Avoid a remedy that is worse than the disease.

The least outlay is not always the greatest gain.

Might makes right.

We must make friends in prosperity, if we would have their help in adversity.

False confidence often leads to danger.

The more honor the more danger.

Every man is for himself.

He is not to be trusted as a friend, who mistreats his own family.

They are not wise, who give to themselves the credit due to others.

He who shares the danger ought to share the prize.

Evil wishes, like chickens, come home to roost.

Our mere anticipation of life outrun its realities.

In quarreling about the shadow we often lose the substance.

Stoop to conquer.

I should indeed be a very simple fellow if, for the chance of a greater uncertain profit, I were to forego my present certain gain.

The hero is brave in deeds as well as words.

Do nothing without a regard to the consequences.

It sometimes happens that one man has all the toil, and another all the profit.

In avoiding one evil, care must be taken not to fall into another.

Every man should be content to mind his own business.

The great do not always prevail. There are times when the small and lowly are the strongest to do mischief.

It shows an evil disposition to take advantage of a friend in distress.

The best intentions will not always ensure success.

Everyone is more or less a master of his own fate.

How can you expect the sheep to be safe, if you admit a wolf into the fold?

Know that not even the stars need to be relit.

Happy is the man, who learns from the misfortunes of others.

Misfortunes springing from ourselves are the hardest to bear.

Men often bear little grievances with less courage than they do large misfortunes.

Those who assume a character, which does not belong to them, only make themselves ridiculous.

Contentment with our lot is an element of happiness.

The desire for imaginary benefits often involves the loss of present blessings.

Count the cost before you commit you.

Be on guard against men, who can strike from a distance.

Use serves to overcome dread.

No one can be a friend, if you know not whether to trust or distrust him.

Fine feathers do not make fine birds.

Every tale is not to be believed.

Necessity is the mother of invention.

A willful man will have his way to his own hurt.

A false tale often betrays itself.

Acquaintance softens prejudices.

Counsel without help is useless.

Straws show how the wind blows.

The dishonest, if they act honestly, get no credit.

Union is strength.

Evil tendencies are shown in early life.

Persuasion is better than Force.

A man is known by the company he keeps.

What is most truly valuable is often underrated.

Youth's first duty is reverence to parents.

Some men are of more consequence in their own eyes than in the eyes of their neighbors.

Self-interest alone moves some men.

Try before you trust.

They, who act without sufficient thought, will often fall into unsuspected danger.

No evil, whether it be small or large, ought to be tolerated.

The safeguards of virtue are hateful to those with evil intentions.

Problems and Problem Solving

Life is made up of several problems. From the time you wake up and until you sleep, you face them almost continuously. However, you may not consider them so because many problems that you face in your daily life do not pose any threat to you or require much thinking, as you learned to solve them routinely and mechanically. For example, although technically it is a problem, every day when you wake up, you do not think about what paste to use or how to brush your teeth because you already know the answer and the procedure. In truth, every decision you make in your life is a solution to some problem you have to resolve. It is also difficult to say at what stage a problem becomes a solution or a solution becomes a problem because it does not take much time for a solution to become a new problem or create new problems. A problem is sometimes an opportunity, but if you are not careful an opportunity can turn into a problem.

What is a problem?

In simple terms, a problem is a question, doubt, situation or issue, which requires an answer or a solution for its resolution. A problem may be real or imaginary and physical or mental. A problem may morph into other problems or grow in complexity, if left unsolved or neglected. How you approach a problem and deal with it depends upon your thinking, your mental makeup and your perspective. You can view a problem from many angles as the following.

- A challenge.
- A question.
- A condition.
- A difficulty.
- An opportunity.
- A warning.
- An eye opener.
- A threat.
- A riddle.
- God's gift.
- Way to success.
- An obstacle.

- A blessing.
- A test.
- A perspective.
- A lesson.
- A weakness.
- A vulnerability.
- Part of your life.

As you can see from the above, depending upon your circumstances, you can view problems in different ways. You may approach them positively, negatively, objectively, or subjectively, according to the situation, and your state of mind. How you view them, make sense of them, and resolve them determine how you experience life and empower yourself to make things possible.

Common steps in problem solving

When there is a problem in your life, what would you do about it? How do you resolve it? Do you feel nervous, angry, suspicious, or do you seek help from others? Do you prefer to confront a problem or escape from it? When a situation becomes serious, do you try to find a solution or lose your focus and feel anxious? Do you feel any responsibility for your actions? Are you sensitive enough to know that you have problems in your life, which need to be resolved? Are you honest enough to acknowledge them? Questions such as these help you to know your attitude towards problems and your particular way of dealing with them. If rightly managed, your problems solving ability and experiences should enhance your self-worth and boost your morale and confidence.

The problems that you face in your daily life fall into many categories, ranging from the casual and simple to the unusual and the most complex. Your problems may be health related, profession related, money related, people related, authority related, aggravated by others, or created by your own actions, beliefs and negative attitude. Some problems you might inherit from birth such as a genetic problem or a problem of inheritance or legacy, and some you may willingly take upon yourself, such as adopting an abandoned baby, ignoring your health, or trusting a person who has a long record of questionable integrity. People become involved in such problems because of altruism, innocence or some hidden agenda. Depending upon the severity and urgency of the situation, you may follow different methods and approaches to solve your problems. How you solve them depends upon several intrinsic and extrinsic factors. However, irrespective of their nature and complexity, or the methods you use, most problem need to go through the following four common phases for their resolution.

1. The definition phase

In this phase, you try to understand and define the problem, by gathering information about it and its history. You ask questions, raise doubts and concerns, and seek clarifications, suggestions and feedback. If the problem is simple or routine, you do not need much effort to define it and find solutions to it. In fact, for many problems that we face we do not collect any additional information, because we already have it. While we do not have to spend a lot of time to gather information for every small problem, we cannot ignore the importance of paying adequate attention to each problem and trying to know it and define it.

Sometimes a simple problem may not be simple at all, but the sign of the onset of a serious problem. This is true in case of many health problems. For example, we cannot take lightly certain symptoms like cough and cold, if it happens frequently, since it may be the sign of a more serious disease. Experience proves that many disasters and accidents could have been avoided by paying attention to early warning signals and taking timely action. Difficult problems need special attention not only because they can upset our lives but also because they can disturb our mental and emotional health. In the definition phase we gather information and make sense of the problem and its possible impact, and to ascertain whether we can solve it. Following are a list of typical questions which you have to consider to know the problem and define it.

- What is the problem?
- Who or what caused it?
- What is its history or antecedents?
- How serious is the problem? What are its implications?
- What are the related issues?
- Is it an isolated problem or part of a much more complex one?

- What are the aggravating factors that may interfere with its resolution?
- What are the implications and consequences if it is not resolved in time?
- Components of the problem if any.
- What do you need to do to resolve it?
- Whether you can solve it on your own or need the help of others?
- Whether there is precedence, or is it a new problem?
- People who may likely to support you and oppose you.
- People who may create further problems.
- People whom you need to resolve the problem.

2. The solution phase

In this phase, you explore various approaches and solutions to resolve your problem and find the right one. You also need to devise a plan or a method to implement it. Depending upon the complexity of the problem, this phase may take time, cost resources and even require the assistance of experts and outside agencies. Finding the right solution to a problem is not always easy, especially if the problem is of technical nature, or has a long history of unresolved issues, or if the solutions may require time and effort to implement. You have to consider the cost implications also, and any side effects and negative consequences that may arise from it. In this phase, your focus should primarily be upon the following.

- The different ways in which the problem can be solved.
- Familiarity with the problem and any prior experience in handling similar problems.
- The number of people needed to solve it.
- The resources that are required to resolve it
- Consideration of cost, time, resources, complexity, effort and effectiveness in solving it.
- How to implement the solution and deal with constraints and contingencies.
- Whether the problem is isolated, or related to other problems, or lead to fresh ones.

At the end of this phase, you should be ready with a solution and a plan. You should have completed your investigation, discussed with the relevant parties and considered the various scenarios arising from proposed solution. You should have also communicated your ideas to the stakeholders and obtained their response, besides making preparations to move forward.

3. The implementation phase

In this phase, you put your plan into action. It is a crucial phase because whatever solution that you might have worked out may either solve the problem or create additional problems or bring into light newer problems you did not perceive before. You may also face problems if your plan is defective or not properly implemented as expected. You may face resistance from people who do not like the solution, do not want to resolve the conflicts or the differences of opinion. In this phase, you have to keep your emotions and the situation under control, use your resources intelligently and efficiently and make things possible. In this phase, you have to focus on the following.

- Details of your action plan.
- Choosing your goals and priorities
- Communicating with people and parties concerned.
- Monitoring and regulating the progress.
- Updating your action plan according to the circumstances.
- Coordination and conflict resolution if others are involved.

4. Post implementation phase

This is the learning phase. In this phase, you review your actions, learn from your experience and take preventive measures to minimize the recurrence of the same problem. The experience you have gained will help you to devise suitable strategies to deal with similar problems in future. If you are working in a group or for an organization, you may share your experience with them and help them to improve their problem solving skills. If you solve the problem successfully your confidence and optimism will improve; but if you have faced setbacks and failures, you may have to manage the consequences arising from them and find a better solution. Each major problem offers you a learning opportunity. Whether you solve it or not, each problem enriches your experience and improves your knowledge and understanding. Some problems may leave a permanent mark upon you even after you resolved them because of their peculiar nature. Your solutions may also affect other people's lives and bring you into conflict with them or create feelings of guilt and remorse in you. When you have to take tough decisions due to the obligations of your duty, you cannot avoid causing unpleasantness to others or facing their displeasure. You must be prepared to manage such situations and minimize their negative fallout.

How to improve your problem solving skills

Life teaches us many lessons. As we progress from childhood to adulthood and old age, our eyes open to many truths of life. As years pass by, some people learn from their experiences and grow in knowledge and wisdom, while some remain stuck in their lives, thinking and attitudes, as if they have frozen their minds and ambition. Many people do not realize that we are part of Nature's learning process. We keep learning lessons until we make progress, perfect our methods, and improve our character and behavior. We are taught lessons, until we learn them. Problems become crises and crises threaten our lives and mental peace, if we do not respond to the problems in our lives with knowledge and wisdom. The quality of our lives and the nature of success depends upon our ability to solve problems. To face the challenges in our lives and resolve them we need a tough mindset, which can be developed only with effort. When you are faced with problems, remember the following.

- Control your emotions.
- Remain positive and hopeful.
- Listen to others, with an open mind, but take your own decisions.
- Do not take anything for granted.
- Pay attention to the details.
- Be flexible in your approach and attitude.
- Be practical and realistic.
- Take control, by doing what is possible and whatever is within your control.

- If others are involved, be considerate and helpful.
- Do not accept surface solutions. Dispute your thinking and judgment to make sure that you are on the right track and your solution is workable.

Different methods to solve problems

How you solve a problem depends upon many factors. Simple problems do not require much effort, but the tough and unusual ones require time, effort and the use of advanced techniques. The quality of your solution depends upon the information you gather and your confidence. Problem solving poses many challenges because our minds are not fully equipped to deal with ambiguity and uncertainty and we cannot easily foresee the impact or the consequences of our actions. Sometimes you may have to rely purely upon your gut feelings or chance. There will be pros and cons to every solution and whatever you do you may be left with the feeling that you could have done better or chosen another alternative. Sometimes circumstances may force you to choose the best of the worst and take responsibility and accountability for it. Some people are exceptionally good and creative in finding uncommon solutions to the problems they face. They are always in demand. You can solve a problem in different ways using different approaches. The following are a few well-known approaches to problem solving.

1. Logical or analytical approach

This approach is also known as scientific approach, in which you rely upon facts, use reason and analysis, keeping your emotions under control and look for solutions, whose effectiveness can be measured objectively based upon certain reliable criteria. Before solving the problem, you gather as much information as possible, breakdown the problem into manageable parts, and deal with them according to the information you gather. In choosing the alternatives, you rely upon facts, experience and verifiable standards, which you can use later to measure your success in solving it. In this approach, you analyze every failure, gather information and use it to improve your methods and solutions. This approach is effective where you can safely rely upon your information and predict possible outcomes based upon your experience. It is also the most reliable method of problem solving and used in a wide range of fields, including science, business and commerce. However, not all problems can be solved this way.

2. Creative approach

In this approach, you rely upon your creativity to find unusual solutions which are not available to your wakeful consciousness, using techniques such as brainstorming, imagination, creative visualization, association, and creative pause. These techniques help you to break through the habitual thinking of your mind and see the problem from unusual perspectives. The general approach is you think about the problem deeply and allow your mind to sleep on it thereby giving an opportunity to your subconscious mind to push the solution or the idea into your wakeful mind. This approach works well when you keep your mind flexible, restful and passive, without judgment and critical analysis, and let the ideas and solutions to flow uninterruptedly and spontaneously. The emphasis is not as much on being right, but on letting the mind think freely and find solutions without the usual mental noise. You may evaluate the solutions only after you are satisfied with the creative phase and found enough alternatives.

Creative approach is useful when you are looking for breakthroughs in your thinking and effort. It does not always guarantee a solution, since the creative process is not under your control. Unless you are looking for a change, it may not be the right approach to resolve routine problems. On the downside, creative solutions may be risky and involve cost and additional effort, since the solutions have not been tested before and you cannot be certain of their outcome. Besides, you may face problems from others who are conventional and do not like to change the status quo or experiment with new methods.

3. Intuitive approach

In this approach, you rely upon intuition and gut feelings rather than your logical mind to solve your problems. In intuition you gain insight into a problem or a situation without using the rational faculties of the mind. In contrast to logical or rational approach, here you do not rely upon your active and rational mind, but allow the solution to arise on its own, from the depth of your consciousness, as premonition, hunch, or gut feeling. The distinction between creative and intuitive approaches is very thin. In creative approach you use both your active mind and sleeping mind to find solutions, whereas in the intuitive approach you do not do any brain storming but allow the idea or the feeling to surface into your consciousness on its own.

According to some people intuition is your mind's automated rapid response system to the problems, threats and situations you face. It saves you from trouble because it has already worked out the solution through a compacted rational process. This is based upon the observation that your intuition works better where you have expertise and prior knowledge. It works well when you pay attention to your own feelings and trust them. Many people do not pay attention to their intuitive thoughts as they remain focused outwardly, or they do not allow intuition to work for them by keeping their minds busy. To make your intuition work, you need to look within, calm your nerves, keep your mind receptive, and pay attention to your own thoughts and feelings. As in case of creative approach, intuitive approach may prove risky and costly. Since it is based upon your intuitive thoughts rather than factual analysis, it may not be appreciated by others who do not share your beliefs or thinking. If the problem is complicated, you may also suffer from self-doubt, uncertainty and may not persuade everyone to proceed with the solution you found.

4. Mastermind approach

Of the many fancy names that have been floated in the contemporary world, mastermind is one. It means many things to many people. It has a mystical aura to it. Some even equate with the universal Mind or God. However, in simple and practical terms, mastermind means a network of people (minds) you unite to form a team that can act as the think-tank for all the members in that group. You may view them as your personal ministers or board of directors. In the mastermind approach, you rely upon them to help you find solutions. The group may consist of members from your professional team, your close friends and associates, or a group you specially assemble for the sole purpose of resolving a difficult problem. In this approach, you may assemble the people and facilitate their meeting, but you will not control or regulate their thinking. You let them speak freely and contribute their ideas and solutions through a collaborative and cooperative approach. The mastermind group may follow certain conventions and rules of engagement, which are agreed upon by them in advance. Hence, their method is not exactly a creative and intuitive process, but an exploratory and rational one.

A mastermind group usually consists of highly talented individuals, each having a mind of their own. Therefore, they may voice different opinions or suggest different solutions to the same problem. Unless you have a mind of your own and know how to deal with ambiguity, their suggestions and solutions may create in you a lot of confusion and lead to doubt and indecision. If you can take care of such problems, the mastermind approach is probably the best of all methods, since here you are pooling the knowledge and intelligence of a diverse group of people and using their collective wisdom to solve your problems instead of relying upon your own.

5. Spiritual approach

If you do not believe in God or supernatural powers, you may skip this section and go to the next. This approach works for some but not for all and not always. None can explain clearly why it is so. It is suitable for only those who believe in spirituality, psychic powers, esoteric rituals and religious practices. People used it in the past successfully to cure terminal diseases, precipitate rains, attract luck, and overcome misfortune, physical and mental disability. In this approach, you refer the problem to God, a higher power, a personal deity, ancestor, angel, saint, or spiritual master and seek his intervention to resolve it. You may also invoke your own soul or your higher consciousness by looking within. You may use prayers, chants, songs, guided meditation, visualization, and invocations, accompanied by rituals, austerities and offerings to communicate with them and obtain their favors. You may also seek the assistance of priests and other intermediaries to help you perform them correctly.

Your success depends upon your faith, sincerity, surrender, devotion, purity of intention, humility and virtues. Many people resort to this approach when everything else fails. It may not always resolve your problems, but it has proven useful to develop strength, ability, courage and hope to live with the problem and experience peace. There are limitations to what any human being can do in certain situations. Our lives and destinies are not entirely under our control. Our knowledge and abilities are also limited. We can find solutions, make decisions and take actions, but we cannot be certain about the results. We cannot look far into the future or predict what may happen. We cannot be even sure how our actions will turn out. Since the world is impermanent, we cannot take anything for granted. In these circumstances, it is better to surrender to a higher power or the universe and pray for the best. Spiritual approach is effective, especially when it is combined with other approaches. You should try it as long as you have faith in yourself and your hidden potentials, even if you do not believe in magic or external powers. You can use it to strengthen your faith or your character.

Problem vs. crisis

If a problem is snowfall, a crisis is a blizzard. If a problem is a question, begging for an answer, a crisis is a conundrum, defying all solutions. When a problem is ignored for long, it becomes a crisis. Many crises in our lives are self created. We allow them to happen, because we think we are too busy, do not have time, presume they will not happen, or too afraid, angry, prejudiced, disturbed or depressed to act rationally and confidently. A crisis is a product of our ignorance, apathy, lack of motivation and neglect. When we do not handle a problem situation in time, it may go out of control and become a source of torment. If we sleep over a small fire in the middle of a dense forest and forget to put it out in time, we may find ourselves in the midst of a violent forest fire.

You can prevent problems from becoming crises by paying attention to them and taking timely action. If you are attentive and proactive, you can even prevent many problems from happening. Thus, readiness or preparedness is part of any problem solving process. From your experience and based upon your specific profession or lifestyle, you can anticipate certain problems and make a provision for them so that when it happens, you are not completely take by surprise. It is like having a tool box in your house to take care of minor household repairs, or keeping a few handles in case there is a power failure. Simple precautions can save you a lot of trouble, like saving for your retirement, controlling your expenditure, taking care of your health, insuring your assets, managing your relationships, doing proper maintenance for your appliances, and keeping your car in good running condition.

Tools and resources

Courage, conviction, positive mental attitude, patience, intelligence, foresight, discretion, balance, detachment, objectivity, openness, readiness, preparedness, foresight are some of the qualities and resources you need to improve your problem solving skills. If you want to improve them and control your life and destiny, you must be goal oriented, attentive, purposeful, serious about your life and actions, disciplined, committed to your purpose, courageous, flexible, willing to take risks, and decisive. Your feelings of self-worth and attitude are equally important so that when a problem arises you will focus on the problem instead of suffering from fear, guilt, and anxiety.

Problems are opportunities, which help you to improve your skills and knowledge. They strengthen you and improve you as you learn from them and become skillful in solving them. Life can be regarded as a series of problems, which give you an opportunity to become a better person. Therefore, you should not escape from them or avoid them as some people do. When you escape from problems, it affects your morale and self-esteem. Problems are going to be part of your life, whether you live normally or escape into a cave or a forest. A better course would be to improve your problem solving skills and improve your chances of success and happiness. Life is a gift. It is an opportunity to experience consciousness and the feeling of being alive and active. To make it worthwhile, and make your existence memorable and unique, you must not let any problem interfere with your wellbeing.

The Pillars of Prosperity

In the final analysis, your true worth as an individual does not depend upon the prosperity you inherit, but the one you create and sustain out of your thoughts and actions, determination and the will to succeed against odds. Even in the latter case, you cannot take full credit for it. You may think that you have toiled alone to amass your wealth and deserve all the credit for your success, but you must remember that countless people and forces must have helped you in your journey to be where you are now. Even if you inherited substantial fortune from your parents or someone else, they too would not have been able to amass it without help from others.

Although, outwardly, everyone seems to be acting selfishly and tending one's own fence, the world is sustained mostly on the principles of generosity, sharing and cooperation. Nature promotes both cooperation and competition for the survival of species. We may draw our own little circles of selfishness upon earth and define our boundaries, but beneath the circles and the walls we build, Nature and the earth unite everyone and everything to the processes of life. Above us, there is the sky that has no boundaries, and in between, there is the air, which we all share. Whether we are rich or poor, high or low, in the game of life we are all interdependent and inter connected. It means that you owe considerable debt to society.

Abundance is a state of mind. It does not necessarily depend upon material wealth, but upon your thinking and attitude. Some people spend their whole lives accumulating wealth, but remain poor in their hearts as they suffer from fear and scarcity. On the other hand, you may find some who are poor, but live with contentment, unburdened by the weight of sorrow or the expectations of society. Whether they have money or not they remain generous, sharing whatever they have, and live with contentment, gratitude, compassion, understanding and appreciation. They help others and feel connected even if personally they are going through difficult times.

Some people open their hearts, as they become successful, while some remain vain and conceited. Some people are unhappy even though by world standards they are rich and successful, while some manage to stay balanced and contended even though they may have limited means. Thus, your happiness does not necessarily arise from your wealth but how you feel about yourself and your achievements. Wealth does not guarantee morality, virtue, humility or good character, while it may give you freedom to make certain decisions and extend your approach and sphere of influence. Wealth creates opportunities, but does not by itself ensure success and fulfillment.

What is the true meaning of being rich? It primarily means having monetary or financial freedom, which may, however, arise variously from abundance, detachment, contentment, or freedom from desires. You can experience the richness of life in many ways, not necessarily by having money or spending it. For example, you can experience it by doing what you love to do, by appreciating the simple pleasures of life, by experiencing the warmth of relationships, by helping others, and by increasing your knowledge and awareness. You should aim not only to accumulate wealth but also to build your character and personality so that you can use your wealth for right purposes with right awareness.

In the following paragraphs, I have identified 15 qualities, which can empower you to overcome your self-imposed limitations and disempowering beliefs to create wealth and manage it successfully. I call them pillars of prosperity, because they are the foundation, upon which anyone can build a wholesome and balanced life. Most of the qualities are interrelated and sustain one another. If you possess them already, you can skip this article. If not, you can cultivate them to channel abundance into your life and enjoy the freedom and happiness it creates. They are listed below.

1. Optimism.
2. Awareness.
3. Discipline.
4. Determination.
5. Courage.
6. Faith.
7. Compassion.
8. Intelligence.
9. Interest.
10. Love.
11. Humility.

12. Simplicity.
13. Generosity.
14. Curiosity.
15. Initiative.

Optimism

It is better to be an optimist rather than a pessimist. Pessimism is required to understand the gravity of a situation, but optimism is required to deal with it. Pessimism helps you to foresee the threats and risks involved, stay within your limits and avoid unnecessary risks, while optimism helps you to find opportunities and possibilities even in the dark corners of misfortune. Most importantly, pessimism helps you to remain within your limits and stay free from trouble, while optimism helps you to test your limits and potentials.

Although for a balanced life, you need both optimism and pessimism, you should predominantly remain optimistic to keep your spirits high and sustain the momentum of your life, motivation, morale and enthusiasm. When you are optimistic, you can effectively manage your negative feelings such as fear, suspicion, hatred and ill will. By framing your experiences and perceptions positively and seeing positive outcomes, you can improve your chances of success and happiness. When you have hope, you see possibilities and opportunities, overcome your fear, believe in yourself and your abilities, and feel encouraged to solve your problems and pursue your goals.

Awareness

Awareness arises from knowledge, observation, attentiveness, contemplation, experience, intelligence, interpretation, curiosity, and learning. Awareness gives you the competitive edge to stay ahead. When you have specialized knowledge, your influence, power and authority increase, as people respect your knowledge and approach you for help and solutions. With increased awareness you gain insight, make new discoveries, patent your inventions and multiply your sources of income. Successful people focus upon three types of awareness, self-awareness, awareness of others, and of the world. All are important. Self-awareness helps you to become a better and capable person, by knowing your strengths and weaknesses.

Awareness of others helps you to choose right people to be part of your life and career, and manage your relationships. The knowledge of the world helps you to protect and promote your interests, explore opportunities, and pursue your goals. Awareness arising from knowledge and insight is necessary to achieve success in any field. Everyone has awareness, but most of them lack depth. To stand above the rest and achieve distinction, you need insight and intuitive awareness, which will help you to manage difficult situations, foresee problems and adapt to situations. You can identify threats and opportunities present in your environment and plan accordingly, and conserve your energy and resources by responding to problems in time.

Discipline

Discipline makes humans different from animals. Animals have a discipline of their own mostly guided by their instincts, but humans have a better capacity for discipline. We can discipline ourselves consciously through self-effort, setting standards and striving to achieve them. Discipline is important to achieve success and happiness. Discipline may cause discomfort, but provides the framework in which you can shape your life and dreams. Success and discipline go hand in hand. Without discipline you cannot prepare well for success or failure. Discipline gives you control over your mind and body and the strength to pursue your goals, persevere, and manage your life. Without discipline, your life is like a boat without the rudder.

Discipline means sticking to a program, staying the course, and having the resolve to reach the end, despite the challenges, threats and distractions. It also means order, control, moderation, balance, and adaptability. If you have discipline, you can balance your expectations with reality, and your actions with your abilities. You can adapt to your circumstances, make sacrifices when required, and if necessary stand alone and fight your life's battles with determination, courage and tenacity. Discipline enables you to control your thoughts and impulses and bring to fruition your hopes and dreams through goal oriented effort.

Discipline improves efficiency and effectiveness, and brings clarity and simplicity into your thinking and methods. With a disciplined mind, you develop tolerance, compassion and understanding and accept failure as a part of your success, learning and improving. You forgive people for their mistakes, weaknesses, and imperfections. As you learn to control your behavior and environment, and direct your thoughts and energies, you realize your cherished goals, and deal with people and your limitations wisely and confidently. A disciplined person knows when to let go of things and when to hold on to them, according to the situation. Therefore, practice discipline for your self-development and to improve your character and behavior. It is the invisible partner in your success. If you have this basic quality, you will succeed any venture and reach any goal.

Determination

You may have goals and plans, and dream wonderful dreams about your future. However, it comes to nothing, if you do not have the determination to carry them out. Without resolve, you cannot beat the obstacles, successfully implement your plans, meet your own expectations, or keep up your enthusiasm, motivation and optimism. Determination means perseverance, a quality that distinguishes a winner from a loser. It is the ability to keep yourself focused on your goals, when the world is crashing around you. It means not losing hope in what you do and your goals, having faith in yourself and your methods and accepting setbacks and failures without being crushed by them. Without determination you cannot go far in your life.

Life is full of problems and obstacles. There are people and forces outside, who want you to fail, or see you humiliated and hurt and stop trying. They do so because they are in competition with you or envy your success. If you are determined, you will not let them win. Your determination arises from your self-discipline, confidence, faith, courage, commitment and self-esteem, according to your beliefs and convictions. If you think positively, you are more likely to sustain your determination even in difficult times.

Courage

Courage is the ability to take calculated risks, face the unknown and unfamiliar when needed, standup to the problems and challenges, and bear the pressures of life by overcoming doubts and negative emotions. It is having the belief in yourself and the willingness to sacrifice immediate gains for the sake of long term goals. Courage is not absence of fear, but the ability to control it and manage it. You are courageous to the extent you control your fear and act. None can remove fear completely from their minds because it is part of our survival instinct. Some fear is considered good for your safety and survival to prevent you from engaging in reckless and irresponsible behavior. It is incorrect to say that a courageous person is never afraid of anything. He knows how to act in the face of fear.

Courage also means the ability to use your will in the face of difficulties and demand the best from your life and actions. When you have courage, you will not set easier goals, undersell your talents and abilities, or settle for the less. You speak for yourself and negotiate with others on your terms. Courageous people are not afraid to make mistakes or correct them, or ask for help when they need it. They rely upon their inner strength when no outside help is available, and forge relationships without the compulsion to control and manipulate others. They also stand for what they believe in, and defend their ideas and thoughts when required. For them victory is an opportunity to celebrate and plan for further victories, while failure is an opportunity to learn and move forward. They continue to advance in life undeterred by setbacks and failures.

Faith

Without faith you can neither achieve success nor wealth nor happiness. Faith makes you strong, heals your past, answers your doubts and prepares you for the battles of life. Your faith is responsible for your beliefs, values, trust, self-confidence, self-reliance, loyalty, commitment, dedication, initiative, responsibility, feeling of assurance and willingness to take risks. When you have faith in yourself, you do not to look others for approval or blame them for your failures and faults. You take responsibility for your life and show initiative, courage, and self-reliance, in taking decisions and actions. You experience confidence, peace, and freedom from anxiety and uncertainty. Your relationships are also shaped by your faith. When you have faith in yourself, you will have faith in others. When you have faith in others, you accept them, without controlling them, and treat them with dignity and respect. The third component of faith is faith in God, which gives you the added strength to pursue your dreams and goals according to your faith and values. It will help you to think beyond yourself, transcend your selfish desires and work for a greater cause that may outlast your life and balance your material interests with your spiritual aspirations. Having faith in oneself is therefore of utmost importance. It is the key to all riches and abundance. How much you can draw from the reservoir of life depends upon what you think you deserve. It is always in proportion to how much you believe in yourself.

Compassion

Compassion arises in the heart of a person who feels and cares for others, and who is willing to share his happiness with others and transcend his own selfishness to help them. Compassion elevates your character and increases your peace and happiness. It arises from sensitivity, empathy and understanding. When you expand your self-concept to include others, you find in it space for them. You should not practice compassion to impress others or expecting rewards. However, when you have compassion, you will seek abundance not only for your happiness but also for the happiness of others, and try to reduce their suffering. As you help people your influence grows, and opportunities increase, while the wishes and blessings of others increase your positive energy. It is the reward of good karma. The universe compensates you for the help you render and the good you do. When you let others share your happiness and success, it multiplies your own happiness and abundance. Through your compassion, you instill hope and faith in others, and inspire them to follow your example. You become a lamp that will bring light and cheer in their lives.

Intelligence

Intelligence is the ability to know, think, understand, and analyze your perceptions and use the knowledge according to your discretion to solve your problems and achieve your goals. Human intelligence plays an important role in several functions of the mind, such as perception, observation, learning, thinking, comprehension, analysis, reason, problem solving, decision making, estimating, creativity, intuition, foresight, discretion, etc. It can be enhanced, polished and molded through study, observation, learning and use. Using it, you can find opportunities and threats present in your environment and increase your chances of survival and success. It also helps you to know the distinction between right and wrong and deal with ambiguity and uncertainty.

There are many types of intelligence, such as verbal, visual, auditory, mathematical, logical, intuitive, etc. Each plays an important role in letting you make sense of the world and interpret your perceptions and experience. They are not separate entities but rather aspects of the same intelligence.

Your intelligence is Nature's gift to you. It sets you apart from others, to the extent you polish it, express it and use it to resolve your problems, control your impulses and emotions, and establish equilibrium in your life and relationships. Use your intelligence to know how to attract right things into your life and keep them for your enjoyment, peace and happiness.

Interest

Interest means what you like, curious about, love or where your mind rests automatically. It is the quality, which attracts your attention, concern or curiosity. When you pay attention to something, it grows in importance and value and becomes interesting to you. It is indeed a form of attachment, or a manifestation of it. All that you create or make happen begins with interest. For example, if you are interested in abundance and positive aspects of life, they will eventually flow into your consciousness and become part of your life. Interest evokes and sustains dedication, concentration, whole hearted attention, passion and enthusiasm. They are the essential ingredients of success in any field. If you pursue in life what you are primarily interested in, your chances of success multiply. When your interests are aligned with your goals, you will experience inner harmony, which gives you a greater ability to express your talents, skills and latent energies.

When your interests are properly aligned, you do not feel conflicted because your mind and heart remain in harmony with each other. They enable you to learn from your experiences, know the possibilities and limitations, remain curious and open minded, accept challenges, take risks, test your limits, explore the unknown and the hidden, and thereby improve your skills and talents. The secret of success, therefore, is to select a career or a profession, which is in harmony with major interests, and pursue them with determination. When you follow your life according to your deepest aspirations, you experience peace and fulfillment and inner harmony. Prosperity arises from dedicated and concentrated effort, which is best possible when you are engaged in doing what you love to do. Therefore, you should aim only for those goals and aspirations which are directly influenced by your major interests.

Love

What you love loves you in return. Sometimes there may be resistance, but eventually if your love is strong, all resistance breaks loose. If you love material wealth, wealth will manifest in your life. If you love relationships, your life will be enriched with relationships. Your knowledge and wisdom grow in the direction of your life. Thus, love guides, directs and influences your life. You enjoy what you love, excel in what you love to do, and care for those whom you love. Your love manifests as acceptance, appreciation, harmony, peace, recognition, loving relationships, caring and nurturing help, and happiness. Your love for things can be selfish or selfless. Selfish love is eventually counterproductive as it separates you from the things you love or those you love.

Many successful people suffer from loneliness since they cannot overcome their self-love and selfish love for material things. Sometimes they love the ownership rather than their possession. They end up owning things but suffer from emptiness as they alienate the people who love them. Your success should not take away from you your capacity to love and appreciate people selflessly, especially those who contribute to your success and love you genuinely. You cannot force yourself to love anything. You have to prepare yourself for it by cultivating the higher qualities of compassion, friendliness, caring, gratitude, sacrifice and selflessness. When you have these, you allow your heart to feel love and extend it to others in your life. If you have love in your heart, you will not suffer from the scarcity of loving and positive relationships or the damage caused by negative emotions. You will enjoy your success by helping and healing people, serving others and creating opportunities for others to succeed in their lives.

Humility

The most difficult thing in the world is to remain unaffected by the rewards of success. Many people lose their balance, after becoming successful. They forget to look back and remember from where they have come. We can always celebrate our success, but it is important that we remember the basic virtues that keep us firmly rooted to the ground. Humility is the most important among them. Without humility, it is difficult to achieve success and much more difficult to sustain it. When success goes to your head, it leads to your downfall. Those who climb the steps of life, without looking down, are bound to fall from the heights at some point of time. It pays to be modest and unassuming to fill the cup of your life with knowledge, experience and abundance. Life is always eager to teach us lessons and those who succumb to pride and arrogance receive many.

Humility means feeling confident without vanity and conceit, accepting challenges unassumingly with courage with faith, and rejoicing in your victories without pride and arrogance. It is to acknowledge those who are worthy of respect and reverence, and learning from others without feeling small and inadequate. Humility is all about balance. It lets you know your strengths and weaknesses and accept them realistically without feeling high or low about yourself. The know-it-all attitude does not help you to forge relationships or improve your knowledge and skills. People, who lack humility, learn their lessons the hard way. If you overrate yourself, you may set unrealistic goals and take wrong decisions. Alternatively, if you underrate others you may make mistakes in choosing right people or using them for right purposes.

Humility enables you to accept suggestions, learn from others, be considerate, thoughtful, helpful and humble in your relationships and communication, and express gratitude for the help you receive and the success you achieve. It lets you keep your feet firmly on earth, and your imagination soar. When you are humble, you do not feel the compulsion to prove yourself or indulge in pretentious behavior. The universe conspires against those, who are arrogant and conceited. It is better to be humble and avoid unnecessary controversies and conflicts on your way to success. The least that you can do in your life is to become an obstacle to your own goals through your negative behavior.

You can express your talents and skills in various ways. Arrogance and pride are definitely not among them. Humility is a virtue, which opens the doors of friendship and appreciation, and secures the help and cooperation of others. If you are humble, you receive help from many because you do not hesitate to ask for help, show your vulnerability, or accept rejection. Since you respect others, they will serve you willingly. You can be proud of your accomplishments, but you should be humble in your thinking, attitude and behavior. You can aim for stars, but with your feet firmly on the ground. To your pride under control, you may rejoice in your victories, but you should remain balanced in defeat. You should have faith in your abilities, but you should not let your self-confidence turn into arrogance and cause your downfall.

Simplicity

Simplicity is like a straight line, or music without noise, or a person without titles. You manifest it in your life when you remove the clutter and keep what is necessary. Simplicity implies ease, straightforwardness, order, organization and clarity in both thinking and behavior. You reach it through mastery, understanding, experience, insight, discipline, wisdom and self-control. If you master it, it serves you well in life, as it improves your efficiency and effectiveness and leads to peace and perfection. If you want to be successful, you should set clear and precise goals, minimize distractions, and follow a strict discipline, using efficient methods and means, and finding straightforward solutions. When you simplify your life, you will have time and opportunity to improve your knowledge and skills, spend time with your friends and family, rest your mind and body, find freedom from stress and strain, do the things you love most and put your resources to more efficient use.

We cannot completely remove complexity from our lives, since we are not in complete control of our lives. The world is complex enough to worry us. We have to deal with people who are by nature unpredictable and complex. Since we do not always have the answers, we cannot help making things difficult and complicated for ourselves. The world is attracted to glitter and glamour. Many people do not even appreciate simplicity. Yet, simplicity is important to keep your focus, maximize your efficiency and effectiveness and conserve your resources. Therefore, try to bring simplicity into your life wherever possible. Focus on the important. Eliminate redundancies. Delegate tasks. Minimize expenditure. Improve efficiency and effectiveness. Avoid micromanaging. Establish rules and norms. Organize everything, and finally, use what is necessary.

Generosity

We are well aware of the corrupting nature of wealth. When success goes into their heads, people lose their balance. When Jesus declared that it would be difficult for a rich man to pass through the eye of a needle, he was not suggesting that prosperity was a curse, but that it could corrupt the minds of people and lead them astray. One of the dangers of accumulating wealth is, it tends to make people too selfish and self centered. All religions urge their followers to be aware of the attachment created by our desire for material things. As our attachment grows and as we accumulate material things, our hearts begin to constrict and we give less and less. Our lives undergo transformation as old relationships fade away, new relationships are formed, new standards of achievement are established in place of the old, and our hunger for further success and achievement grows in intensity.

All wealth belongs to God. In fact, material wealth is a trap, set to test the nobility and refinement of our character. When abundance flows into our lives, we become its temporary trustees. We have a right to enjoy it and share it with others, but we cannot cling on to it forever. It does not belong to us in the strict sense of the word, because God is the true Owner of everything and someday we have to return to Him what belongs to Him.

There is a law of compensation operating in the universe. It is what we can loosely translate as the law of karma. What you give, you will receive manifold. What you receive, you have to give back at some point of time in your life. If you hold on to things, which belong to the universe, you may likely reap its negative effects. Spiritual wealth is perhaps more important than material wealth and we cannot accumulate it enough, if we are attached to material things and remain under the influence of our egoistic and selfish thinking.

Abundance flows into your life because of the generosity of God. When you receive it, it becomes your prime responsibility to permit its free flow back into the universe so that its movement is not impeded and its purpose is not defeated. The riches that come into your life are not meant for you alone, but for all those, whose welfare has become your responsibility and whose progress in life depend upon you.

We have to remember that our success is not achieved by our individual effort alone, but with the help of many. The support and generosity of many make possible the dreams of one. Even the group, nation, society, or community, to which we belong, play an important role in our survival and success. It is not necessary that only those whom we know help us. People whom we have never met and never seen play their role in shaping our lives through their thoughts and actions. Therefore, it would be unwise on our part not to share our fortunes with others and carry the karmic debt we incurred beyond this life.

The true purpose of prosperity is to overcome attachment to material things and give expression to the highest aspirations in you, as you free yourself from the petty demands of your egoistic self and become a self-aware individual, with a refined character, noble attitude and an expansive mind and heart. Your material wealth will not become an obstacle on your path to salvation only when you learn to control it rather than be controlled by it, and make it a source of happiness and solace to others through giving and sharing. This way, you carve your path to the heavens and earn your right to pass through the "needle."

Generosity should be practiced with regard to not only material wealth but also other aspects. You can do it by sharing your thoughts and ideas with others, helping them solve problems, find resources or information, or sharing your love and happiness. You can be generous in your appreciation and support and cooperate, and collaborate with others since cooperation and collaboration are aspects of generosity only.

Curiosity

Curiosity means eagerness, enthusiasm, desire and interest to know about something. It is the main driving force in our progress and that of our civilization. It plays an important role in the growth of young children as they want to know about everything and keep asking questions and seeking answers. It is not confined to humans only. Even animals possess some curiosity. They want to know what is happening around them, where they can find food, and whether they are safe or not. In humans it serves as an important motivating factor. It prompts us to go out of our comfort zones and explore the world to satisfy our needs and adapt to it.

There is also a negative side to it. In the hands of unscrupulous people, curiosity can turn into prying and meddling, and cause a lot of grief to others. Positively speaking, it increases our knowledge and awareness, prompts us to seek new relationships and opportunities, know the world, stay in the present and solve our problems and ignorance by being creative, inquisitive and inventive.

Because of curiosity people venture into the unknown and the unfamiliar, and try to unravel the secrets hidden in the world. In a proper frame of mind, it sustains our interest, propels us into action, and fills our minds with wonder and enthusiasm. As we become adults, we become less interested in the world and less curios. We take things for granted and become preoccupied with our routine lives, whereby we stop learning and growing. Therefore, it is important to keep our curiosity alive and use it to achieve excellence and superior knowledge. Revive your childhood curiosity to know yourself and your potentials, and keep learning and expanding your knowledge and awareness.

Initiative

Initiative comes with the freedom to think and act. It implies leadership, ambition, interest, enthusiasm, control and commitment. In a competitive environment, it puts you in control of your actions and ahead of others. It is a rare quality, which is found mostly in entrepreneurs, authors, scientists and resourceful individuals who want to achieve excellence in their field. Success is achieved mainly through intelligent and self-motivated effort. Extraneous factors may play a role in testing and strengthening your resolve, but without interest and initiative you cannot progress far. People and circumstances may encourage you or inspire you to achieve success, but ultimately you have to take the initiative to control your life and actions. Successful people know that they have to find motivation and purpose within themselves and rely upon their talents and skills to achieve success.

Hence, they take responsibility for their actions and lead themselves without waiting for inspiration or instruction from others. Since they are self-directed individuals, they do not blame others for their failures. They own their failures and learn from them. Since they show courage and initiative and are unafraid of taking risks, they distinguish themselves as leaders, pathfinders and torch bearers. They become popular for their initiative and effort in helping others and helping themselves.

Conclusion

Remember these fifteen qualities which can change your life. Write them down a piece of paper and keep it within your gaze for frequent reference. Your life will change to the extent you manifest them in your life. If you practice them sincerely, they can transform your life beyond your imagination. I have no doubt in my mind that these qualities can pave the way for your excellence in any field, elevate your consciousness, build your character and help you to transcend your lower nature. Therefore, practice them regularly, finding opportunities in your daily life. For your convenience, I am restating them here.

- Optimism.
- Awareness.
- Discipline.
- Determination.
- Courage.
- Faith.
- Compassion.
- Intelligence.
- Interest.
- Love.

- Humility.
- Simplicity.
- Generosity.
- Curiosity.
- Initiative.

Planning Your Vacation

Planning is an important activity which can make the difference between success and failure. Successful people find their purpose, set their goals and plan for them. Planning is the first part. After planning comes implementation, which is even more important. However, your implementation depends a lot upon your planning and foresight. If you choose a wrong path or a wrong vehicle, you may not reach the destination. It is the same with planning. Unless you plan well, you cannot reach your goals. Many big projects and grand schemes fail because of lack of proper planning.

Planning means you should foresee how to reach somewhere in time and space or achieve something in the journey of your life with a meaningful map. It is about how to find, organize and use your resources within the usual constraints, rules and regulations to achieve your goals or fulfill your desires. Many people plan their journeys and vacations, but do not plan properly for their future. They drift along and waste a lifetime of opportunities before they find themselves unhappy or in situations they dislike. I am using here vacation as the basis to present some aspects of planning, but you can use them to plan for anything. This article touches only a few elements of planning, but it is still useful to anticipate and troubleshoot known problems and risks in any undertaking, and deal with contingencies.

Planning reduces anxiety

Life is unpredictable. You cannot accurately predict how your life or events in your life will turn out. While we cannot completely foresee into the future, we can bring some predictability into our thinking and actions through proper planning. You may not be able to predict future, but you can certainly make intelligent guesses and estimate probabilities and possibilities based upon risk analysis and other factors. Depending upon your nature, planning can either reduce or increase your anxiety. It is said that Sigmund Freud, the father of modern psychology, used to suffer from anxiety before traveling.

Some anxiety before going on vacation is normal, because travel implies change in your surroundings and moving out of your comfort zone, which may be your home or workplace, to a new and different place. If you are planning to go on vacation to an entirely unknown place or a foreign country, which you have not visited before, you are bound to experience anxiety. However, if you plan well you can reduce your anxiety greatly. Planning is the antidote to fear, anxiety and stress, which you experience as you prepare for your journey.

Planning means knowing and organizing

In simple terms, planning means drawing a roadmap with landmarks and estimates of time and resources to reach them. Technically, it involves goal setting, resource allocation, resource prioritization and resource utilization. The resources can be time, money, people, skills, or raw materials. In vacation planning, you have to consider several resources, which you may use or require to make your vacation pleasant and trouble free. It is one thing to wish for a dream vacation and another to make a realistic and practical plan to make it happen. If you want to go on a hassle free vacation to exotic places and enjoy your vacations, you need to plan carefully, gathering as much information as possible and making wise choices. You must know beforehand how much money you have, and how you should stay within your budget, avoid the usual risks and manage the contingencies.

In vacation planning, you need to be familiar with the places you want to travel and possess some basic skills in scheduling, budgeting, time management, forecasting and event coordination. You have to be good at adaptation, improvisation and communication, so that you can cope with the challenges and contingencies that may arise during your vacation. The same principles apply to plan any activity. If you are traveling with your family, your family members become your team. If you take responsibility for their journey and comfort also, you have to take care of their needs and problems while planning to make sure that neither you nor they would suffer from any negligence and carelessness!

Planning with purpose

When it comes to planning your vacation, you should not take anything for granted or rely upon your memory, even if you are blessed with high IQ. Otherwise, you may find yourself in embarrassing situations. For example, a friend of mine bought an airline ticket to travel to India. To save some money, he opted for boarding the plane from a nearby city rather than city where he lived. On the day of his journey, he drove about a hundred miles to reach the airport. At the airport, during the check in he found that he forgot to bring his old passport which contained all the visas which he required to travel. Eventually, he had to request one of his friends to bring the passport by road. To avoid such problems and make your travel and stay as comfortable as possible, you should prepare in advance a comprehensive checklist of the things you need to do and the items you need to carry.

The purpose of going on vacation is to relax and enjoy. No one would like to see their vacation turn into a nightmare, because of negligence or mistakes. You can take care of many problems and risks by preparing a checklist. The vacation checklist will empower you to keep your planning under your radar and save you time, money and effort. With Its help, you can minimize oversight and enjoy a memorable and happy vacation. Your travel checklist can be as simple or as detailed as you want it to be, depending upon where you go, how long you stay and what you intend to do during your free time. A simple checklist will suffice if you are going on a short vacation or if you are familiar with the place you are planning to visit. However, if you have not visited the places before or if you are traveling with others for whom you are responsible, you may require a detailed checklist. Most importantly, your checklist should always be in writing.

Planning with foresight

In planning, attention to detail is very important. You must visualize as many details as possible and anticipate all possible scenarios. Before you start working on your check list, you have to familiarize yourself with the places you are planning to visit. You have to be aware of the risks involved and possible remedies. Using your ingenuity and imagination, you have to find out what you can expect from your vacation and what type of arrangements and planning you need to make the vacation pleasant and trouble free. If you are visiting more than one location, you have to collect information about each of them. If you or any member of your traveling group has special food requirements, you have to find places, where you can find such food. Nowadays, Internet provides free information about almost every place in the world which is worth visiting. You can not only know about the place, but also see a few colorful images that give you a fairly good idea of what you are going to see. You can check the travel websites and location specific tourism websites, which provide lot of detailed information about the local hotels, bars, restaurants, tourist attractions, car rentals and other relevant services. You can even book your reservation from them or contact the customer service to find our more details. If you are a member of clubs or organizations such as American Automobile Association or Travel Clubs, you can contact them for information and help regarding travel, lodging and boarding, insurance, maps, discounts and visa arrangements.

Preparing the checklist

The following checklist can help you to cover all the basics and plan for your vacation.

- Destination.
- Climate.
- Date and duration of travel.
- Clothing (which essentially depends upon what you intend to do and in which climate.) and other items that are needed on vacation such as baggage, shoes, sunglasses, cameras, binoculars, etc.
- Number of people intending to travel and specific issues associated with them, such as health issues and special needs.
- Available travel options and intended mode of travel. Also consider whether you need insurance to drive a rental car or whether your existing insurance covers it. Buying insurance from a rental car company can be more expensive than the rent itself.
- Available stay options and intended places of stay. If you plan to camp outside, you may have to make special arrangements. If you plan to stay in hotels, you may need to book in advance and look for good deals.
- Amount of money required to travel and how you intend to carry it. Also, you need to know whether

you can use your credit cards at the places you are traveling or you need special arrangements. If you are planning to visit foreign countries, it is essential to plan this part carefully to avoid slippage in converting your money into local currencies and the possibilities of fraud.

- Local customs and habits, places to visit, hours of operation, health facilities, security aspects, telephone facilities, emergency contact numbers, etc. If you do not plan this properly, you may end up standing in long queues or missing important sites and events altogether.
- The overall objective of your vacation. Is it simple relaxation you are expecting, a family get together, or a learning opportunity for you and your children?
- Arrangements needed at home during your vacation. There can be myriad things that need attention and care, while you are on vacation, such as security, housekeeping and arrangements for your mail or your pets or your garden.
- Contingency planning to take care of the unexpected and any emergency situations that may arise.
- Also to avoid last minute confusion and stress, you need to take care of the following.
- Packing your travel bags well in advance.
- Keeping your money ready.
- Paying your pending bills and arranging payments that may become due during your vacation.
- If your kids are accompanying you, you may have to plan for their absence and homework assignments.
- Checking your passports and visas for inconsistencies and expiry dates.

In conclusion, it is important to plan for everything and take nothing for granted. When you go on vacation, you step out of comfort zone and your daily routine. You will be spending time among total strangers and deals with a number of issues and risks. Therefore, it is very important that you plan for your vacation so that you can return from it with positive memories and pleasant experiences.

Positive Mental Attitude

Today's sorrow hides in its bosom the joys of tomorrow. Adversity is the soil in which you sow the seeds of success. The rains that came today and ruined your paths would soon make the earth green and abundant. In the womb of loss is the seed of gain. The storms and floods that devastate life on earth also enable us to start life afresh. The night that invokes in us fearful thoughts, also reveals to us the beauty and majesty of the star filled heavens.

Life is what we make of it.

Life is as we think about it.

Life is what we want it to be.

Life is a mixture of colors that we choose and put on an otherwise empty canvas. We see what we want to see, accept those we believe in and ignore those that do not interest us. This is the wisdom of the ages, ancient as well as modern.

Therefore, think positively. Even amidst difficulties hope for the best. Keep courage. With faith in your heart and confidence in yourself, you can overcome your problems. Know with certainty that at the end of darkness there can only be light.

Your suffering is a part of your spiritual evolution. It sets in motion a purifying process, which ultimately leads to your awakening and enlightenment. If you look at the world with thoughts of love, full of compassion and understanding you do not live in despair. If you look at yourselves, with understanding and acceptance, you will not find any reason to be unhappy.

How often do we spend our lives, feeling unhappy and inadequate about ourselves? How often do we defeat ourselves with thoughts of self-criticism? How often do we hurt others with anger and frustration? How often do we silence our courage and confidence with negative thoughts, and how many relations do we lose, by our judgmental and critical nature?

A positive mind accepts life as it happens and accommodates every event and circumstance with a positive interpretation, however difficult it may be. In the mind of a positive person darkness is dissolved in the light of wisdom. Everything finds in it a cause to celebrate and reason to stay.

A positive mind is a liberated mind. If you want to be a true optimist, liberate yourselves from all forms of pettiness and selfishness. Happiness can be an invention of the mind that can see light on the other side of darkness. Invent your happiness through positive thinking. With your feet firmly on the ground and your head held high, fight the battles of life.

An optimist's world view

We can make ourselves happy or unhappy out of the same situation. We have the capacity to impart meaning and significance to the events and situations in our lives. At each turn in our lives we have to make choices and find direction. On earth we are creators, creating our lives and destinies and shaping our reality according to our thoughts and desires. Our experiences are part of the great story that we create in our minds about ourselves and the world around us. Our moods, emotions and feelings do not depend upon what life offers to us, but on how we receive the perception and make sense of it.

Happiness, unhappiness, courage, timidity, love, and hatred, are the illusions and indulgences we create in our minds in pursuit of our desires and dreams. It is according to our thoughts and desires that we make choices and indulge in actions to reach our goals and enjoy pleasures and comforts of life.

A positive person reacts with consideration and wisdom to the events in his life. He controls his reactions and interpretations and there by his feelings and emotions. He knows well that he can control his thoughts and behavior, but not the world. He also knows that to be happy and contended, he must learn to find opportunities and possibilities in problems to learn from them and keep hoping and striving until the door of wisdom and success open to him.

Optimism is not escapism

Thus, he takes personal responsibility for his choices, actions, and the consequences he faces, without blaming others. Shielded by positive attitude, he safeguards himself from the negative and the harmful. He remains immune to his enemies and critics as he forgives them with compassion and understanding. When sorrows knock him down, he lifts himself up by his own thoughts. He does not wait until the end of the tunnel to discover the beauty of light. In darkness he looks at the stars and assures himself of the coming dawn, and if there are no stars he finds comfort in the healing and relaxing power of the silent night.

Positive thinking is not wishful thinking. It is neither self-deception nor rationalization. A positive person is not an escapist, who deludes himself with fantasies. He knows how to deal with the world and guard his interests. When events do not happen as expected, he knows what to do and where to look for answers. In difficult circumstances, he knows how to make sense of them and deal with them. This is the secret of positive thinking. It helps you to nurse your wounds when you are hurt by adversity and strike back when you find an opportunity.

Therefore, think positively with your feet firmly on the ground. Learn to look for the hidden purpose in the events and circumstances of your life and the brighter side them. Even if you have a strong reason to be unhappy, know that it will be temporary and you will soon overcome it. Whatever be the circumstances, difficulties, and problems, keep faith in the positive outcomes. Balance your negative thoughts, doubts, and fears with hope, courage, confidence and gratitude.

To be positive towards others, you have to learn to think positively about yourself. You must forgive yourself, heal your past and accept yourself without guilt or remorse. When you love and accept yourself, you will be able to extend the same attitude towards others. You will forgive people, and tolerate their imperfections and shortcomings.

Protecting Your Health

You can regard health as a gift from God or as a gift that you can give to yourself. You can be wealthy as well as healthy, provided you live a balanced life. Whatever may be your goals or priorities, being healthy is far more important than being just wealthy. If you have to choose between the two, you know what should be the right answer. If you have wealth, you will have better access to health resources and control over your lifestyle choices. However, wealth alone would not ensure good health or happiness.

One of the wonderful aspects of life is that people can make themselves happy, even if they are poor and live in difficult conditions. Happiness arises not only from having things you desire, but also being in the right mood at the right time. Health and happiness are interconnected, but the same is not always true regarding wealth and happiness. We also know that a healthy person, who is poor financially, is much happier than a wealthy person, who is in poor health.

Social factors and your health

With the advances in science and technology, we have learned to cope with many health problems. The world now has more doctors, hospitals, medicines, and health facilities. With new noninvasive techniques, many surgeries have become painless and require less recovery time. The average life span of people in many countries has almost doubled, while cures are found for many deadly and incurable diseases.

However, at the same time, the world has grown complex and our lives have become stressful and difficult to manage. People are now suffering from many health problems like obesity, growing incidence of heart diseases and diabetes, and increasing healthcare costs. Children and adults alike are now vulnerable to global pandemics such as swine flu. Drunk driving, binge drinking, and driving while texting have become major health hazards.

In the last few centuries, our world has undergone a tremendous transformation. Environment has become more unfriendly due to wars, over exploitation of natural resources, drought and lack of regulation in several parts of the world, while our lives have become more unstable with increased cost of living. Smoking, drinking and overeating are now major problems in many nations. People are presently consuming more alcohol, drugs, and unhealthy food than at any other time in history. Obesity is a major issue, while increasing number of people are forced to live in poor dwellings and in unhygienic conditions because of over population.

Living in too crowded cities and working in aggressively competitive environments is not at all easy. It alienates people from people and leaves them feeling isolated, anxious and agitated. Such challenges in our lives create a lot of pressure on our minds and bodies and make us vulnerable to many health hazards. In many cases they also lead to harmful behavior and mental illnesses. These problems make one point very clear. We need to protect our health and take care of our environment and living conditions. While we cannot control the external factors that affect our health, other than avoiding them or shielding against them, we can improve our health by taking control of our minds and bodies and making healthy lifestyle choices. We can manage not only our health, but also our attitude towards it.

Some people are physically healthy, but mentally depressed about everything in their lives. Neither money nor health can make them happy. Relationships do not bring them solace. On the other hand, there are some, who are physically unhealthy, but learn to cope with it in positive ways, living within their limitations, with contentment, determination, and enough energy to remain active and hopeful. Our happiness in life ultimately boils down to our attitude, thinking and behavior. It is important how we make sense of the world and ourselves, what we believe and pursue, and with what frame of reference we live and experience life.

Recognizing your role in your health

We may not be able to control on our own what happens in the Arctic or the Antarctic, the oceans, or the dense forests of Amazon, but we can keep our homes, and surroundings clean. We can keep our lawns green, avoid using harmful chemicals and fertilizers, practice good housekeeping, use environment friendly products and teacher our children how to keep their rooms and surroundings clean. We can stop littering public places, and natural habitats, and resist the pollution of our farmlands and backyards by not letting the energy companies dig wells or set up wind turbines. You can take such actions within your control to keep the environment clean.

You can also follow a similar approach with regard to your personal health, doing what you can with what you have. Your health is shaped largely by your own thoughts and actions. Others may play a role in motivating and guiding you. Sometimes you may fall sick due to external conditions. However, for the most part of your life your health depends upon the choices you make and the habits you cultivate.

Clean habits, discipline and positive thinking contribute to a healthy lifestyle. With them you have better control over your health than any environmental factor. You should not neglect your health because you are perfectly healthy. It is when you are perfectly healthy you should be more concerned about it and take preventive measures to avoid health risks and keep yourself in good shape. Your body is like a vehicle or a machine, which needs regular care. You can protect it from wear and tear, disease and injury using the following suggestions.

- Exercise your body regularly, at least three times a week.
- Exercise according to your age and health conditions.
- As grow older, make health the number one priority.
- Read at least one article on health every day. It will make you health conscious.
- Cultivate positive mental attitude. Studies prove that your beliefs contribute to health and Wellbeing.
- Avoid talking about sickness or sick people unless it is extremely necessary.
- Use positive affirmations to heal yourself.
- Practice moderation in your habits and lifestyle choices.

- Eat a healthy and balanced diet according to your lifestyle and body requirements.
- Keep your body, house and surroundings clean.
- Give your mind and body adequate rest and relaxation.
- Keep yourself busy with some activity.
- Have regular and periodical medical checkups to know what is going on.
- Choose your doctor carefully because your beliefs about your doctor can affect your health and recovery time if there is any illness.
- Help others since it makes you feel good about yourself.
- Build dependable, and working relationships that restore your faith in the humanity.
- Respect your body's strengths and weaknesses and protect it from extreme conditions.
- Choose proper healthcare insurance and keep your healthcare costs under control.

Five golden rules of health

In addition to the above, you may pay attention to the following five golden rules of health.

1. Accept the changes that come with age: As time goes by, your body undergoes many changes. You cannot do much about it, other than accepting it and responding to it in healthy ways. Resisting the aging process would only make you unhappy and frustrated. Therefore, accept the changes that arise from aging and mold your life and activities accordingly.

2. Honor the limitations of your body: Your body is an efficient biological machine, which gives you an opportunity to live and interact with the world. However, it has many limitations as it cannot withstand extreme conditions. Hence, you should practice moderation and remain within your limits in eating, drinking, sleeping, doing exercise, having sex, or driving a car.

3. Do not take your health for granted: Do not act or behave as if you are made of steel and iron, and your body can withstand whatever you do. Even if you are healthy and successful with a busy daily schedule, protect your mind and body from abuse and neglect.

4. Follow a proactive approach: You can be proactive in your health matters and save yourself a lot of trouble. Preventive healthcare is not seriously practiced in many countries, because of the costs and regulations enforced by the insurance companies. Many doctors hesitate to propose even routine tests, since they do not want to displease the insurance companies or explain to the patients the extra costs they have to bear. In many cases, the annual checkup is not done to detect problems but complete a formality. Many problems remain undetected during your visits to doctors unless you are willing to bear the costs outside the scope of your insurance. In these circumstances, you have to keep a close watch on your health and consult your doctor if you feel you have a problem.

5. Make your health a priority: To protect your health, always be a health conscious person. Pay attention to your health needs. Read books and articles on health and keep yourself well informed. Listen to your body attentively and respond quickly to the messages and signals it sends out.

Simple Pleasures of Life

We hardly live in the present. What we experience in the present is usually superimposed by the memories of our past. We cannot experience anything and make sense of it, without labeling it, categorizing it, comparing it or contrasting it. Here comes the most significant existential problem of our lives. We experience reality through the mind and it does not perceive reality accurately, as it is subject to many restrictive and disruptive mechanisms. In this our past becomes the filter, the accumulated knowledge, through which we experience the current reality. How we experience the world or the reality depends upon what we already know or what we have already experienced. Hence, it is seldom the real reality.

When we live in the prison cells of our past, looking at the world through the windows screened by our desires and expectations, there is hardly much scope for enjoying the spontaneity and beauty of life. Jiddu Krishnamurthy, an Indian spiritual master, once said to the effect that there was no true observation if there was an observer. You are the observer who determines what you want to observe from the choices that are presented to you by situations and circumstances.

If you observe with your baggage of memories, desires and expectations, you interfere with the purity of your observation and put a smokescreen of your interpretations between you and the observed. It is true because when you see everything from the colored lenses of your past, there is no actual seeing, but a validation of what you have already seen. He also said that when you looked at something, you were conditioned not to see the thing itself, but invoke a copy of its image stored in your mind and treat it as real.

Thus, for example, when you see a rose, you do not see the rose, but an idea of it or an image of it that is already present in your memory. When one falls in love, one does not fall in love with the real person, but an embellished image of that person colored by beliefs and assumptions. Hence, those who fall in love hardly see any flaws in their loved ones. It is also why human love fades away quickly as reality settles in and both sides begin to see each other's flaws clearly and objectively. We are conditioned to perceive the world this way. It is normal and natural to use our past knowledge and our learned behavior to deal with our current reality. It is how our minds choose to do their jobs efficiently and facilitate our survival and continuity.

It is also true that the knowledge that you store in your mind is but an accumulated knowledge. It is the sum of little pieces of information, which you gather from your perceptions and experiences and store in the vaults of your memory, primarily through your senses, which are in themselves limited and imperfect. You cannot rely upon it because it is colored by your beliefs, judgments, values, desires, and understanding. It is also shaped and influenced by the weight of the authority, which you respect and follow. With Its help, you can know only what you already know or what you desire to know. It is not capable of letting you know the unknown, the unfamiliar, or what cannot be fit into its constructs. Hence, as Krishnamurthy said, as long as we are in the field of the known and within the boundaries of our minds, and rely upon our memories, we do not see the truth, without the adulteration of our minds, or experience it accurately.

To a person familiar with the metaphysical aspects of life, this is a profound revelation. If we observe ourselves carefully to know how we live and experience the reality around us, we realize that most of the time we lead repetitive and monotonous lives, reinforcing our current beliefs and knowledge rather than trying to know anything new or transform our awareness. In this scenario, every new experience that we undergo remains an altered version of what we already know or what we have already experienced. Through a maze of conceptualized knowledge and belief patterns, we waddle through life, staying within our comfort zones, dealing with the familiar, and cultivating rigid mindsets. If you are familiar with the concepts of object oriented programming, you will realize that the human mind follows a similar pattern. It uses the same objects and a few design models to interpret and classify information and make sense of the world. It is as if we have created a framework, in which we want to fit in everything, however unrealistic and difficult it may be. We do not realize that we become prisoners of our own minds and worldviews, from which we cannot escape unless we are willing to break the walls that we raise. When we are forced by circumstances or chance to step out of our comfort zones and daily routines to deal with the unknown and unfamiliar, we suffer from fear and anxiety or try to escape from it.

I have explained in a previous article that to ensure your survival and keep you well informed of the threats and opportunities present in your world, your mind performs many functions routinely, and thereby saves you from information overload. Since it is impossible to do everything in a short time, it employs several filtering mechanisms, generalizations and over simplifications to minimize effort, maximize efficiency and conserves resources, without disturbing your feelings of continuity, stability and wellbeing. As a result, you do not pay enough attention to many feelings and sensations that arise in you or the situations that happen around you. If at all you do, you perceive and interpret them according to your beliefs, values, standards, assumptions, existing knowledge and states of mind.

Your cognition or how you make sense of the world also depends upon many factors. The world that we see and accept as real is an assumptive world. You may see the same object, but perceive it differently at different times, depending upon what is going on in your mind. When you look at things you do not look at it with complete surrender, as if you are looking at it for the first time, as if you have never seen it, or as if it is unique and different from all that you have known and experienced before. It happens because the mind makes sense of the world with existing images and memories stored in it rather than the actual images perceived.

The moment you perceive an object, it is superimposed by an image or memory that is already present in you. Since your perceptions are mostly colored by your thoughts, imagination, and memories, a lot of knowledge, impressions and memories that are stored in your mind are mere constructs rather than accurate copies of the objects and situations you experienced. You may rely upon such knowledge for your continuity and survival, but you cannot count on its accuracy or authenticity. It is your version of the past that happened, not necessarily what really happened. It is as you remembered it and not what might have originally happened. If the incidents happened in the remote past, you might have even rewritten them and altered them to fit them into your current belief system, self-image, and worldview.

Thus, we go through life in predictable but self-limiting ways, confining ourselves to the known and the familiar, losing things the moment we perceive them, and letting our past images and impressions aid our perceptions to create a believable reality. To focus upon things, in which we are particularly interested, we allow our minds to ignore all that we deem unnecessary, inconsequential, or irrelevant. While such selectivity helps us to resolve the problem of information overflow, it also limits our experiences, our perception of the world and our ability to understand it. Unfortunately, there is no way we can perceive the world and experience it differently, except through our minds and senses. Until we find an alternative either spiritually or scientifically, we are subject to the limitations and conditioning they impose upon our consciousness, behavior and perceptions.

It is not easy to go against Nature, or the deeply ingrained behavior that stems from your conditioning. Since, the mental processes that control your understanding are also guided by the same factors that influence your perceptions, you may not be even aware of your perceptual errors, logical fallacies, and cognitive distortions, or acknowledge them. However, your mind can be trained and reconditioned to act in desirable ways. By understanding your erroneous thinking, biases and logical fallacies, you can overcome its natural weaknesses and habitual thought patterns and learn to see the things in the field of your observation with greater clarity, understanding, objectivity, and appreciation. You can live more consciously, actively and adaptively to appreciate life and the world around you in wherever situations you may find yourself.

Your happiness must arise from within as a natural condition, in response to the simple joys of life and the little pleasures that make up most of your life. You will not be able to appreciate them if you are too busy or tied up with certain goals and expectations that are not within your easy reach. To be happy naturally, you have to slow down, lift your head and start looking around. Then you will realize how much life happens around you and how much of it you are just letting by, overlooking them rather than looking at them. In your journey of life, you may become stuck in problems and situations, but the world does not stop for you. It moves on, since you have little control over it and you cannot impose any conditions upon it. You can only take from it what you can find in it, as it opens to you in the moments that make up your life. It is how you can make peace with the world around you and find happiness within yourself as well as in the world.

Your happiness does not arise from the external things but from your conditioning. You make yourself happy by finding happiness in the things you seek or by finding freedom from the things you seek. Many people try to find happiness outside, in things and people to whom they develop attachment. For them life occasionally happens when they go on vacation, spend time with loved ones or stay in some exotic location. Their happiness remains short-lived, because it is tied to certain notions, desires, conditions and expectations that are disconnected from their regular lives. Your happiness cannot be sustained for long by the things of the world but by your ability and willingness to appreciate life as it happens. This is the truth. Unless you are a happy person by nature, nothing can make you happy, and unless you are mentally prepared to accept the world on its terms and create happiness from ordinary circumstances and simple pleasures of life, you cannot remain happy for long.

If you have become too dependent upon the world and people for your happiness, it is time you wake up your senses and enrich your life with the simple pleasures of your daily life, shifting your attention, from having to being, from feeling important to staying attentive, and from seeking attention to being perceptive. People go to faraway places to relax and enjoy their vacation. It is definitely a good way to break the monotony of your life. However, should you limit your happiness and enjoyment only to few such occasions? Do you have to spend a whole year doing dreary work to enjoy just a few days of rest and relaxation?

The answer is certainly no. Happiness exists not in the things, but in the seeker. A person can be happy by just staying at home or by flowing with the moment. What is important is your state of mind. If you are disturbed or unhappy you cannot enjoy any vacation or experience peace and relaxation. Therefore, you should learn to be happy naturally, wherever you are, finding opportunities to invent peace and happiness. You have to train your mind and senses to make the very process of living a source of enjoyment. It is immaterial whether you are rich or poor. What is material is whether you know how to appreciate life as it happens and how you can enjoy the simple pleasures of life, by becoming sensitive to the environment in which you live.

A sunset is a sunset, whether it happens in front of your house or on a snowy mountain. Perhaps you may not get a good view of it or you may never see it, but it still is a sunset. There is no point in wishfully thinking about the summer you are going to enjoy in an exotic place when and if you get that bonus, promotion or leave, while it is winter here and snow has covered the ground. You can learn to appreciate what comes your way or what happens to you, suspending your judgment and keeping your mind open and receptive. You can enjoy the snow when it snows and the rain when it rains, instead of thinking of summer when it is snowing, and wishing for snow when the summer is hot and humid.

You do not have to spend a lot of money to enjoy your life or go to faraway places to appreciate the beauty and grandeur of Nature. It is good if you can afford it, but, right here and right now, you can enjoy whatever you have and whatever is given to you. What is required is sensitivity, a loving heart and an appreciating mind. Even the silence of a street or a secluded place in your house can put you in touch with the peace that you may experience when you watch an expansive ocean or a mountain range. Do not ignore familiar things or people just because you know them. You can always find in them something new and fresh, and each time you meet people you can learn something new about them or their behavior.

By observing the world around you, with loving attention, and appreciating the presence of the most ordinary things within your immediate environment, you can stretch your mind, expand your awareness and find freedom from your dependence upon particular things and conditions for experiencing real joy and happiness. By observing the beauty of a flower, the innocence of a child, the serenity of a sleeping baby, the wisdom of an aging face, the anxiety of a flying bird, the placidity of an afternoon sky, the mysterious silence of a starry night, or by simply tasting your favorite coffee, tea or beverage, you can experience the simple pleasures of life here and now. All of it is possible with a few simple guiding principles such as the following. You can improvise them or make your own.

- Happiness is a state of mind. It arises from within.
- The world does not make you happy. You make yourself happy.
- You can create or invent your own happiness
- It is the sense of freedom which fuels your happiness and relaxation.
- Take a few deep breaths and pay attention into your senses.
- Make things and people important and worthy of your attention.
- Each day you spend is a special day.
- Take the child in you along with you when you go into Nature.

Stop Blaming Others

Blaming others for one reason or the other is common behavior in which most people engage. It is an important aspect of human relationships. The closer people get the more likely they will indulge in it for even trivial reasons. A daughter may blame her mother for spoiling her weekend because she asked her to stay at home and clean her room, which she has not cleaned in a month. She will keep blaming her mentally and silently until she gets over with it. After growing up she may blame her parents again for not giving her enough attention or not appreciating her choices. A bored and lazy husband who spends most of his time watching television and eating unhealthy food may blame his wife for his lack of success or peace of mind or for their increasing debts. Open any television news channel, and you will see how we have internalized blaming in our culture and behavior. Children blaming parents, parents blaming their children, mangers blaming their team members and team members blaming their colleagues, people blaming their leaders, leaders blaming their opponents and critics, teachers blaming students, students blaming teachers, neighbors blaming neighbors, these are common facets of life, in which we not only reveal our hidden resentments but also our tendency to let out our fears and frustrations through blame and criticism. We do not spare even God from this blame game, even though we have never seen Him directly and do not know much about Him.

It is easier to find a scapegoat or blame others, with or without reason, whereas it requires a lot of courage to own your faults and accept responsibility. We appreciate such people, but rarely do it in our lives. We may do it rarely but not habitually or as an expression of our essential nature. We are conditioned to seek approval and appreciation of others. Hence, in public we do our best to put on the best possible behavior and meet with the expectations of those whose relationships we value. However, when are frustrated or angry, we use the same human weakness to control others and make them feel guilty or submissive. Sometime, people need to be told what is wrong with them or how they can improve. Constructive criticism is useful and necessary to nurture relationships, build trust and improve ourselves and others. However, it should be done without envy and without any ulterior motive to control people, break their morale or make them feel small and guilty.

Unfortunately, many people do it habitually to vent their own anger and dissatisfaction, settle their scores, feel good about themselves, or just seek attention. Unjustified criticism is modified anger, expressed by the human ego for its own ends. In the end, it does not do any good. It may provide a temporary outlet to vent your negative emotions, but it also attracts a lot of negativity and interferes with your progress and happiness. Most of the time, those who habitually blame and criticize others end up alone. As they cannot think positively, they also miss many opportunities in life. If you criticize others, others will reciprocate with criticism and do not acknowledge your skills or talents. Many great people spend a whole lifetime and end up going to their graves without ever showing their skills or proving their greatness, because they cannot help blaming and criticizing others. If you want to avoid that fate, you should stop thinking negatively about others or blaming them. Here are a few suggestions to help you do it.

1. Accept responsibility for your actions: You may not be aware, but it is true that you are responsible for whatever that happens in your life. You are the author of your life and the creator of your reality. Every event and moment of your life is created by you, with your thoughts, intentions and actions. You have that spark of divinity in you, which gives you an unlimited ability and a wonderful opportunity to mold your life and carve your cherished path. You are endowed with the power to direct your life, using your intelligence and exercising your free will. You can use it effectively to mold your life and the shape of things yet to come. The environment in which you live, the people that come into your life, the problems you encounter as you pass through the portals of life, the successes and failures you experience in your endeavors are creations of your own consciousness, under the influence of desires. You may blame a thousand people, but your life is your responsibility. At any point in your life, you have the freedom to choose from the options the world presents to you. You can choose your actions as well as your responses. You have the power to control your thoughts and words and use them in whatever way you want. Certain aspects of your life may not be in your control, but you can always adapt to them and minimize their impact and interference. Whether it is solving problems or choosing your goals and priorities, you have the freedom to use your intelligence and exercise your will. Therefore, if something goes wrong, instead of blaming others and outside forces, ask yourself how you precipitated it and how you can resolve it.

2. Examine the motive: Why do you blame others? Sometimes you may do it for valid reasons, but it may be a reflection of your inner unhappiness. Before you begin to blame others for whatever mistakes they might have made or the criticism they deserve, examine your own motives. Search your heart and be truthful and honest to yourself. We blame people for several reasons. Some are valid, and some are not. If you blame others habitually, you have to follow the thought process that fuels your anger and understand the source of it. Is it the suppressed anger towards your parents and authority figures, self-hatred or hunger for attention? Until you find the root cause, whenever the thought of blaming someone arises in your mind you should do the introspection. Ask yourself, "What do I get by blaming others? What is the pay off?" Is it coming out of your frustration with your own life?

Sometime we also tend to blame others out of deep seated prejudice or past resentment. Once you form an opinion about a person, it is difficult to erase it from your mind. Your opinion of a person becomes a filter in your mind and any information you receive about that person becomes filtered by your past impressions. Hence, it is so difficult for each of us to change our opinions about anything or anyone. Therefore, we tend to criticize those whom we dislike, even if they are innocent. We cannot reverse this pattern of thinking in a short time, but we can control it gradually with determination and by understanding our own thinking and behavior. Introspection is the key to any self-improvement. You have to analyze your own self-talk and realize how frequently you blame yourself. The remedy lies in becoming more comfortable with yourself. If you feel that you need to help someone with constructive criticism, you may do so with right motives, for right reasons, and with no hidden or ulterior agenda.

3. Know the consequences of negativity: If you think negatively or indulge in negative actions you will attract negative situations into your life and suffer from their consequences. The same principle applies to positive thoughts and actions, which will attract positive forces into your life and create happiness, peace and prosperity. The results may not manifest immediately or as you expect, but eventually your dominant thoughts and emotions will precipitate reality in ways you may not even recognize. Blaming is a negative act of hatred and ill will. You can expect from it negative consequences only, not for those whom you blame but for yourself. When you blame others you attract many negative forces into your life, besides damaging your relationship with them, their supporters and well-wishers. No one likes to be criticized, even if they are wrong. Therefore, it is better to remain positive, fair and objective, when you have to criticize someone or fix accountability as part of your responsibility and obligatory duty. Criticizing people you care is a delicate act, which requires a lot of skill and compassion. You have to know how to convey unpleasant facts to them without breaking their heart or dampening their spirits. If you do not care about them, then you should not even bother to criticize.

4. Learn to forgive: Harboring negative feelings towards others and nursing angry and resentful thoughts in your mind is not good for your health or mental peace. Intentionally and unintentionally people commit mistakes. In this they are not much different from you. We cannot always ascertain correctly why people act in certain ways under pressure and what makes them lose control. When we are angry or frustrated, we cannot think fairly or objectively about other people. We are also influenced by our own irrational thoughts and beliefs, which makes it difficult for us to forgive others or think about them positively. If you are prone to blame and criticize others, you should examine your motives and learn to forgive others. It will do you a lot of good, as it will cleanse the negativity that has accumulated in your mind. Ask yourself what purpose does criticism serve in your life, and which one is better for you, criticizing or forgiving. Much of our criticism is unnecessary since it serves no real purpose, other than making your feel important or ignoring the reality.

I had a relation who criticized others when they were absent. When the same people were present, he would pretend as if he had no rancor. Sometimes, he would go out of the way to please them and praise them. I told him several times that for his own mental peace he should either forgive them or talk to them directly to resolve their difference. He listened to my suggestion, but never followed it. He was not deceitful, but lacked courage to tell them the truth or express his genuine feelings. For your own good and self-esteem, it is better to forgive people than to blame them or criticize them. You may not be able to avoid meeting bad people in your life, but you can mentally forgive them and let them go. Instead of carrying the negativity about them, you can dissolve that burden in the ocean of your inner compassion. Forgiveness opens your heart and makes you feel lighter. People deserve forgiveness because we are imperfect and prone to make mistakes. We all deserve kindness because we go through a lot of suffering in our lives. When you forgive others, you open your heart to the universe and make peace with it. You reinforce your best thoughts and behavior. It elevates your consciousness and character and moves you closer to your soul. Besides, those who are touched by your act of kindness may reciprocate and forge a positive relationship with you.

5. Understand the human nature: If your mind is filled with past injustices and negative memories about others, you will find it difficult to be at peace with even yourself. The more you think about them negatively, the more miserable you will feel about yourself since no relationship is one-sided. I have a friend who cannot trust anyone because he cannot think positively about them. His negativity affects his relationships, as he cannot avoid expressing it in subtle and nonverbal ways in his conversations. If you find people who blame others habitually, know that it stems from a general resentment they feel inside towards the world which they think has wronged them. If you suspect that people out there are ready to hurt you or exploit you, you will become hostile, suspicious and defensive. Carefully analyze what thoughts and impressions come to your mind spontaneously when you remember people. Ask yourself why you feel in certain ways about certain people. Sometimes your negative feelings may arise because you envy their success or feel small in their presence. If you are successful, people who are not so successful as you get easily hurt by your words or actions even if you do not intend to hurt them. The problem is not what you have done or said, but what they felt and thought happened. Their intention is to make you feel small and guilty so that they can feel that you are their equal.

Every human being is a mixture of both positive and negative qualities. Both light and darkness exist in us. Your relationship with others depends upon with which side you interact and which side of yours you bring into focus. In this regard, you have a choice. You can focus only upon the positive, or only upon the negative, or upon both and learn to remain in balance. In social situations, people usually display their good nature, but as they are drawn deeply into relationships, their darkness begins to come out. Hence, after an initial period of bloom and burst, most relationships wither. Therefore, you should have a good understanding of human nature and learn to discern people according to their behavior. You can avoid those who are extreme in their behavior, but in case of others you should use your own discretion to determine how much distance you should keep from them and what type of relationship you should have with them. Focus upon both their positive and negative qualities to know what to appreciate in them and where to keep a safe distance from them.

6. Respect others' rights and their individuality: Many times people blame others with a superior and holier-than-thou attitude. This behavior is more visible in communities that are guided by social conventions, racial and class distinctions. It is incorrect to assume superiority based upon some social, cultural or economic criteria and use it as a justification to blame or criticize others. It is equally wrong to suppress the voices of others because they disagree with you. Freedom of speech is also not a license to blame others or promote your beliefs by a holding a superior attitude. If you treat people as your equals and respect their individuality, your attitude and behavior towards them will be more civilized and flexible. You will be balanced and respectful, even when you have to criticize them for a reason. You will also treat them with dignity, respect and consideration, as you would like to be treated by them. With an open and receptive mind, you will consider their explanations objectively and give them an opportunity to defend their position on equal terms. Aggressive people do not recognize the rights of others or show any respect for their views and opinions. They try to negotiate and have their way through confrontation and authoritarian methods. While at times they may succeed, in the end they lose all support. On the other hand, assertive people remain firm in their resolve, but recognize the rights of others to defend themselves. Therefore, treat people as your equals, recognizing their right to opinion, while asserting your own, and use criticism in collaborative ways to build understanding and relationships. Treat the people fairly knowing that they have the same problems and concerns like you and deserve an opportunity to voice their problems and express their concerns.

Qualities of Successful People

Success means many things to many people. For some it means having wealth. For some it means having a good life. For some it means winning a game or championship. In general, success means achievement, fulfillment or accomplishment. It is moving from point A to point B, if B is what you wanted to reach. Thus, you may say success is to get what you want, realize your dreams or goals, become what you wanted to become, or live the way you desired to live. You may achieve success by reaching short term goals, such as writing a report or organizing an event, or by realizing you long term goals, such as finishing a thesis, earning a degree or winning an Olympic gold medal.

Success is a never ending process. You may rejoice in the glory of your success, but you cannot stay in it forever. Once you succeed in any venture, you move on towards another goal, project, or milestone. On the one hand, success boosts your morale, self-esteem, influence and status. On the other, it breeds insecurity, anxiety, greed and ambition. As we succeed and taste the rewards of success, we want to always remain successful. It is how we become addicted to the sweet taste of success and drawn increasingly into worldly life. However, because of our limitations, the competitive nature of our existence, and the demands success places upon us, not everyone can always remain successful.

Managing success

People vary in their ability to respond and manage success. Under its weight, some lose their balance, some their direction and some their humanity. Some become self-destructive and sabotage their own success, while some remain levelheaded and humble. For some success becomes a trap as they are caught in the web of their own delusions, or use their success to exploit others and extend their power base. However, some use the opportunity to extend their influence and reach out to others to help them and share with them the rewards of their success.

A lot depends upon how success is achieved. If it is achieved through shortcuts and evil means the rewards of such success may not be sweet, since eventually the sins of such actions will bear fruit and turn success into suffering.

Those who achieve success the hard way, become more resilient and competitive as they learn from their failures and successes and thereby prepare themselves for further success.

When the vision is small, people spend more time celebrating small victories and feeding their egos. For them success becomes a distraction and even an obstacle to greater success. Some people are happy even with small achievements, while some are eternally unhappy even if they are highly successful in the eyes of the world. It is important to remember that success is a means to happiness, but not an end in itself. You should aim for success as part of your self-expression, to realize your higher needs of belongingness, freedom, and service, and to feel good about yourself and your accomplishments.

A Successful person

Success is largely a product of many qualities and personality traits, such as imagination, courage, determination, initiative, focus, discipline, perseverance, flexibility, enthusiasm, intelligence, tolerance, humility, sociability and optimism. Successful people are known for their achievements as well as their distinguishing characteristics, which are described below.

- They have goals and plans and work for them. They know what they are supposed to do and where they would like to see themselves in future.
- They take responsibility for their actions and decisions, and keep improving their performance and skills.
- They acknowledge their limitations and know how to work around them.
- They accept their mistakes and failures as learning opportunities and part of their progress.
- They know that they can control their thoughts independent of others and circumstances and act accordingly to keep themselves motivated and positive.
- They are not easily deterred by problems and challenges. They accept them as opportunities to work towards their goals.
- They do not take things for granted. They do not underestimate the problem they face. They believe

- in proactive approach to deal with the problems they face.
- They may be emotional and at times easily give in to strong emotions. Sometimes, people may take advantage of the trust and faith they repose in humanity. However, they are realistic and practical in their approach to problems and human relationships.
- They have high self-esteem and believe in themselves and their ability to reach their goals.
- They specialize in their work and stand out for their knowledge experience and insight.
- They usually spend time doing what they love to do.
- They are hard working and rely upon their strengths and interests to achieve success.
- They build wealth by balancing their income and expenditure and saving wisely.
- They are generous and contribute generously to good causes and help others.
- They believe in certain values according to their upbringing. Sometimes society may not appreciate their values or lifestyles, but they believe in them anyway, since they are not afraid of living according to their personal beliefs and convictions.
- They establish relationships and alliances with people, with matching interests, to help each other.
- They protect their health and know its value in life.
- At times, they do not easily forgive or forget. They also take both competition and enmity seriously.
- They keep pushing themselves and those who work for them to achieve their goals.
- They are mostly self-motivated and self-directed.

Success is largely shaped by sustained hard work and goal oriented approach. People are successful to the extent they have clear and precise aims and purposes in life, and to the extent they are serious about achieving them. Successful people know how to guide their thoughts, correct their actions and improve their performance with positive mental attitude, perseverance, discipline and concentration. They are frank in their opinions and humble in their attitude and possess people and communication skills. They take responsibility for their actions and stand up to their problems.

Having goals

Having clear goals and clarity of purpose is important to achieve success in life. Once you know what you want, you can pool your resources and work for it, with suitable plans and strategies, dealing with problems and challenges along the way, constantly analyzing your actions and learning from your mistakes, and making suitable changes in your plans and methods as you keep moving forward. There are three major steps in achieving any success: know what you want, find the right way to achieve it, and do not rest until you achieve it.

To succeed in any effort, whatever may be the goals and tasks you choose, you must build your thoughts in the direction of your vision and resolve all related doubts and conflicts. If there is confusion in your thinking, there will be confusion in your results. If you sustain your enthusiasm, put in extra effort, go the extra mile, and inspire others with your conviction and positive attitude, you will attract many people and positive forces into your life, who will help you on your way to success.

Sharing your success

To make others your partners in your success, you have to make it relevant and useful to them and their success also. They should be able to see clearly the benefits they may derive from it. When you convince them that you are not the only beneficiary in your success and you are willing to share its rewards with them, you will secure their cooperation and collaboration as they will willingly come forward to help you and work with you. When you reach your goals you will not be alone, but surrounded by a number for well wishers, with gratitude in their hearts. Hence, wherever possible, extend the scope of your goals to include others. Make them a part of your vision for success, and your extended team. Give them an opportunity to celebrate your victory rather than envy it.

Success is the sweet reward of hard work, enthusiasm, positive mental attitude, knowledge, skills, wisdom, service, sacrifice, discipline, self-control, good relationships, character and integrity. All the factors are important, including the last two, which many ignore in their eagerness to achieve success, and thereby cause themselves a lot of grief. You should not only aim to achieve success, but also prepare yourself for it mentally, so that when it happens you will enjoy its rewards, without losing your balance, and without self-destructive habits and thoughts.

Managing success

In simple terms success means reaching goals or fulfilling your desires. You may not always succeed in fulfilling your desires or reaching goals. There will be times when you will be met with disappointments. On such occasions, whatever successes you might have achieved in the past might look meaningless. What this means is that your past successes do not necessarily make you happy forever. You will be happy for some time and then move on to scale another height or reach another goal with renewed hope and enthusiasm. While it helps you to move forward in life and try for more success, it creates uncertainty, and potentially makes you vulnerable to failure and disappointment. The best way to deal with this problem is to cultivate equanimity and treat both success and failure equally with a philosophical attitude as signposts in the journey of life, knowing that you are not defined by neither of them but by your actions, intentions, and convictions.

Working with Long Term Goals

Having goals and working for them is a powerful way to find direction, success and fulfillment in life. It is through clear and specific goals that you lead a purpose driven life and bring control and order into an otherwise chaotic and uncertain life. There are many types of goals. In this discussion, we will focus mainly upon long term goals. By long term goals, I mean goals that may take several years to materialize and shape one's life and destiny significantly.

Successful people use goals to regulate their lives. They know where they want to be one year from now, and ten years from now. Many people do not prefer setting goals in their lives because they do not want to live by a rigid framework of goals, priorities and daily tasks and become mechanical in the process, losing their freedom and spontaneity and dealing with the pressures and expectations it creates.

However, to achieve success in life, goals are important and necessary. By creating empowering goals, you can change your life forever. Your goals can expand your vision, inspire your thinking and keep you motivated. When you feel challenged by them, they bring out the best in you. They help you to transcend your limitations and weaknesses, and realize your true potential and competence. As you get into the habit of achieving your goals, they build your self-esteem and self-confidence and push you to test your limits.

Goals can make an ordinary person extraordinary and the impossible possible. They can transform your dreams and desires into reality. If there is one sure way to achieve success, it is this. Create well-defined goals and live for them, as if nothing else matters. Think of them constantly day and night and saturate your mind with the thoughts about reaching them, no matter what the challenges are.

Everything becomes possible for those who live with such an attitude. Neither loneliness nor boredom nor failure can stop them. Like soldiers in the battlefield of life they march on, undaunted by the challenges they face, with their gaze firmly fixed on the target. They remain flexible, but firm, realistic, but determined, and positive, but well prepared. Every success and accomplishment in life begins with a clear aim. Your goals inspire you and remind you of the life you want to create and experience, which in turn inspire you to reach them. Your desire to reach your goals fuels your success, and your success in turn fuels your ambition to set further goals.

Success is not the result of luck or chance, but mostly an organized effort, in which luck and chance augment the effort. When you do not have well-defined goals, you squander many opportunities that come your way as you may either miss noticing them or fail to utilize them due to lack of prior preparation. Without goals and plans, you will ignore your true potential and waste away your talents and skills or use them for mediocre work, without giving yourself any chance to truly excel. Such aimless life adds to your misery and feelings of emptiness. Without goals, a writer would probably end up as a teacher and a player as a spectator.

Working with long term goals

We should not only have goals, but the right ones that are in harmony with our essential nature and dominant desires and dreams. A goal is a pointed desire filled with a purpose and plan. The following suggestions are useful in setting effective lifetime goals that would lead you and inspire you to test your limits and realize your potentials.

1. Align your goals with your life's main purpose: When it comes to setting lifetime goals, you have to follow a two step process. In the first step, you have to find out the true purpose of your life, and in the second, you have to set your goals to make it possible. It is not easy to find the true purpose of your life, because you have to use both your heart and mind to know exactly what drives your passions and emotions and what you ultimately cherish in your life, transcending your beliefs, conditioning, and prejudices. You will come to know the true purpose of your life by doing introspection and ascertaining the following.

- What you like most.
- What you value most.
- What you think most of the time.
- What you desire strongly.
- What you admire in other people.

The two-step process described above in setting goals is important to achieve success in your life. When you know the purpose of your life, you can organize your goals around it and use your resources to reach them. You can also prioritize your goals according to their importance, and devise suitable action plans to accomplish them. Your life's purpose is central to everything you do in your life. You should know it by knowing what your heart wants, what your strengths, talents and predominant desires tell you and the kind of life you want to lead. If you set your goals without knowing it, chances are you may not feel committed to reaching your goals and you may not enjoy your success even if you realize them.

2. Make your goals clear and specific: The more precise your goals are the more pointed your aim will be, and your chances of success will be even greater. Hence, when you set your goals remember the acronym, SMART, which stands for Specific, Measurable, Attainable, Realistic and Time-bound. When you set your goals, each of these criteria is important. There are definite advantages in creating and using SMART goals. Firstly, you know clearly what you want to accomplish and in what timeframe. Secondly, you can send a clear instruction to your subconscious mind to manifest them. Thirdly, you can draw clear and precise plans with attention to detail. Fourthly, if others are involved in your effort, you can let them know clearly what you expect from them and what they can expect from you. Fifthly, you can measure and monitor your progress and performance by establishing clear standards and milestones. Finally with clear goals, you can clearly visualize the end you want to achieve and motivate yourself to stay on course.

3. Make your goals sound positive: Your goals should be not only SMART but also positively worded, because they should convey what you intend to do and where you want to go, rather than what you want to avoid or what you do not want to reach. Your subconscious mind has to be given a clear message and kept free from any confusion that may arise from negative messages. If you tell your subconscious mind what you do not want to achieve, very likely it will manifest its opposite. It happens because your subconscious mind does not understand negative words. Thus, for example, if you repeat to yourself, "I do not want to increase my weight," your subconscious mind will interpret it as, "I do want to increase my weight," and will act accordingly. Therefore, use positive words to describe your goals to convey what you intend to do and achieve rather than other way round. Construct them in such a manner that they inspire you and motivate you to remain committed to them.

4. Prioritize your goals: Not all goals are equally important. It is also not possible to accomplish them all at the same time. When you have multiple goals aligned to a central purpose, you have to prioritize them according certain criteria, such as their relative importance, availability of resources, and any constraints and conflicts that may arise. For example, if you have a goal that depends upon another important goal for its completion, you cannot focus exclusively upon the first without completing the second. At times, you may run into resource shortages and you may have to finish your goals and tasks in phases. Prioritization will help you to address such problems and avoid any confusion, or conflicts that may arise in the execution of your plans. It will also help you to conserve your resources and proceed with your tasks smoothly.

5. Write down your goals: A better way to create SMART goals is by writing them down. When you put your goals into writing, you form a clear picture about them in your mind. Any doubts or confusion you may have about them becomes cleared. With the clarity you gain, you can make them more concrete and specific. Written goals also help you to remember them better and avoid any errors that may arise due to memory lapses. Most importantly, by referring to them frequently, you can send a clear message to your subconscious mind and induce it to manifest them in its own mysterious ways. Hence, write down your goals as clearly and vividly as possible and keep them in a safe place for ready reference.

6. Affirm your goals: Refer to your written list of goals frequently until they are firmly etched in your mind. Carry the list with you and go through it whenever you find time. The purpose is to make your goals a part of your active memory, so that they influence your thinking, awareness and behavior. If you keep repeating the goals mentally to yourself, your goals gather strength and begin to attract positive forces. You will also become more committed to them, while your chances of achieving them increase greatly. To make the process even more effective, you can practice visualization along with affirmations. Some people also express gratitude at the end of each affirmation appreciating and acknowledging the help and the blessings they receive from others in their effort.

7. Overcome your fears and doubts: When you are setting your goals, you are influenced both by positive thoughts of hope and confidence and by negative thoughts of fear, anxiety, doubt and disbelief. The latter are caused by your self-limiting beliefs arising from low self-esteem and negative self-talk, which interfere with your ability to choose effective and empowering goals according to your skills and potentials. As a result, many people lower the bar and set low targets that may not challenge them enough or draw the best out of them. Your life is guided by hope on the positive side and by fear on the negative side. You have to know how to think through them and find your strengths. Fear prevents you from being yourself and from using your talents and potentials to express yourself. It protects you from possible harm, but at the same time prevents you from seeking goals that define you. Fear comes to you in many forms, and increases in intensity in proportion to the problems and failures you face. Fear of failure, fear of rejection, and fear of losing money, status, or prestige act as mental blocks and prevent you from setting and pursuing legitimate goals. You can overcome your self-limiting thoughts, doubts and fears, with positive affirmations and reasoning, and choose your long term goals according to your strengths, skills and abilities.

8. Accept responsibility: Your goals make sense only when you take responsibility for them and act responsibly. Responsibility means taking ownership of your goals and actions and accepting the consequences arising from them. Whether you know it or not, and willing to accept it or not, you are responsible for everything that happens to you. You can blame others, but that does not change the truth that you are responsible for your life and destiny. In choosing your goals or pursuing them, you should not lose sight of it. Your life is like a horse. You are the rider. If you want to ride the horse and control its movements and direction, you must hold the reigns. You can take the help of others, but you cannot transfer the ownership of your life to others unless you want to lose your freedom and live like a prisoner. When you take responsibility for your life and actions, you also become responsible for your successes and failures. You will not waste your time or blame others for the outcomes. You will learn from them and use your knowledge and experience to polish your skills and improve your effectiveness. You will develop new ideas, attitudes, and new ways of doing things and finding solutions. Most importantly you will earn the trust, appreciation and cooperation of others.

9. Try to push your limits: Generally, people have a tendency to follow a routine life, perform routine tasks and resist change, because they prefer avoiding the anxiety, pain and discomfort that arises from pursuing the unknown and the unfamiliar or the untested and the unpredictable. Hence, they habitually prefer sticking with their routine ways of thinking and doing, and thereby limit their opportunities for growth and achievement. The best way to counter this is to think of what you can do in the context of your circumstances, strengths and weaknesses, and find better ways to express your creativity and improve your efficiency and effectiveness. For example, if your goal is to start a business, find out what others have done in the same field and try to do better. See whether you can find any new ideas and concepts that will help you to improve your performance and stay ahead of the competition. The idea is you should always explore ways and means to go the extra mile by improving your performance, pushing your own limits of performance, taking small incremental risks and, if necessary, stepping out of your comfort zone. With this strategy, you will increase your competitiveness and excel in any field you choose. You can apply this simple rule to other areas of your life and give yourself an opportunity to transcend your limitations and exceed your own expectations.

10. Seek the divine help: If you do not believe in God, you do not have to follow this. However, if you believe in God, you can reduce much of your fear and anxiety, by seeking His help and making Him a partner in your efforts. You can offer your actions as well as their results to God and let him take care of the rest. Remember that God Himself is duty bound. Although He has no particular desire and no interest, He does keep goals to ensure the order and regularity of the world and the continuity of our existence. Nothing works without God's will and power. We can take credit for our actions, but the real force and strength to perform them come to us from God only. Therefore, you should live with humility and the sense of surrender, making goals and interests subservient to the will of God, and perform your actions as a form of worship. With such an attitude, you can live without fear of failure or anxiety, and yet aim for your goals, with the assured feeling that you are not alone in your journey of life.

Goals are important and necessary

Goal setting is a disciplined mental process, in which you succeed to the extent you manage the rules applicable to your profession or task, commit to the discipline, and overcome your routine thinking, and mental blocks. Your goals serve you as the lamp posts that lead you towards your future. They sustain your forward momentum and keep your hopes and dreams alive. They also serve as milestones in the journey of your life, providing direction and predictability to your plans and actions. Having goals is the best way to get things done. Working for them is the best way to remain occupied meaningfully. It is the first and the most important step in achieving success. When you have clearly defined goals, you will find it easier to make your way through difficulties. When you pursue them with faith, resolve, courage and confidence, you will overcome obstacles and prove to yourself that you are a winner in the battles of life.

Overcoming the Monotony of Life

When you are caught in an endless flow of routine, you suffer from monotony, despair and the frustrating and unsettling feeling that fate has handed you a raw deal. As you grow accustomed to the same pattern of life day after day and lose your zest for life, you may feel trapped and helpless in the hands of a twisted fate, although fate has nothing to do with it. Stuck in the same habitual thought patterns and incapacitated by fear and uncertainty, you will continue to follow the same lifestyle and pursue the same interests as if you have no alternative and you are born to endure rather than appreciate the life that happens to you. Even if you chance upon opportunities to change your life and find a new direction, you will not feel comfortable with the idea, because you would not like to disturb the illusion of comfort and security your routine life offers and expose yourself to the risks and uncertainties any change may precipitate.

A routine life may give you a false feeling of security but does not offer much scope for success or happiness. Occasionally, when you see people, who are more successful and influential than you, you may wishfully think of the opportunities you might have missed, suffer from envy, or blame those who you think did not do enough to help you succeed. A routine life without direction and dynamism is a sign that its bearer has reached a plateau in life and possess neither courage nor conviction to change its course and momentum, or utilize the opportunities life has to offer. Many people live such a life and complete their existence upon earth without leaving a trace.

When you do not have faith in yourself, you let things happen to you, not because you have outgrown the need to control, but because you have lost the will and the vision to mold your life according to your wishes. When you become a spectator of your own life, you live passively and defensively in a little circle of your own, with resignation or resentment, making routine decisions, trying to please others to win their approval, afraid of stepping out of your comfort zone and feeling uneasy at the mere thought of dealing with anything that might upset your routine life.

Many people are stuck in their lives, because they do not believe in themselves and cannot decide by themselves, overwhelmed by their own self-defeating thoughts and beliefs, and living as if they are born to suffer and they have no alternative to what has been going on in their lives. They habitually blame someone or something else for their problems, to free themselves from their own feelings of guilt and inadequacy, and usually end up feeling miserable, lonely and defeated.

Having the hope and desire for a better life is a sign of positive mental attitude. It keeps people alive and expectant. However, to sustain hope you should have faith in yourself and in your ability to change your life and manage the change you create, without expecting fate or an external force or circumstance to intervene and change it for you. The first step to become unstuck and take control of your life is to realize the need for change and take definitive action to make it possible. It is possible when you change your thinking and attitude by changing the way you talk to yourself, and gain control over your actions and responses.

Symptoms of being stuck in monotony

Here are a few characteristic features of those who are habitually stuck in their comfort zones and prefer staying there, out of fear or habit. You may also use them to know whether you are limiting your abilities and success, with self-defeating thoughts and negative attitude.

1. You stick to your old friends and do not prefer finding new friends or building new relationships.
2. Since you hesitate to ask others for help, especially those with whom you are unfamiliar, you prefer performing your tasks alone.
3. Even if you are bored or unhappy with your present job, you are not prepared mentally to look for a new job or learn new skills.
4. You prefer availing the same third-party services, go to the same restaurants or visit the same old places during vacation.
5. When you have financial difficulties, you prefer limiting your expenses, rather than looking for ways and means to increase your income.

6. You do not want to change your methods, thinking, or lifestyle, even if you are dissatisfied with many aspects of your current life.
7. You speak or think mostly about your achievements or missed opportunities instead of the current reality.
8. You prefer solving your problems conventionally, using known and safe methods, rather than innovative and creative solutions.
9. You are uncomfortable with unfamiliar people and places.
10. You hesitate to speak for yourself or express your ideas for fear of criticism or ridicule.
11. Due to lack of confidence and fear of rejection or loss you either avoid negotiations or settle for less, rather than trying to secure your interests and claiming what is yours.
12. You do not assert yourself or speak about yourself comfortably, even when it is strongly required.
13. You prefer living like a person without means, even though you earn a decent income, because you think you do not deserve riches or happiness.
14. You are uncomfortable with thinking big, buying expensive things or using quality services, which you believe only the rich can afford.
15. You are uncomfortable dealing with people, who do not belong to your caste, race, nation, religion, community or profession.
16. You indulge in negative thinking, complaining about things and criticizing people for no particular reason.
17. You want to be perfect in everything you do or you would not do it at all. Your passion for perfection arises from your need to seek the approval of others and avoid their criticism.

Imagine a person, who was living inside a dark dungeon for most of his life because he was too afraid to go out and face the world, and suddenly one day, driven by curiosity, he decided to go out and see the world for himself. Now, imagine what would have happened to him when he climbed out of the dungeon and stepped into the beautiful world outside. For a while, he might be bedazzled by the brightness of the sky, but once he opened his eyes, he would experience immense freedom upon seeing the beauty and radiance of an entirely different world. A similar kind of experience awaits those, who venture out of their comfort zones, overcoming their fears and limiting self-talk. They will not only discover their true potentials and abilities, but also find new possibilities and opportunities that will help them to achieve success and happiness.

Breaking free from comfort zone

If you want to break free from the monotony of your life and see the brightness of your life and the numerous possibilities that await you, you must be willing to break out of the dark dungeons of your own fears and habitual thoughts and set yourself free from your self-limiting thoughts. To let your life flow in the direction of your dreams and desires, you should let go of the illusion of security and comfort that you build around yourself. Here are some ways, in which you can do it. .

- Change your thinking.
- Change your responses.
- Change your negative self-talk.
- Begin to take action in your zone of influence.
- Learn to take calculated risks.
- Establish clearly defined goals, following your interests.
- Try to go out of your comfort zone to experience things you have not tried before.
- Increase your knowledge, by taking up some courses if necessary.
- Practice assertiveness.
- Increase and improve your relationships to spread your zone of influence.
- Accept failure and rejection as a part of success and as a learning opportunity.
- Expand your mind, by remaining open minded and non-judgmental.
- Try experimenting and new ways of doing things whenever possible.
- Practice possibility thinking.
- Learn to negotiate on your terms.
- Do not be afraid to ask for help or seek assistance.

The Power of Positive Affirmations

Affirmations are useful and effective to control your thoughts and change your behavior. Since they operate in the domain of your consciousness, you can use them anywhere and anytime to influence your thinking and behavior according to the needs and demands of your life or the situation. They are the best means to bring desired changes in your behavior, without stress and anxiety, and without the need to make major adjustments to your current lifestyle.

Using strong and powerful affirmations you can dismantle your self-limiting beliefs with empowering thoughts and motivate yourself to become a different person. You can change your behavior and habitual responses and reinforce them for lasting effect. Using them, you can also overcome your fears and negative self-talk, and learn to think positively about your goals and abilities, letting your mind explore new possibilities and opportunities with the newly found freedom. Most importantly, you can use them to saturate your subconscious mind with the outcomes you want to manifest.

How to create positive affirmations

Affirmations are positive statements with specific personal and emotional appeal. They have to be relevant to your life and problems and framed according to your specific needs and goals. When you affirm them, they should be able to invoke vivid and powerful images in your mind and remind you of the specific goals, desires and the improvements you want to manifest. To make them effective, inspiring, and worth remembering you have to use simple words and phrases that are commonly used and well understood. You should frequently repeat them or meditate upon them until they are firmly etched in your memory. The following guidelines help you to create powerful affirmations.

- When you create affirmations, use only positive words and adjectives. For example, "I am happy," "I can control my emotions."
- Avoid using negative statements that use "no" or "not." We have already seen that the subconscious mind does not understand negative words and may even manifest its opposite.

- Make your affirmations concrete, convincing and realistic, using descriptive words that invoke your imagination and sensory experience.
- Keep your affirmations short, and specific, using easy to remember words and phrases.
- Create your affirmations in the present tense so that your subconscious mind will take them literally and manifest them effectively.
- Include words that convey positive emotions and powerful feelings so that you can make them sound convincing and credible to your subconscious mind.
- Use the first person in creating them since they are meant for you.

Rules for using affirmations effectively

Once you create suitable affirmations using the above stated guidelines, you have to use them properly and regularly to achieve desirable results. The following suggestions can make your affirmation effective.

- Repeat them frequently until they become part of your subconscious mind. You should remember them at least two or three times a day, once in the morning after you wake up, once in the afternoon, and the third time before you sleep.
- Read them aloud if necessary. If you have voice recorder, create an audio file of your affirmations and listen to them regularly. You can even make slideshow or a video.
- Practice visualization, along with your affirmations. Visualize the end clearly and vividly, using your imagination and vivid details.
- Keep a file of images that correspond to your affirmations and frequently refer to them. You can use old magazines and Internet to gather your images.
- Mix your affirmations with powerful positive emotions and feelings.
- Use the power of belief for better results. Believe that your affirmations are already working and manifesting desired results.
- At the end of each session, express love and gratitude to God and thank the invisible forces He

set in motion mysteriously to manifest your desires and affirmations.
- Carry the list of your affirmations with you wherever you go. Write them down on a piece of paper or on index cards and frequently refer to them. You can also put them in your laptop or mobile phone.

Affirmations help you to deal with your weaknesses, destructive habits, disempowering thoughts, negative emotions and self-talk, which weaken your resolve or prevent you from being effective in using your talents and skills to your best advantage. Using them you can change your outlook and attitude, overcome inner conflicts and psychological problems, harness positive emotions, improve your health and fitness, and people skills. By implanting them firmly in your active memory, you can motivate yourself to deal with emotional problems and troubling memories

Therefore, use affirmations to transform your life, reach your goals, stretch your limits and overcome your fears. Create powerful affirmations and repeat them frequently to improve your energy and enthusiasm, build emotional resilience and self-esteem, and change your values and beliefs. Using them, counter your weak thoughts and self-doubts, and instill courage and confidence. Make them your principles to fuel your subconscious mind and manifest the hidden design of your life. Put them to effective use to overcome the barriers and mental blocks that interfere with your success and inner transformation. Be the dream you desire to become.

How to Improve Your Self-Esteem

Nandita came from Bangalore. When she was a child, she always felt bad when she had to travel by train in the economy class to visit her grandparents who lived in New Delhi. During her journeys, whenever she had to walk by a first class coach, she would feel uneasiness and avoid looking at the passengers who were traveling inside. She did not know then that the people who traveled in them were not necessarily rich and might be travelling at the expense of their employers, customers, or the government. Her parents were rich enough to afford first class fare, but they wanted her to travel in the economy class and save money which could be used for a better purpose when she was with her grandparents. They also wanted her to know the value of money and the virtue of humility.

The economy class compartment was like a mini India on rails. It offered a grand spectacle of people from all wakes of life, who were hard working, spoke different languages, and accepted the conditions life offered to them with dignity and tolerance. When they saw a young person traveling alone, they readily offered whatever food and treats they had and made her feel at home in their company. However, none of it gave her solace as she felt that finding herself amidst them lowered her status, while she deserved to be in the first class with better people.

Nandita was a normal child. She grew up to become a chief technology officer in a prestigious technology company. She now travels regularly in the business class, and has lot of friends, and admirers. She still feels that her achievements are few, her looks are average, and she is not attractive enough to deserve a happy marriage or a good looking husband. She constantly keeps looking for approval and appreciation from her peers and colleagues and feels depressed when it is not forthcoming. Nandita has all the things in the world, other can only dream of. Yet, she is not comfortable with her achievements or her looks. Her problem is not about having or not having riches, status, or looks, but low self-esteem, which is common to many people, who feel limited by circumstances and personal drawbacks and judge themselves negatively and rather harshly in their own esteem. They focus upon what they do not have or what they lack, which makes them unhappy. It is a burden, like the cross of Christ, which many people carry in their hearts for their whole lives. They suffer from an emptiness, an inner vacuum, that cannot be filled by any amount of riches or achievements. Since the problem is internal, they alone can resolve it.

Self-esteem is the way you feel about yourself, treat yourself and measure yourself against the standards set by society or your peers. It is how you define yourself and hold yourself in your own esteem and how you relate to the world and others. It is not only how you value yourself but also how you think others perceive you. Your self-esteem does not have to depend upon reality. It is what you make of it and how firmly you believe in it. In most cases, it is an illusion you solidify and preserve due to the value system and the authority of parents peers you replicate in yourself.

Without feeling good about yourself, it is painful and difficult to continue your existence. Everyone expects to be treated well, but most do not realize that more important than how others treat them is how they treat themselves and how much respect they give to their own thoughts and opinions. When you feel rejected or disapproved by your own judgment, you make life difficult for yourself and others. To avoid the feelings caused by it, you erect your own walls of defense, which makes it even more difficult to address the real problem and resolve it.

Your well being, inner happiness, attitude, thinking, actions, expectations, relationships, failures, accomplishments, social skills, courage and confidence depend on your self-esteem. It influences the way you respond to your life's challenges, other people's opinions and your own inner critic, who keeps nagging to you constantly about how incomplete and inadequate you are according to the best standards he chooses for you. You inner critic is your friend as well as your enemy. Whenever you make mistakes, his voice grows louder and he keeps reminding you how far you are from the ideal life and behavior you are expected to cultivate.

You may get away from unpleasant friends and relationships, stay away from threatening or disturbing situations, but you cannot escape from your core beliefs about yourself and your inseparable inner critic. Your experiences shape your values, beliefs, and the way you think and feel about yourself. In this regard, societal and parental influences play a crucial role. They create your inner critic and bring him to life, with commands and instructions that become part of his value system and thereby yours. Neither our education system nor our competitive environment directly addresses this problem.

Your self-esteem is a product of your circumstances. However, it does not mean that you can do nothing about it. You can improve your circumstances by improving your self-esteem. Here lies the hope as well as the solution. People with low self-esteem tend to show some of the following behavioral patterns.

- They develop low expectations about themselves.
- They believe that they do not deserve good life.
- They try to impress others, if necessary by putting themselves down.
- They are quick to blame themselves and feel guilty about it.
- They avoid taking risks, since they lack self-confidence.
- They suffer from fear of failure and fear of rejection.
- They seek the approval of others to compensate for their feelings of worthlessness.
- They give more weight to the opinion of others since they do not believe in themselves.
- They do not make effective leaders as they try to impress everyone.
- They become too defensive or aggressive in conflicts and discussions.
- They suffer from self-doubt, fear, anxiety and stress.
- They enter unhappy and unequal relationships.
- They find it hard to persevere and keep up their resolve.
- They react emotionally rather than rationally in difficult and challenging situations.
- They hesitate to express themselves honestly in the company of others.
- They rarely live in the present.
- They have a problem saying 'no' to others.

- They have a problem accepting 'no' from others.
- They are easy to influence, dominate and control.
- They accept low pay and unhappy work situations since they undersell themselves and settle for less.
- They are their own worst enemies, since they sabotage their success with self-destructive thoughts.
- They minimize their successes and exaggerate their failures, which reinforces their low self-esteem.

Self-esteem is a product of experience and circumstances. Very early in your life you form an opinion about yourself, which stays with you and becomes a part of your consciousness. Unless you change your thinking and attitude, it remains there and influences the course and direction of your life. If a child's self-confidence is constantly eroded through mindless criticism, negative comments, ill treatment, and unjustified comparison with others, eventually the child would suffer from low self-esteem and carry that feeling into adult life. If parents discriminate between their children and show partiality, it can impair the self-esteem of those who are less favored as they attribute the reasons for their parents' partial behavior to their own inadequacies.

A person's self-esteem may fluctuate from time to time, depending upon circumstances. People who migrate to other countries, either as refugees or in search of livelihood, people who live as minorities in their own countries and suffer from social disabilities and discrimination, people who are deprived of their jobs or income or status by circumstances, may suffer from temporary loss of self-esteem. So is the case with people who go through a bad marriage or an unhappy divorce. Unless a person is equipped with optimism and resilience, repeated failures, setbacks and abuse by others will erode his or her self-esteem greatly.

Basic honesty and unconditional self acceptance are the keys to a healthy self image. For someone who has been tormented for years by self-doubt and nagging poor self-image, such blessings are hard to come by. The process of restoring your self-esteem has to begin with a brutally honest self-evaluation, followed by a course of action that should be implemented honestly and sincerely with great commitment. The following are a few proven ways by which you can deal with the problem of low self-esteem.

- Believe firmly that you deserve a good life and you are entitled to the best things in life like anyone else. Developing this conviction is not easy, but it is the key to restore your self-esteem.
- Develop a list of your strengths and weaknesses, with complete honesty. Focus upon your strengths to boost your self-confidence and use them frequently to express yourself and remind yourself that you have talents and abilities which set you apart as an individual.
- Dispute with your inner critic with healthy rebuttals until they become automatic responses to any negative thought that may arise in your mind.
- Develop a healthy and flexible mindset to deal with failure and rejection, by refusing to take them personally.
- Avoid the language of musts and shoulds in your thinking and communication.
- Learn to take risks, with a positive mental attitude.
- Empower yourself, by taking small and incremental risks such as trying a new restaurant, talking to a stranger, asking someone for a date or speaking in public.
- Accept what you are and what you can do, without judging yourself harshly.
- Focus on your achievements and your blessings.
- Whatever you do, give your best, without being driven by the need to be perfect or correct. Focus on doing the task, rather than achieving the result.
- Let go of your past and the unpleasantness that exists in your mind about people and situations. Forgive those, who treated you rather unfairly in the past.
- Pay attention to your health and physical appearance and keep yourself physically fit.
- Use positive affirmations and visualization techniques to boost your confidence and self image.
- Learn to accept yourself unconditionally, suspending your judgment.
- Keep your mind focused on positive thoughts.

- Specialize in some branch of knowledge, without the need to be prefect or impressive.
- Improve your professional skills, and general knowledge of places, people and human behavior. It will boost your self-confidence and social skills.
- Learn to deal with friends on your terms as your equals, without expectations and the need to win their approval
- Cultivate assertiveness, either by reading self-help books about the subject or by taking class in assertive training.
- Avoid comparing yourself with others or the need to put down others to make yourself feel good.
- Practice mindfulness and learn to watch your actions and reactions, with complete awareness.
- Finish what you begin, however challenging may be the task.
- Read the biographies of people, who persevered during tough times, without losing faith in their abilities.
- Learn to love yourself unconditionally.
- Develop a non judgmental attitude, by controlling your habitual thoughts and reactions. Use the daily news or a similar program on television to cultivate non judgmental observation and awareness.
- Celebrate your success and learn from your failures.
- Help others, without expecting anything in return.
- Cultivate self-awareness, through observation and attentiveness.
- Get into action habit. Become more productive. Make yourself more useful to others. Find opportunities to prove your worth.

Self-esteem is all about feeling good about yourself and your achievements, without the compulsive feeling to impress others or depend upon them. You can achieve it by disputing with your inner critic, changing your rigid mindset, accepting yourself unconditionally, overcoming your obsession with perfection as compensatory behavior to impress others, suspending your judgment about yourself and the world, focusing upon your strengths, and learning to cope with your successes and failures with a positive mental attitude. Most important of all, you should believe that you are unique human being, with many strengths, skills, and positive qualities, who deserve a better life and the comforts the world has to offer. No one can make your feel anything unless you accept it and allow it to happen. No one can make you feel inferior or unworthy, unless you accept it and believe in it. Your beliefs and attitude are important to your self-esteem. Therefore, follow the guidelines mentioned here to empower yourself and rebuild your self-esteem, strength and confidence to manifest the destiny for which you are born.

Recommended Reading

Abundance / Prosperity

McColl, Peggy. 21 distinctions of wealth: attract the abundance you deserve, Hay House, 2008.

Butler-Bowdon, Tom. 50 prosperity classics: attract it, create it, manage it, share it ; wisdom from the best books on wealth creation and abundance, Nicholas Brealey Publications, 2008

Hicks, Esther an Jerry. Money, and the law of attraction: learning to attract wealth, health, and happiness (The Teachings of Abraham). Hay House, Inc., 2008.

Hill, Napoleon ... [et al.]. How to prosper in hard times : blueprints for abundance by the greatest motivational teachers of all time. Jeremy P. Tarcher/Penguin, 2009

Kessel, Brent. It's not about the money: unlock your money type to achieve spiritual and financial abundance, HarperOne, 2009.

Orman, Suze. The courage to be rich: creating a life of material and spiritual abundance. Riverhead Books, 2002.

Allen, Marc, The greatest secret of all: moving beyond abundance to a life of true fulfillment. New World Library, 2008.

Losier, Michael J. Law of attraction: the science of attracting more of what you want and less of what you don't, M.J. Losier, 2006.

Hicks, Esther and Jerry. The vortex: where the law of attraction assembles all cooperative relationships, Hay House, Inc., 2009.

Adversity

Stoltz, Paul G. and Weihenmayer, Erik. *The Adversity Advantage: turning everyday struggles into everyday greatness*, Fireside/Simon & Schuster, 2006.

Sydow, Clas von; preface by Csikszentmihályi, Mihály and Klein, George; translated. *Live Now: inspiring accounts of overcoming adversity*, Prometheus Books, 1997.

Stoltz, Paul G. *The Adversity Quotient @ Work: make everyday challenges the key to your success--putting the principles of AQ into action*, Morrow, 2000.

Stanley, Charles. *How To Handle Adversity*, Walker and Co, 1999.

Joni Tada, Eareckson. 31 days toward overcoming adversity, Multnomah Publishers, 2006.

Feldman, Gail C. *From Crisis To Creativity Taking Advantage Of Adversity*, BookPartners, 1999.

Salmansohn, Karen. *The Bounce Back Book: how to thrive in the face of adversity, setbacks, and losses*, Workman Pub. Co., Inc, 2007.

Farbe, Barry J. *Diamonds Under Pressure: five steps in turning adversity into success*, Berkley Books 1998.

Cohen, William A. *Wisdom Of The Generals: from adversity to success, and from fear to victory: how to triumph in business and in life*, Prentice Hall, 2001.

Affirmations

Gawain, Shakti. Reflections in the light: compiled by Grimshaw, Denise, Nataraj Publications; Distributed to the trade by Publishers Group West.

Franken Al. I'm good enough, I'm smart enough, and doggone it, people like me!: really, Dell, 1992.

Hay, Louise L. I can do it! : How to use affirmations to change your life, Hay House, 2004 .

Dyer, Wayne W. Living the wisdom of the Tao: the complete Tao teaching and affirmations.

Hay, Louise L. Self-esteem affirmations [sound recording], Hay House, 1990.

The Don't Sweat Affirmations:100 inspirations to help make your life happier and more relaxed by the editors of Don't Sweat Press; foreword by Richard Carlson, Hyperion, 2001.

Chopra, Deepak. The soul of healing affirmations [sound recording]: A-Z guide to reprogramming the software of the soul, Rasa, 2008.

Career Development

Fields, Jonathan. *Career Renegade: how to make a great living doing what you love*, Broadway Books, 2009.

Arruda, William & Dixson, Kirsten. *Career Distinction: stand out by building your brand*, J. Wiley & Sons Inc., 2007.

Miller, Gordon. *The Career Coach: winning strategies for getting ahead in today's job market*, Currency/Doubleday 2001.

Craddock, Maggie. *The Authentic Career: following the path of self discovery to professional fulfillment*, New World Library, 2004.

J, Ella L. & Bell, Edmondson with Villarosa, Linda. *Career GPS: strategies for women navigating the new corporate landscape*, Amistad, 2010.

Hess, Peter M. *Career Success: right here, right now!*, Delmar, 1999.

Bench, Marcia. *Career Coaching: an insider's guide*, Davies-Black Publications, 2003.

Taguchi, Sherrie Gong. *The Career Troubleshooter: tips and tools for overcoming the 21 most common challenges to success*, AMACOM, 2006.

Dealing with Fears

Bourke, Joanna. *Fear*, Shoemaker Hoard: Distributed by Publishers Group West, 2006.

Bourne, Edmund & Garano, Lorna. *Coping With Anxiety: 10 simple ways to relieve anxiety fear & worry*, New Harbinger, 2003.

Moehn, Heather. *Coping With Social Anxiety*, Rosen Pub. Group, 2001.

Martin Shepard. *Dying: a guide for helping and coping*, G.K. Hall & Co., 2000.

Lucado, Max. *Fearless: Imagine Your Life without Fear*, Thomas Nelson, 2009.

Watt, Margo C. & Stewart, Sherry H. *Overcoming the Fear of Fear*, New Harbinger Publications, 2008.

Becker, Gavin de. *The Gift of Fear: survival signals that protect us from violence*, Dell Publishing, 1998.

Hendricks, Gay. *The Big Leap: Conquer Your Hidden Fear and Take Life to the Next Level*, HarperOne, 2009.

Effective Listening

Robertson, Arthur, K. *Listen For Success: A Guide To Effective Listening*, Irwin Professional Pub., 1993.

Madelyn, Burley-Allen. *Listening: the forgotten skill: a self-teaching guide*, John Wiley & Sons, 1995.

Shipside, Steve. *Effective Communications: get your message across and learn how to listen*, Dorling Kindersley, 2007.

Van Slyke, Erik, J. *Listening to Conflict: finding constructive solutions to workplace disputes*, AMACOM,, 1999.

Goulston, Mark; foreword by Ferrazzi, Keith. *Just Listen: discover the secret to getting through to absolutely anyone*, American Management Association, 2010.

Kratz, Dennis, & Kratz, Abby Robinson. *Effective Listening Skills*, McGraw-Hill, 1995.

Opitz, Michael F. *Listen Hear! 25 Effective Listening Comprehension Strategies*, Heinemann, 2004.

Lebauer, Susan R. *Learn to Listen, Listen to Learn 1: Academic Listening and Note-Taking*, Pearson ESL, 2010.

Eye care

Zinn, Walter J, Solomon Herbert. Complete guide to eye care, eyeglasses & contact lenses. Lifetime Books, 1996.

Cross, Warren D. and Jr., Lynn, Lawrence. Your vision: all about modern eye care. MasterMedia Ltd., 1994.

Grossman, Marc and Swartwout, Glen. Natural eye care: an encyclopedia: complementary treatments for improving and saving your eyes. Keats Publishing, 1999.

Moodie Christine. The five-minute eye makeover. Crown, 1992.

Rubin, Melvin L.and Winograd, Lawrence A. Taking care of your eyes: a collection of the patient education handbooks used by America's leading eye doctors. Triad, 2003.

Friedlaender, Mitchell H. and Donev, Stef. 20/20: a total guide to improving your vision and preventing eye disease. Wings Books, 1994.

Goals

Tracy, Brian. Goals! : how to get everything you want--faster than you ever thought possible. Berrett-Koehler, 2003.

Ziglar, Zig. Book on CD 2. Goals [sound recording]: [setting and achieving them on schedule].Simon & Schuster Audio ; Nightingale-Conant, 1995.

Schienle, Kathleen. Achieving goals : define and surpass your high performance goals.Collins, 2005.

Smith, Andy. Achieve your goals: strategies to transform your life.Dorling Kindersley, 2006.

Bateman, Barbara D., Herr M. Cynthia. Writing measurable IEP goals and objectives. IEP Resources, 2003

Davidson, Jeff. The complete idiot's guide to reaching your goals.Alpha Books, 1998.

Loneliness

Cacioppo, John T. and William Patrick. *Loneliness: human nature and the need for social connection*, W.W. Norton, 2008.

Dumm, Thomas. *Loneliness As A Way Of Life*, Harvard University Press, 2008.

Kiley, Dan. *Living Together, Feeling Alone: healing your hidden loneliness*, Prentice Hall Press, 1989.

Brassell, William R. edited by Tilley, Leslie. *Belonging: a guide to overcoming loneliness*, , New Harbinger, 1994.

Lynch, James J. *A Cry Unheard: new insights into the medical consequences of loneliness*, Bancroft Press 2000.

Memory

Parkin, Alan J. *Memory, a guide for professionals*. J. Wiley, 1999.

Lorayne, Harry. *Ageless Memory: simple secrets for keeping your brain young*, Black Dog & Leventhal Publishers, 2007.

Hagwood, Scott. *Memory Power: you can develop a great memory-- America's grand master shows you how*, Free Press, 2006.

Small, Gary with Gigi Vorgan. *The Memory Prescription: Dr. Gary Small's 14-day plan to keep your brain and body young*, Hyperion, 2004.

Small, Gary. *The Memory Bible: an innovative strategy for keeping your brain young*, Hyperion, 2002.

Carter, Rita. Mapping The Memory: understanding your brain to improve your memory, Ulysses Press, 2006.

Gordon, Barry & Berger, Lisa. *Intelligent Memory: improve the memory that makes you smarter*, Viking, 2003.

Felberbaum, Frank with Kranz, Rachel. The Business Of Memory: fast-track your career with supercharged brainpower, Rodale, 2005.

Whitaker, Julian with Dace, Peggy. The Memory Solution, Avery Publishing Group, 1999.

Mental peace

Sarma, Kama. Mental resilience: the power of clarity : how to develop the focus of a warrior and the peace of a monk. New World Library, 2008.

Omartian, Stormie. Finding peace for your heart: a woman's guide to emotional happiness. T. Nelson Publishers, 1998.

Lind-Kyle, Patt. Heal your mind, rewire your brain: applying the exciting new science of brain synchrony for creativity, peace, and presence. Energy Psychology Press, 2009.

Ellis, Richard. Practical Reiki: focus your body's energy for deep relaxation and inner peace. Sterling, 1999.

Glovinsky, Cindy. Making peace with the things in your life: why your papers, books, clothes, and other possessions keep overwhelming you and what to do about it. St. Martin's Griffin, 2002.

Gibson, Katherine. Unclutter your life: transforming your physical, mental, and emotional space. Beyond Words Publications, 2004.

Jeffers, Susan. Embracing uncertainty: breakthrough methods for achieving peace of mind when facing the unknown. St. Martin's Press, , 2003.

Pierce, Linda B. Choosing simplicity: real people finding peace and fulfillment in a complex world. Gallagher Press, 2002.

Negotiations

Roger, Fisher. *Getting to Yes: Negotiating Agreement without Giving In*, Penguin, 1991.

Krannich, Ronald, L., Caryl, Krannich Rae. *Dynamite Salary Negotiations: know what you're worth and get it*, Impact Publications, 2001.

Bazerman, Max, H. & Neale Margaret H. *Negotiating Rationally*, Free Press, 1994.

Claude, Cellich, Jain Subhash C. *Global Business Negotiations: a practical guide*, Thomson/South-Western, 2004.

Kramer. Henry S. *Game Set, Match: winning the negotiations game*, Alm Publications, 2001.

Goodman, Peter J. *Win-Win Career Negotiations: all you need to know about negotiating your employment agreement*, Gut Instinct Press, 2001.

Shell, G. Richard. Bargaining *for Advantage: Negotiation Strategies for Reasonable People*, Penguin, 2nd Edition, 2006.

Babcock, Linda and Laschever, Sara *Ask for it: how women can use the power of negotiation to get what they really want*, Bantam Dell, 2008

Positive thinking

Peale, Norman Vincent (1898-1993). The power of positive thinking. Simon & Schuster, 2003.

Gerald, Amanda. The power of negative thinking: coming to terms with our forbidden emotions, Madison Books, 1999.

Quilliam, Susan. Positive thinking. DK Publication, 2008.

Hay, Louise L. and friends. Everyday positive thinking. Hay House, 2004.

Hansard, Christopher. The Tibetan art of positive thinking: skillful thought for successful living. Atria Books, 2005.

Peale, Norman Vincent. The amazing results of positive thinking. Simon & Schuster, 2003.

Thomson, Geoff. The elephant and the twig [electronic resource]: the art of positive thinking. eBook. Summersdale, 2000.

English, Martin. How to feel great about yourself and your life: a step-by-step guide to positive thinking. American Management Association, 1992.

Reading Skills

Diffily, Deborah and Sassman, Charlotte. *Managing Independent Reading: effective classroom routines, Scholastic*, 2005.

Mikulecky, Beatrice S. & Jeffries, Linda. *Reading Power: reading for pleasure, reading comprehension skills, thinking skills, reading faster,* Longman, 2005.

Branstetter, Kacy. *Master Skills Reading*, American Education Publishing, 1995.

Konstant, Tina. *Speed Reading*, McGraw-Hill, 2003.

Abby, Marks Beale with Mullan, Pam. *The Complete Idiot's Guide to Speed Reading*, Alpha, 2008.

Wechsler, Bernard H. & Bell, Arthur H. *Speed Reading For Professionals*, Barron's, 2006.

Frank, Steven. *Speed Reading Secrets: read faster, remember more, and get great grades,* Adams Media Corporation, 1998.

Stephen, Howard Berg & Conyers, Marcus. *Speed-Reading the Easy Way*, Barron's Educational Series, 1998.

Relaxation

Craze, Richard. *Relaxation*, Contemporary Books, 2003.

Benson, Herbert & Klipper, Miriam Z. *The Relaxation Response*, Avon Books, 2000.

Bob Sharples. *Meditation & Relaxation In Plain English*, Wisdom Publications, 2006.

Davis, Martha & Eshelman, Elizabeth Robbins & McKay, Matthew. *The Relaxation & Stress Reduction Workbook*, New Harbinger Publications, 2008.

Editor: Blumenfeld, Larry. *The Big Book of Relaxation: simple techniques to control the excess stress in your life*, Relaxation Co., 1994.

Shealy, C. Norman. *90 Days to Stress-Free Living: a day-by-day health plan including exercises, diet and relaxation techniques*, Element, 1999.

Levey, Joel. *The Fine Arts of Relaxation, Concentration & Meditation, Revised: Ancient Skills for Modern Minds*, Wisdom Publications; 3rd edition, 2003.

Lazarus, Judith. *Stress Relief & Relaxation Techniques*, Keats Publications, 2000.

Sherman, Carl and the editors of Prevention Magazine. *Stress Remedies: hundreds of fast-relief tips to relax your body, calm your mind, and defuse the number one cause of everyday health problems and chronic disease*, Rodale Press, 1997.

Wilson, Elisabeth. *Stress-Proof Your Life: smart ways to relax and re-energize*, Perigee, 2008.

Adamson, Eve. The everything stress management book : practical ways to relax, be healthy, and maintain your sanity, Adams Media, 2002.

George, Mike. *Learn to Relax: a practical guide to easing tension & conquering stress*, Chronicle Books, 1998.

Self-esteem

McKay, Matthew, Fanning, Patrick. Self-esteem. New Harbinger Publications, 2000.

Sherfield, Robert M. The everything self-esteem book: boost your confidence, achieve inner strength, and learn to love yourself. Adams Media Corp., 2004.

Murk, Christopher J. Self-esteem : research, theory, and practice. Springer Pub. Co., 2nd edition, 1999.

McKay, Matthew ... [et al.]. The self-esteem companion: simple exercises to help you challenge your inner critic and celebrate your personal strengths. New Harbinger Publications, 1999.

Ellis, Albert. The myth of self-esteem: how rational emotive behavior therapy can change yourlife forever. Prometheus Books, 2006.

Palladino, Connie D. Developing self-esteem: a guide for positive success. Crisp Publications; Distributed by Career Research & Testing, 1994.

Gust, John; illustrated by Radtke, Becky. Enhancing self-esteem: a whole language approach. Good Apple, 1994.

Cypert, Samuel A. The power of self-esteem. American Management Association, 1994.

Cleghorn, Patricia. The secrets of self-esteem: make the changes you want in your life. Vega, 2002.

Ewitt, John P. The myth of self-esteem: finding happiness and solving problems in America. St. Martin's Press, 1998.

Branden, Nathaniel. The six pillars of self-esteem. Bantam Books, 1994.

Subconscious mind

Murphy, Joseph (1898-1981), edited and revised by Pell, Arthur R. The power of your subconscious mind. Prentice Hall Press, 2008.

Friedman, Sidney. Your mind knows more than you do: the subconscious secrets of success. Blue Dolphin Publications, 2000.

Murphy, Joseph (1898-1981). Miracles of your mind. Hay House, 2006.

Wise, Anna. Awakening the mind: a guide to mastering the power of your brain waves.Jeremy P. Tarcher/Putnam, 2002.

Murphy, Joseph (1898-1981), revised by McMahan, Ian D. The amazing laws of cosmic mind power. Reward Books, 2001.

Tallis, Frank. Hidden minds: a history of the unconscious. Arcade Publications, 2002.

Success

Pincott, J. editor. *Success: advice on achieving your goals from remarkably successful people*, Random House Reference, 2005.

Canfield, Jack with Switzer, Janet. *The Success Principles: how to get from where you are to where you want to be*, HarperCollins Publishers, 2005.

Hill, Napoleon. *The Law of Success: in sixteen lessons: teaching, for the first time in the history of the world, the true philosophy upon which all personal success is built*, BN Publishing, 2007.

Arthur, James Ray. *The Science Of Success: how to attract prosperity and create harmonic wealth through proven principles*, SunArk Press, 2006.

Maxwell, John C. *Success 101: what every leader needs to know*, Nelson, 2008.

Taylor, Sandra Anne. *Quantum Success: the astounding science of wealth and happiness*, Hay House Inc, 2006.

Pearsall, Paul. *Toxic Success: how to stop striving and start thriving: getting what you want without losing what you need*, Inner Ocean, 2002.

Ferriss, Timothy. The 4 – Hour Work Week: Escape 9-5, live anywhere, and join the new rich. Crown Publishers, 2007.

Thought power

Browne, Mary T. The 5 rules of thought: how to use the power of your mind to get what you want. Atria Books, 2009

Besant, Annie W. (1847-1933). Thought power, its control and culture. Theosophical Pub. House , 1973.

Wind, Yoram (Jerry), Crook, Colin, with Gunther, Robert. The power of impossible thinking: transform the business of your life and the life of your business. Wharton School Pub, 2005.

Jordan, Bernard E. The laws of thinking: 20 secrets to using the divine power of your mind to manifest prosperity. Hay House, 2006.

Ventrella, Scott W. The power of positive thinking in business: ten traits for maximum results. Free Press, 2001.

Schuller, Robert Harold. Power thoughts: achieve your true potential through power thinking. HarperCollins, 1993.

Rando, Caterina. Learn to power think: a practical guide to positive and effective decision making. Chronicle Books, 2002.

Pure Life Vision Books

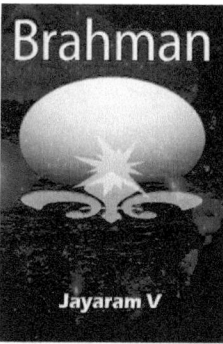

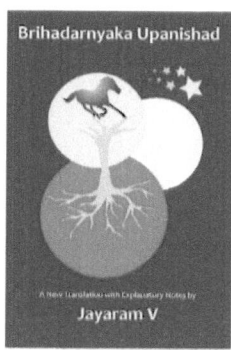

To order please visit

http://www.purelifevision.com

www.ingramcontent.com/pod-product-compliance
Lightning Source LLC
Chambersburg PA
CBHW020349080526
44584CB00014B/951